SOCIO-ECONOMIC PROFILE OF RURAL INDIA

Volume Two

NORTH-EAST INDIA

Socio-Economic Profile of Rural India

Vol. I : SOUTH INDIA
Andhra Pradesh, Karnataka, Kerala, Tamil Nadu

Vol. II : NORTH-EAST INDIA
Assam, Manipur, Tripura, Nagaland

Vol. III : NORTH-CENTRAL & WESTERN INDIA
Punjab, Haryana, Himachal Pradesh, Gujarat, Maharashtra

Vol. IV : EASTERN INDIA
Bihar, West Bengal, Orissa, Uttar Pradesh

About the Editor

C. Ashokvardhan, an IAS officer of 1980 batch, belongs to the Bihar Cadre of Service. He was awarded Gold Medal for his Master's Degree in Political Science from Patna University, Patna. He obtained his Ph.D. in Personnel Management and Financial Administration from Patna University, Patna. Before joining the IAS, he was on the faculty of Political Science at Ranchi College, Ranchi and Patna College, Patna. He wa receipient of several awards and honours during his distinguished academic career. He has also visited many foreign countries on different occasions like study tour and training.

Among several responsible positions with State and Central governments, Dr. Ashokvardhan has held posts of SDO of Godda, Bihar, Vice Chairman of Ranchi Regional Development Authority; Collector of Sitamarhi District; Additional Secretary of Department of Revenue & Land Reforms; Additional Member of Board of Revenue; Secretary of Department of Parliamentary Affairs; Secretary of Deptt. of Secondary Education and Secretary of Department of Raj Bhasha, Government of Bihar. He was appointed as a Member of Committee on the Revitalisation of Land Revenue and Land Records Administration in India (Ministry of Rural Development, Government of India). He has contributed a paper entitled "Continuity & Change in Tribal Tenancy Laws in Bihar: A Review of Transfer Provisions" as a Member of an Expert Group, formed by the Department of Rural Areas and Employment, Government of India. As a member of an Expert Group set up by the National Commission for SCs and STs, (GOI) to study issues related to land rights, he has contributed a paper entitled "New policy options for tenancy reforms in Bihar'. He has also served as member of Committee on Consolidation of Land Holdings and Committee on Tribal Land Alienation and its Restoration, formed by Ministry of Rural Development (GOI).

Currently, Dr. Ashokvardhan is the Additional Member, Board of Revenue, Government of Bihar. He has several publications to his credit, including books entitled *Land Record Management in 14 States of India*, and *Readings in Land Reforms*.

SOCIO-ECONOMIC PROFILE OF RURAL INDIA

VOLUME TWO

NORTH-EAST INDIA

(Assam, Manipur, Tripura, Nagaland)

Edited by

C. ASHOKVARDHAN, *I.A.S.*

Published for
Centre for Rural Studies
L.B.S. National Academy of Administration, Mussoorie

by

CONCEPT PUBLISHING COMPANY, NEW DELHI-110059

Cataloging in Publication Data—DK

Courtesy: D.K. Agencies (P) Ltd. <docinfo@dkagencies.com>

Socio-economic profile of rural India / edited by
V.K. Agnihotri.
v. cm.
Includes bibliographical references.
Includes index.
Contents: v. 1. South India — v. 2. North-east India :
Assam, Manipur, Tripura, Nagaland
ISBN 8170227429

1. India—Social conditions. 2. India—Economic conditions. 3. India—Rural conditions. 4. Rural development projects—India. I. Agnihotri, V. K. (Vivek Kumar), 1945- II. Lal Bahadur Shastri National Academy of Administration. Centre for Rural Studies.

DDC 330.954 21

ISBN 81-8069-145-4 (Vol. 2)
ISBN 81-7022- 742-9 (Series)

First Published 2004

Published and Printed by
Ashok Kumar Mittal
Concept Publishing Company
A/15-16, Commercial Block, Mohan Garden,
NEW DELHI-110059 (India)

Phones : 25351460, 25351794
Fax : 091-11-25357103
E-mail : publishing@conceptpub.com

FOREWORD

North-East India consisting of the States of Arunachal Pradesh, Assam, Manipur, Meghalaya, Mizoram, Nagaland and Tripura has immense diversity; linguistic, cultural, social and religious. This region is home to 209 scheduled tribes in addition to a number of distinct ethnic groups not officially recognised. Yet this region is also homogeneous in that social stratification found in other parts of the country is not present in the North-East. The tribal population forms only one-fourth of the population of the North-East, despite the fact that in four States including Mizoram, Meghalaya, Nagaland and Arunachal Pradesh, they constitute as much as 90 per cent of the population. The North-Eastern region remains an economically backward region even within the general framework of under development in the country. The entire North-Eastern India is identified as an economically backward region and there have been efforts to channel funds to hasten development. But the State, public and private sectors have been largely unable to generate or initiate widespread entrepreneurship in the region. Compulsions of geography, lack of infrastructure, a weak economic base and lack of resources for investment have thus far retarded growth.

The region, therefore, stands as one of the backward areas of the country with peculiar problems for economic development. The agricultural sector remains predominantly traditional, cultivation practices not having seen modernization thus far. Although the economy of the region is primarily agrarian, its full potential is yet to be attained. A very large portion of the hill areas in the North-Eastern India has no cadastral survey, so there are no records of rights over land. In most cases land vests in the village community or clan. Without any recorded individual rights a very serious obstacle is placed on any possible source that could encourage the flow of credit from any institutional investors to infrastructure or indeed to the cultivators. Shifting cultivation has through the ages been the main means of securing a livelihood for most tribes of the north-eastern hills and a substantial portion of the total hill population still depends on it exclusively for its survival. On an average, 3,869 sq. km area is put under shifting cultivation every year and an estimated 4,43,336 households earn their livelihoods from it. It is today not only a source of livelihood but also has acquired high cultural importance among the peoples of the North-East. The extent of area under shifting cultivation is maximum in Nagaland followed by Mizoram and Manipur.

Indeed, the abundant resource base in this region has the potential to generate adequate employment. However, it needs imaginative planning and reforms in prevalent policies. Even within the region, the socio-economic conditions of people in the hilly areas and plains differ considerably. The natural resources of hilly areas are under-exploited compared to the exploitation of natural resources in the plains. North-East India thus presents a remarkable case of industrial backwardness in the midst of abounding resources. The area has substantial potential for industrialization based on minerals, agriculture and forests. The industrial sector has mainly grown around tea and timber in Assam and mining, saw mills and plywood factories in other parts of the region. Since both the agriculture and industrial sectors are yet in premature stages of development, the pressure for employment is mainly on the service sector. The constitution of a North Eastern Council in 1971 by an Act of Parliament for the economic and social development of the region has to some extent helped promote planned and coordinated development of the region.

The decentralized politico-administrative set-up in the North-East is also different from the rest of the country. Most of the States are governed under the Sixth Schedule of the Constitution of India which provides a framework of autonomy for protection of indigenous tribes and to prevent their exploitation by more advanced social groups in the tribal areas.

The North-East region if properly marketed can attract investment because it is rich in mineral resources and plentiful in energy sources, some yet to be exploited. An example is the mighty river Brahmaputra and its tributaries, forming the largest perennial water system in India with an immense potential for energy, irrigation and also transportation. North East India could develop into India's Power house. Besides, it has fertile stretches of land stretching along Brahmaputra Valley. It is also a storehouse of Horticulture products, plantation, the crops, vegetables, spices and rare forest products. It has abundant forest resources and can offer attraction for tourists and ecologists because of its natural scenic beauty as well as rich cultural heritage. The region also boasts of easily available skilled and reasonably priced manpower. The North-Eastern region can be especially attractive to foreign investment as it is close to Myanmar, the gateway to the economically vibrant ASEAN countries. It has the potential to emerge as the strategic base for foreign and domestic investors wishing to tap this rich South East Asian market. It is also in the neighbourhood of the SAARC countries of Bhutan, Bangladesh and Nepal and can take advantage of international trade through SAPTA (South Asian Preferential Trade Agreement).

This book is the second volume of the series *Socio-Economic Profile of Rural India*. The authors of different State papers of this volume are senior bureaucrats and academicians. Many of the authors are directly involved in policy formulation at different levels of Government of India. Undoubtedly, the State papers prepared by them are of high quality being enriched by inputs from long experiences in the field of rural development. I express my gratitude to each of them for each of their contributions.

The task of publishing the volumes of Socio-Economic series was initiated by the Village Study Unit (VSU), later merged with Land Reforms Unit to form Centre for Rural Studies (CRS). I congratulate Shri Amarjeet Sinha, IAS, who was the Coordinator of VSU, when the task of publishing Socio-Economic series was initiated. The efforts of Manoj Ahuja, IAS, the present Coordinator of Centre for Rural Studies and Shri Subhransu Tripathy, Assistant Professor, Centre for Rural Studies to bring out this book are worthy of praise. I look forward to the publication of the remaining volumes in this series.

5.4.2002

Wajahat Habibullah
Director
Lal Bahadur Shastri National Academy
of Administration,
Mussoorie-248179 (INDIA)

CONTENTS

EDITORIAL NOTE

The Micro-Universe

This slim volume is an exposition of the socio-economic scenario in some of the States of the North-East, as seen through the eyes of some I.A.S. officers on training in a typically North-East field situation, at different points of time. While we are free to make certain generalisations from the micro-universe under study, we should not be oblivious to the micro-universe as such, characterised by its own individuality and myriad nuances.

This micro-universe presents, not boastfully of course, the face of a village, tanned by misery and deprivation. There exist social taboos which block a rather modern outlook and thinking and there are pockets of utter resourcelessness, where primitive economy has come to stay. There is a terrain, which prevents the use of scientific implements and says "No" to big industries. There is a sky which in an hour of vengeance, sends floods and destruction. But there is a forest covers too, the rarest of the rare, producing bamboos, to say the least, those products are sold to fetch food. There are cows and pigs as also silk-worms. There is a loom in the household to weave out a shawl. There are stray patches of manure and fertilizer and there is a beam of hope to see the results. There is credit, too, to be spent on marriages and funerals and also the lethargic tribal who sleeps at home, while the womenfolk work.

There is, nonetheless, the unmistakable dawn of awakening. Children go to schools. The health worker pays visits. Drains in stones are carved – the mini waterways. There is a gradual shift to terrace cultivation. The advent of IRDP & JRY, with all the promises. The village council and their writ. There is communal harmony and no caste. Urbanization, at places. Infrastructure expands its base. Irrigation potential increases. Horticulture looks up. The North-East Council pumps in funds and incentives leading to diversification and to markets.

The probationers' study unfolds this very living and colourful panorama of the North-East, in select village. It presents a socio-economic structure responding to change and to improvement. What is evident is a slow but steady transformation from a primitive and limping to a vibrant economy.

About the Region

As we all know, the North-East has distinct regional personality. The general economic profile of this region is one of extreme backwardness reflecting by and large a low level of living standards. The infrastructure remains under-developed. Intra-regional links are weak. Paradoxically, the region is one which has immense resource potential but the technical know-how is still deficient. There lies the need for entire region to work towards an integrated approach in transport, phone, irrigation and flood-control, management of forest resources and supply of food and essential commodities.

Topographically, the different areas in the region are similar, each has a hilly terrain interspersed with flat valleys. All the areas have heavy annual rainfall and have large areas under forests. Except for the rivers of Tripura, most of the rivers draining the various areas of the region flow through more than one State. Though the various units are endowed with natural resources like oil and gas, coal, silmanite, limestone, bamboo, good quality timber, hydro-power potential etc., the level of exploitation of these resources is commonly very low.

Though agriculture is the only source of livelihood to majority of the people, rational land utilisation was not possible due to difficult terrain. Tribals throughout the region practice shifting cultivation of old form. This actually means excess labour for low yield and wastage of land due to lengthy cycles. Again agricultural processes are disturbed by taboos, beliefs and customs. The main features of shifting cultivation are rotation of fields rather than crops; clearings by means of fire; absence of draught animals and manuring; use of human labour only; employment of dibble stick or hoe; short period of occupancy alternating with long fallow periods. After the clearings are abandoned, the cultivators shift to another clearing, leaving the old one for natural recuperation. This explains the use of the term 'shifting cultivation'. It however does not imply that the homesteads are also shifted to the new site along with the shifting of cultivation. More often than not, the homesteads are not shifted.

North-East India with a remarkable variety of agro-climatic zones ranging from the tropical in the plains to the temperate in the high hills has a wide range of possibilities of agricultural, and animal husbandry development. Though the agricultural sector accounts for more than 60 per cent of the net domestic product, it has not exposed to scientific methods of agricultural such as multiple cropping, relay cropping, soil conservation, water management, use of chemical fertiliser, pest and plant control, etc. The region is suitable for growing a variety of crops – pine-apples, banana, papaya, oranges, etc., but due to lack of processing and marketing facilities, their cultivation have remained unrealised. Conditions are also favourable for the cultivation of commercial crops like coffee, cashewnuts, ginger, black pepper, etc. In spite of sufficient pasture available, the animal husbandry is not developed. The livestock population is considerable but the quality is unsatisfactory. The region needs proper guidance and facilities for higher training in agriculture.

As Assam and Meghalaya are rich in mineral resources, the prospect of mineral based industries are bright in these States. Coal though has high sulphur content is excellently suitable for the production of coal gas and coal tar. The use of coal for thermal power generation can easily lessen the power crisis. The limestone deposits of Southern Meghalaya can be used for flux and chemical industries like soda ash, caustic soda, calcium carbide, etc. The deposits are suitable for cement industries also. Sillimanites of Sonaphhar have a great scope for the manufacture of high grade refractory. Separation of corundum from Sillimanite can easily establish an industry. The clay deposits of Meghalaya and of Mikir hills are suitable for white wares, stoneware pipes, and sewer which have a good demand in this region. The sand glass deposits of the Khasi hills can be used for ordinary bottle glass, window glass.

Forests supply a variety of raw materials for pulp, paper and newsprint industry, hard fibre board and insulation board industry, match industry, medicinal plants, oil, resin, dye industry, etc. Forests of Assam supply large quantities of timber, bamboo, grasses, canes, firewoods, medicinal plants and a number of other products. The pine and bamboo of Maghalaya provide scope for the establishment of a big paper mill while timber trees can establish an integrated building and furniture industry. The forests of Manipur and Arunachal Pradesh have vast scope for match industry, say mills, paper and pulp industry, chip board and hard board plants, etc. The forests of Nagaland, Tripura and Mizoram can be used for the production of small goods in cottage industry.

With 12.5 million hectares of forests, North-East India shares about 17 per cent of the country's total forests. The percentage of forest area to total area is 49. Of the regional forests, Arunachal Pradesh shares about half, and Assam more than a fifth. The percentage of forest areas to total areas varies greatly from 17.7 in Nagaland to 72.7 per cent in Arunachal. The per capita distribution of forest lands varies from 0.19 hectares in Assam (higher than the all-India average of 0.14 hectares) to 13 hectares in Arunachal Pradesh. Only Assam and Tripura have considerable reserved forests, 55.5 per cent and 53.8 per cent of the total forests respectively. Others have only about 10 per cent of their forests classed as reserved.

The reserved forests of Assam are confined to the following three areas: foothills of the Himalayas in the Bhabar and Terai tracts, Northern slopes of the Meghalaya's plateau and the hills surrounding the Barak valley. The upper Assam forests are evergreen with broad leaves and the lower valley forests are deciduous, dominated by *sal* trees. The Barak valley forests predominate in bamboo. The *sal* forests of the Garo hills and of the Northern Khasi hills and the pine forests of the central Khasi hills are rich forest resources. Meghalaya is rich also in medicinal plants. Most of the forests of Manipur are of mixed type. However, on the basis of climatic conditions, they are of four types: (1) tropical semi-evergreen forests in the western part of the State, (2) tropical moist deciduous in the south-eastern corner of the State, (3) sub-tropical pine forests in southern and north-eastern parts, and (4) dry temperate forests surrounding the Imphal valley. There are large areas of bamboo in the western part of the State. Most of the reserved forests of Nagaland are in Kohima district and one block in Tuensang district. All the protected forests are in Mokokchung district. Most of the reserved forests of Tripura are of mixed type. About three-fourth of the forests are covered either with patches of bamboo or with any jungle grass which are of little use of man or beast. Forests of Arunachal Pradesh are tropical evergreen, temperate evergreen, conifer and alpine. Trees found only at the foothills of the territory are commercially exploitable. Except a few areas of pine trees on high ranges, most of the forests of Mizoram are composed of bamboo. Taking together, only the forests of Assam, Meghalaya and Arunachal have useful timber trees. North-East India is rich also in wild lives.

A very large portion of the hill areas in the North-Eastern India has not been cadastrally surveyed, with the result there is no record of rights over land. In most cases, land rights vest either in the village community or clan. In some cases the rights vest in the Chief or Siem or head of the clan. In strictly legal terms, individual land rights exist in the flat areas of Dimapur Sub-Division of Nagaland, tribal reserve of Tripura and perhaps in the permanently cultivated flat land of Mikir Hills which had at one time formed a part of Sibasagar district of Assam. Non-existence of recorded individual rights puts a very serious restriction on the flow of agricultural credit to the cultivation from any institutional agency, be it a bank or a co-operative society. Under such circumstances, mortgage of land in favour of the lending agency cannot be legally created, and land is normally the security for the loans advanced. Thus, the application of conventional norms of security automatically excludes almost the entire hill tribal area of the region from getting agricultural credit from the banks and the co-operative credit societies. This is exactly the reason why the Lead Bank Scheme has not been able to make any headway in the North-eastern India. The restrictions, whether legal or customary, credit operational difficulties for the banks financing the agricultural credit in the matters of acquisition and disposal of agricultural land. It is, however, agreed that there is hardly any need for agricultural credit for shifting cultivation, but then the same is vitally necessary in areas and pockets where irrigated rice in being permanently cultivated, and in case of fruit orchards, if not for animal husbandry.

North-Eastern region receives a good amount of rainfall annually. However, distribution of rainfall over time and space is very uneven which is quite copious from June to September, i.e. monsoon period. About 64 per cent of the annual rainfall is received during this period. As result floods are almost a regular annual phenomenon. At the same time, the post-monsoon rainfall (October-December) and winter rainfall are very scanty limiting the scope for agricultural activities during the *rabi* season. Arunachal Pradesh, being located in the Himalayan range, receives highest precipitation with average annual rainfall of 3294 mm followed by Assam and Meghalaya States 2184 mm. The remaining parts of the region, viz., Nagaland, Manipur, Mizoram and Tripura receive much lesser rainfall, i.e. only about 1851 mm. In fact, in this sub-division there are many rainshade and scanty rainfall areas.

In view of the limited potential of the organised industrial sector to absorb increase in the labour force, small-scale industries and the rural non-farm sector will have to play an important role in generating additional employment. There would be substantial employment creation through rural works programme. In addition it is expected that if the traditional skills of rural artisans are upgraded and their competitiveness is improved, the rural industrial sub-sector would provide more permanent avenues of employment.

The relevant questions are about the type of rural industries to be started, their location, and their organisation as viable units, etc. For this purpose techno-economic surveys of rural areas should be planned to assess the needs and potentialities of various regions. As we observe that the bulk of processing or products turned by agriculture has been done in urban based industries. A programme of rural industrialisation envisages processing of agricultural produce near the place of origin, so that rural labour gets employment thereby. Not only this, ancillary and feeder industries should also be located in or near the rural areas. Such a programme of rural industrialisation requires a number of supporting administrative, technical, financial and organisational measures.

A programme of rural industrialisation should consider the feasibility of setting up the following four types of industries: (a) processing of agricultural produce which may include rice milling, cotton ginning, preparation of milk and milk products, oil extraction, and manufacture of sugar etc.; (b) fruit and vegetable processing, which includes packing, canning and preservation of fruits and vegetables, preparation of jams, pickles and other food products; (c) industries to utilise agricultural by-products like molasses, baggase, rice husk, broken rice, jute sticks, tea waste etc. Such industries offer good scope for employment of rural labour force; and (d) development of village handicrafts and cottage industries. The handloom industry is the largest single cottage industry in terms of employment. Sericulture is another area, which has tremendous scope of expansion and employment.

The village industries can also manufacture agricultural implements. In addition, a number of ancillary and feeder industries can help to manufacture such goods, which may ultimately be produced in the large scale sector. Certain parts of agricultural machinery or other equipments may be produced as per specification in rural areas. The States can also play an important role in rural industrialisation by providing infrastructural facilities in the form of rural electrification, irrigation and transportation which itself has large employment opportunities.

For securing the balanced development of the North-Eastern region the North Eastern Council was set up under an Act of Parliament in 1971, as an advisory body to assist the constituent units in matters of common interest in the field of economic and social planning, inter-State problems relating to transport and communication and any matter relating to power or flood control projects of common interest. The main functions of the Council are to formulate a unified and coordinated regional plan for that area (the States and the Union territories governments also formulate their separate State plans) with regard to matters of common interest and importance and advise on priorities of the projects and the schemes included in the plan, determine their phasing, their implementation and decide their location. In this way the Planning Commission is seeking to bring about necessary plan, which is intended to provide much of the regional balancing. For starting a project the Council utilises the different agencies of the State/Union territories government to whom the funds are advanced through the Council's plan. The Council is also required to be in contact with the government of the State/Union territory of the region, the Ministry concerned with the project at the Central level and Planning Commission for successful and effective implementation of the project.

The Council's plan is that it is not a regional plan in the true sense of the term, but is mainly a set of regional schemes relating to power, transport and communication, agriculture and allied programmes, marketing and training facilities intended to benefit a group of the States in the region by seeking to provide collectively, certain facilities which individually these States at their present state of development cannot afford.

Since the Council can sponsor and finance the projects, which are of regional importance and supplements the developmental activities undertaken both under the State plans and the national plan, bulk of the Council's investment has been in power and transport sector as noted earlier. They constitute the basic infrastructure creating an environment for development of other sectors. It is in these fields that a cooperative approach, recognising their mutual interdependence is of paramount importance.

The Council's function should not be limited up to mere allocation of funds for various schemes and supervision on the progress of a project but must have a constant watch on the problems, which may arise, and consequently suitable remedies to be provided to solve these problems. The Counsel's role in arranging scarce raw material, technical know-how, skilled manpower should be more purposeful and of much use in successful implementation of a project. The State/Union territory government should also show more interest in quick implementation of the projects by allotting required land area and other facilities because these projects are being introduced for their own benefits.

Engagement of the council in every field of planning even where the State governments have their well established departments would create a doubt in the minds of people that the NEC is super-regional body adopting authoritarian attitude in sanctioning schemes/projects. Such type of involvement may be avoided except where it becomes essential in the interest of the region as a whole or in the interest of two or more States of the region. A doubt may also be raised that how long the financial powers assigned to the Council would not set in motion the process of erosion of financial autonomy of the States of the region. Such doubts would never get a surface if the Council continues to act as an advisory body for the planned development of the region. It would be better if the Council confines its activities on the projects on inter-State importance, regional importance, extension of infrastructural facilities, arranging technical education, resource survey, exploitation of natural resources available with fullest cooperation of State governments and their maximum utilisation for development of the region. All this will be helpful in a balanced regional development without creating a controversy of genuineness of the Council for the development of the North-Eastern region.

STATE PAPERS : A RESUMÉ

The State papers included in this volume relate to Assam, Manipur, Tripura and Nagaland. It will be worthwhile shedding some light on the contributions made to the volume with regard to certain essential facts of the socio-economic domain.

I. Assam

The concept of commercialisation of agriculture has not yet taken its root in the villages. Average landholdings are small with a high percentage of fragmentation. Therefore, agriculture is not considered economically viable and productive. Most of the villages face the wrath of flood every year rendering agriculture uneconomical. Other support systems including irrigation, use of fertilizers and pesticides, HYV seeds are minimally used in the villages. Except for tea cultivation, most of the produces are basically consumption oriented.

If the harvest is good the farmers earn some surplus but the problem arises when flood or other factors affect the farm resulting into heavy losses. That is to say, the farming activity does not give the farmers staying capacity. This is especially true in the case of jute.

Most of the villages do not have co-operative society, and hence, the products are sold to middlemen (*marwaris*) at the *hat*.

The agricultural wages range between Rs. 15 and Rs. 20 per day depending upon demand (though the wages are slightly more during sowing and harvesting seasons).

Though most of the households possess cows, milk is not very popular and the yield per cow is quite low. There are no improved breeds (like *jersey*). Bullocks are used for ploughing purposes.

Few villagers rear pigs. Pig is more prevalent among Mishing tribes. Goats are reared for meat purposes. Poultry is very popular among the villagers. In most of the villages, the people are engaged in Pisciculture in the ponds since fish is the most common food relished by the Assamese.

After agriculture, the next highest proportion of workers is engaged in livestock, forestry, fishing, hunting, plantation, orchards and allied activities. There is a considerable number of agricultural population in upper Assam and Cachar who are tea garden labourers. Tea cultivation in Assam occupies about 1657 sq. km with a labour force of 5.5 lakh (1971) working daily.

In most of the surveyed villages, rural industries were found at the very primitive stage. Traditionally, weaving of Mekhla Chadara has been a common custom practiced by Mishing society. Mekhla Chadara is a traditional handicraft and involves weaving of cotton and development of beautiful designs in a wide range of clothes. The other items produced are riha, churia, cheleng, borkapor, gamosa etc. The implements used, besides looms are ugla, mako, spinning wheel etc. Generally, throw shuttles loom, loin loom, and ply shuttles loom are used for weaving. The first one is found in every Assamese household while the second is common among the hill tribes. The Bengali weavers mostly use pit looms. The ply shuttle loom is of recent origin and is an improved type of traditional loom. Interestingly most of the raw materials are imported from outside the State. The average income of a weaver is generally around Rs. 25 a day.

Sericulture has an important place in the rural economy of the State. The villagers produce three principal varieties of silk, pat, endi and muga.

2. Manipur

The main occupation of the people in the villages of Manipur is agriculture. In the hill pockets it is cultivation of rice by means of shifting cultivation. They practice *Jhumming* in areas around the village. There is no fixed area for cultivation as the sites are shifted year after year. The distance of the *jhum* land can be anything between 2 km to 10 km.

As is evident from the Khemkan report (Thoubal district), seeds mainly come from the previous year's stock. Fertilisers and pesticides are purchased from the Thoubal bazaar. Tractors are taken on hire basis. No supply of HYV seeds is reported from Dongjang in Churachandpur, nor there is any use of fertilisers, pesticides and tractors in this village. Seven households in Dongjang use bullocks, which are borrowed at the rate of Rs. 500 per acre. Similarly, no scientific technology is employed in Thanlon (Churachandpur district). The only inputs are personal seeds and human labour. In Tangpijol (Churachandpur), the seed varieties are all traditional ones having low yield which goes down in subsequent years. The use of fertilisers, small implements, power tillers, buying of water for irrigation, hiring of labour is totally absent. In Parbung Lungthulien and Senvon (Churachandpur district), there has not been any conscious effort to adopt better technologies. There is no concept of mechanised farming in Chandel and Ukhrul districts as well.

No irrigation facilities are available to the cultivators in most of the villages in Manipur. This is the case, for instance, with the cultivators of Vanchengphai in Tamenglong district. They depend entirely on rainfall for cultivation. In Nungsai-Chiru village of the Senapati district no irrigation facilities exist. However, in Hundung (Ukhrul), canals, streams, tanks and ponds are available for this purpose. In Tolloi (Ukhrul), irrigation is done only through channels by the gravitational method.

The major problems confronting agriculture in the universe area are as follows:

1. The soil is acidic in nature. This leads to low availability of phosphorus, which gets fixed, thus leading to low response to fertiliser. Due to heavy rains and consequent leaching of silica, there is high concentration of iron leading to iron toxicity at places.
2. High rainfall and humidity create a favourable environment for a wide range of pests, diseases and weeds. Similarly, climate creates problems in the storage of grains and hay-making etc. Double-cropping is non-existent. Undulating topography, hill slopes and varying altitudes also create problems for the agriculture.
3. *Jhum* cultivation is associated with many social and cultural patterns, customs and habits.
4. The dearth of proper technology as well as poor utilisation has greatly limited agricultural production. Appropriate technology to tackle with area-specific problems is still not fully available.

A good potential for horticulture exists. If properly taken care of, it can provide good supplementary occupation to villagers. The land, mostly in the backyard is used to grow papaya, guava, jackfruit, banana, 'yongchak' etc. mostly used in self-consumption. Horticulture, on a commercial scale has not yet been tried.

The present condition of the livestock may be termed as below average in the universe area. Milk is not popular among the tribals. The unproductive cows are slaughtered for beef. There is immense scope, however, for the development of piggery.

There are a few carpenters, wool-knitting units etc. and a saw mill in Tungjoy (Senapati). The village being basically non-market oriented, these carpenters and wool-knitters restricts themselves to meeting the demands of the villagers only. In Moltuk (Chandel) handicrafts exist in a small way. Carpentry, bamboo works and blacksmithy come as subsidiary sources of income in Parbung, Lungthulien and Senvon (Churachandpur). The income is highly variable and is directly proportional to the interest taken by the government agencies. The articles produced by the cane and bamboo works in Thanlon (Churachandpur) and mats, baskets, winnowing fans, bamboo curtains, sieves, *murhas*, chairs etc.

Promotion of agro-based industries is a must in this area as it would make decentralised planning a reality and thereby help in formulating a plan strategy based on local resource endowments and felt needs of the people in the area. It would promote local entrepreneurship, generate employment, arrest mindless migration to urban areas and also check concentration of economic power through diffusion of the ownership of means of production.

The study area is marked by low credit absorption capacity, lack of banking habit among the people and overall unsatisfactory law and order situation. The recovery of the loan advances is only in the vicinity of 6 per cent. Hence banks have adopted a rather cautious approach to lending and have lost zeal and initiative. The banks have perforce to finance IRDP only under obligation. Bank dealing is confined by and large to non-tribal groups. As the credit needs are of unproductive purposes, the possibility of getting loans from either banks or cooperatives diminishes. Therefore, the money-lender flays a crucial role. In the past, DWCRA has not been implemented properly because some years back the money was used by the villagers for getting electricity connection/paying electricity bills. DWCRA requires a sincere monitoring and regular flow of credit by the banks. The women's groups should be educated not to spend the money on feasts/festivals/electricity connections, rather they should take up some income generating activities which can give employment to other villagers.

One of the basic pre-requisites of poverty eradication is reorientation of agricultural relations so that ownership of land is shared by a larger section of population. In Tangpijol, the land ownership pattern is customary in nature and entire village land is vested in the chief. The Manipur Land Reforms and Land Revenue Act does not extend to hill areas and unless this Act is extended there is no question of land reforms. There is no incentive to the individual farmer for making any improvement on land or for taking up modern technology. It is difficult to obtain long-term or short-term loan as the farmer cannot offer his land for security. The shifting nature of cultivation and absence of individual land ownership has a direct bearing on poverty alleviation programmes.

There is a growing tendency among the tribals to send their children to the main land for higher education. Further many tribals have realised the importance of movable assets like livestock and poultry, which can be their own.

The villages have excellent potential in the areas of horticulture and animal husbandry. These need to be tapped to improve the economy of the village.

Development of forests is another means by which the villages having forest cover can have greater economic growth. Tree plantation for timber and fire-wood in the vast private and common village lands will bring prosperity in the future.

If the villages are electrified, power supply can be used for powerlooms, fruit processing, bamboo chipping and paper rolling industries.

Local resources may have to be tapped in a meaningful manner to increase employment avenues. Small units of bamboo chipping, or of preparing pineapple juice etc. are feasible as a plenty of both bamboos and pineapples are available locally.

3. Tripura

Tribals in Tripura do not stay in a village kind of human habitation in the traditional sense of the term as applicable in the plains areas. Instead, they live in closely knit, mostly single community human congregation called *Paras* which are remarkable different from the villages. These *paras* have several distinguishing features such as high mobility on account of *jhumming*, inherent desire of seclusion from urban cultures, self-administration etc. Majority of the *paras* were set up by different Roajas (heads/choudharies) and they derive their names from these Roajas. The age of their setting up varies from 15 years to 100 years back. Majority of the *paras* are either in reserve or protected forests or on Khas land. Most of them are having single community either Peang or Jamatia or Noatia etc.

Agriculture is the mainstay of Tripura's economy, paddy being the principal crop. It is cultivated twice a year in a flat land. The paddy of April/August is *Aush*, that of August-November is called *Aman* and that of December-March is called *Bora*. *Jhumming* or shifting cultivation is practiced in the tribal pockets of the State.

Nevertheless, the agricultural output has not been, over a period of time, in consonance with an increase in demand. An increase in agricultural output has been offset by a sharp rise in demand resulting from the growth of population and the desire of the urban people for a better life.

About 76 per cent of the people directly depend on agriculture for their livelihood and 67.48 per cent of the total workers are engaged in farming, shifting as well as settled. About 70 per cent of the State revenue is also earned from agriculture. The total area of the State is 10,43,696 hectares. Only little more than 20 per cent of it is sown with crops while about 60 per cent is classified as forestland. Uncultivated and fallow land cover about 20,000 hectares and most of it is in fact under permanent pastures and grazing lands, much of which have been overgrazed.

The cultivable land in the State can broadly be divided into two categories, viz. *lunga* land and *tilla* land. The former is a plain tract normally located between two hillocks and the latter is undulating and sloping land situated on highlands. The *lunga* land is already under the plough while the *tilla* land is partly under the area of the *jhumiyas* and is partly being reclaimed for plough cultivation. About 40 per cent of the total land of Tripura is made up of valley basins, plain tracts, mid-uplands. Most of it is found in the West Tripura district.

The area irrigated in Durgapur (North Tripura) is 31.4 hectares which is only 5.3 per cent of the total area and 6 per cent of the net sown area. In Lebachhara (South Tripura), most of the land is under rainfed cultivation with single cropping irrigation facilities in Chenchuria (West Tripura) are quite poor. The facilities included a deep tubewell constructed by the Government and a Cherra (small stream) passing through the village.

The average yield of low variety paddy per acre in Kanchan Bari (North Tripura) is 25 maunds. The price per maund is Rs. 80. Hence returns per acre is Rs. 2,000 out of which Rs. 805 goes to inputs. In case of HYV paddy, the production per acre is 1800 kg so the returns per acre are Rs. 3600. The cost involved is Rs. 1100. Hence net profit per acre is Rs. 2500.

In Holakhet (South Tripura), apart from paddy, the production levels of potato also are in excess of the village demand.

The area under paddy in Chenchuria accounts for 77 per cent of the gross area of 790.576 hectares followed by area under 'Mesta' (21%). The area under vegetables, oilseeds, fruit orchards and rubber account for 3 per cent of the gross cultivated area only.

Due to lack of irrigation and good quality of seeds, the production of wheat, pulses and mustard is quite low and unprofitable. There is a scope to increase the productivity of these crops by adopting modern technology.

There is enormous scope for improving irrigation facilities in the villages through the provision of seasonal bandhs and irrigation channels.

Livestock if developed properly will go a long way in reducing the pressure on agriculture. In fact, it is the only way to reduce poverty in the area as otherwise the area does not hold much promise. With large scale demand, marketing is no problem.

Livestock development combined with horticulture will definitely lead to the emergence of a truly mixed farming in the State.

Rural industries in the surveyed villages of all the three districts of Tripura include weaving, cane and bamboo work and certain miscellaneous industries.

The Manipuries in Durgapur (North Tripura) are engaged in weaving which is a traditional pursuit. Weaving is done by the Manipuries for meeting their own needs but there are some families which are selling the cloths in the market also. The common products are bed-sheet, towel, pachra etc. With necessary official support, weaving may become a good economic activity. There are about 100 weavers in Kanchanbari (North Tripura). In June 1990, the Tripura Handloom and Handicraft Development Corporation, a Public Sector undertaking of the Government of Tripura, set up a weaving centre, to impart training to women interested in learning afresh or developing the skills they already possessed. There are two schemes of the Rural Development Department to assist tribal weavers in supply of yarn at 75 per cent subsidy and supply of free yarn. The non-tribals are assisted by the Industries Department in upgrading their pit loom. Daily earnings of a weaver range from Rs. 9 to 15 depending on the skill.

This is a vanishing skill in Lachuchhara because of low returns despite hard labour.

Handicrafts are a part and parcel of the tribal Iife. All tribal families in Gandachera (South Tripura) produce some kind of handicraft. By and large, the handicrafts produced are textile, basket, wood-work, cane and bamboo articles, dari and so on. Most of their own garments are produced by them. Many of the articles produced are sold in the nearby market. Birchandra Manu (South Tripura) has no industry except weaving.

The area under study is badly in need of financial assistance. Nonetheless, repayment position *vis-a-vis* Bank credit being tardy, it is neither forthcoming nor being channelised into meaningful pursuits.

Employment Generation Programmes (EGPs) have helped in mitigating rural poverty in Tripura to some extent. In lean seasons, people find it difficult to get employment. EGPs provide employment to the needy and also create some durable community assets in the process. The Government has been able to make positive impact by providing gainful employment to the people, creating rural infrastructure and providing basic amenities to the people.

The assets created under the JRY are relatively durable in nature as compared to the other employment generation programme SREP as there is sufficient provision for the material component in the JRY. SREP also has been effective in meeting the employment needs of the poorer sections of the village in lean seasons.

In the uncultivable, amenable areas, rubber plantations can be taken up under the technical guidance of the Tripura Rehabilitation Plantation Corporation (TRPC). Due to the lesser gestation period required and the long productive life, it is most suited to the tribal people.

Sericulture activities can be taken up in suitable pockets on an experiment basis, to begin with.

Due to indiscriminate felling, the forests cover has gone down drastically in the recent years. Afforestation under the employment generation programmes, viz. NREP, SREP etc. be taken up with fuel, firewood and timber plants.

The large scale immigration of displaced persons has so changed the demographic profile of the State that the Bengalis now outnumber the tribals. This demographic change has led to the intensification of the pressure on lands. The lands of the tribal people are also being alienated to the Bengali settlers. It cannot be disputed that the interests of the tribals have been affected by the settlement of the refuse in the State on a large scale. At this moment when the tribals have been showing much interest in settled wet rice cultivation in place of shifting cultivation, the non-availability of adequate amount of valley lands (*Lunga*) has emerged as the biggest constraint. It is also alleged in certain quarters that the development expenditure meant for the tribal people exclusively have been diverted to the area where benefits accrue mainly to the non-tribals. Thirdly, as the Bengali settlers are generally more advanced culturally, they naturally dominate over the tribal people in political, social and economic fields.

Women enjoy a very respectable position in the Tripura society. They do contribute to the family income by day labour and by weaving of bamboo baskets etc. They get equal wages as men for doing day labour. The women cover their head with sari while talking to the elders, but do not practice parda system at all. There is coeducation in the school. The girls are given the same food as their brothers.

People do not follow their religious customs very diligently. The Hindus do not follow many of the rituals as their counterparts follow in the mainland. In fact there are very few temples in the sample universe. The Manipuri community has a hall, for instance, in Ichabpur village (Pakhirbada sample area), which they use as a temple. The Muslims do not have many rituals after birth or death of a person. Except for very aged men, nobody has the typical Muslim appearance. Nobody has beard or the tuft of hair under the chin or wears the typical Muslim cap. The women do not wear purda. They are dressed in the villages under study.

4. Nagaland

In the light of the turbulent history of the State a socio-economic study reveals unique characteristics in this area. The village economy is an agricultural one. The traditional system of leadership and ownership and control of land continues to hold force to this day. Generally, there is a little economic inequality.

Absolute poverty is not to be seen anywhere. The poorest of the poor has enough to eat and live. The standard of living of the villagers is on the whole quite high. Within the last two decades or so, much development has been achieved in road network, water supply, electricity supply, health care and education. However, much more yet remains to be done. Corruption and nepotism are the bane of the society and have come to stay.

Traditionally, Naga villages have been autonomous almost insular socio-political units. With the establishment of the modern political system consisting of a relented legislature and assembly constituencies, as also the present facilities for transport and communication, this insularity is being eroded. However, the village still retains, to a large extent, the decisive say in internal matters. Every landless family was allotted a plot by the Government and the family managed to build its house on it. There are 564 households. The main building materials in use are timber, bamboo, mud and plaster for the walls, thatch or more often CGI sheets for the roof and mud plaster or wooden planks for the floor. A few of the villagers have built RCC houses. Only about 50-60 houses still have thatched roots. Barring the RCC and Assam type houses, others are self-constructed.

Average yield of rice is reported to be about 7 to 8 quintals per acre: The pattern of land distribution in Nagaland in general, but in Angami areas in particular, is probably the best and the most egalitarian existing anywhere in India. There are no landless poor and no agricultural labourers. Everyone owns the house and the land he lives in and works on. In addition, if anyone is willing to cultivate any more land, he can utilise the community land for the purpose. The rich people who are large landholders also lease out land to those who do not have enough, but the rents are nominal. Tradition normally determines the values of land, which is, oriented to status rather than productivity and paid rents are determined entirely by tradition. No doubt, there are inequalities of income and standards of living, but there has been till now, very little accumulation for investment and the productive system has remained almost static over a very long time.

Rice is mixed with maize, chillies, potatoes, squash, sorghum and some varieties of oil seeds. All this is done by *jhum* cultivation. The *jhum* cycle is now 8 years long, i.e. they start working in jungle at the same place, which was worked eight years ago. Nobody has ventured to do Panikheti partly because of lack of sufficient water sources. No initiative for construction of water harvesting structures has been seen and perhaps that would lead to some structural difficulties within the village. There is a kind of vicious circle in the sense that water sources are required for terrace cultivation to be possible but the very fact of *jhumming* leads to lack of permanent attachment to any particular piece of land. This precludes any effort for water harvesting structures catering to any piece of land. Further *jhumming* having been the practice since time immemorial and people have a strong disinclination to any change. Added to all this is the fact that terrace cultivation would mean immense hard work at the beginning.

Two styles of agriculture are practiced, namely terrace rice cultivation and *jhum* or dry rice cultivation. Unlike other Naga tribes, the Angamis and the Chakessangs have been practicing terrace cultivation since immemorial.

From the rivulets and water splashes, the main sources of irrigation, channels of enormous length are dug to carry water and overflow the terraces. Bamboo pipes sometimes serve as supplementary irrational means down the slopes where terraces are located.

Land ownership, its classification and measurement is very difficult in Nagaland. No cadastral survey has been done in the past. Thus there are no authentic data on the land ownership system, landuse pattern, tenure and tenancy pattern. The culture system is based on traditions, which in turn are governed by the customary law.

Almost all Naga ladies know how to weave their *meghla* and shawl and hence do the same at home. The loom used is an ancient one. It is made of bamboo. However the produce generally finds a market only within the State. The market for Naga traditional handicraft has never been explored. One of the factors which makes weaving and spinning products very expensive. The loom used is traditional and inefficient — practically no improvement has been made in its design over the years. Each tribe in Nagaland has a distinctive shawl.

People are not vegetarian by way of habit. While pork and rice forms the staple diet, almost every other meat is also considered edible. Generally each house has a small number of pigs and hens. Some piglings and calves are bought from the plains of the Assam. The cows generally yield very little milk and 3 to 4 litres/day would be the average. A Government Veterinary Doctor visits the village from time to time.

Nagas believe and observe cleanliness. For this they have used the natural and animal source also. The incident of malaria is low, the infant mortality is less than the national average and other tropical diseases are unheard.

In northern part of the State, sanitary conditions like pucca toilets, drainage etc. would have to be improved.

The medical facilities available to an average Naga are of a very low standard. There is a strong need to open new health centres in the State.

The village society consists of family units, which are grouped into several exogamous units known as clans. The clan is spread over several villages of the tribe, but the members of a particular clan living in a village are added to belong to one *khel*.

Though much cohesion exists even at the village level and community feeling is very strong, the clan is the unit which is most important. The prestige of a man partially depends on the prestige of the clan and on the reverse a person, through accomplishments contribute to the honour of the clan or spoils name by negative acts. During life-cycle rites like birth, marriage and death, the clan as a whole shoulders the responsibility through immediate relatives obviously do it to a greater degree.

Naga society is highly egalitarian as is evident from the absence of hierarchical caste structure as also any rules or regulations advocating discrimination to any group of people living in the village, even the Non-Christian participate in the social and political affairs of the village.

Panchayati Raj system as applicable to the rest of the Country is not existing in Nagaland However, the Angami Society has been traditionally a very democratic society. Grass roots democracy at the village level is truly visible in Kohima district. In Nagaland traditional village councils have been given a legal sanction by passing of a legislative act, called the Village Area Councils Act under which the village functions. They lay down rules and see that they are followed to settle disputes arising among individuals and families in the village.

The administrative functions of the village council include liaison with the district administration, construction and maintenance of community assets, planning the use of resources such as land, forests, water sources etc., that belong to the community as a whole, and management of the village fund. The traditional functions of the village council includes representing the village in tribal meets, arbitration in internal disputes, performing the required role in feasts and festivals, etc. There is a judicial board, which is part of the council, and this board decides cases of civil and criminal nature under the unwritten customary law.

The principle of administration of the village states, the heredity system and the divine nature attached with the kingship/chieftainship, the representative character of the village councils etc. are basically same in all the Naga tribes. However, in application of actual laws in the day-to-day administration, there are variations from tribe to tribe.

The Village Development Board (VDB) of Nagaland is perhaps the only one of its kind in India. It is a unique experiment in bringing about development in the rural areas of the State. At the heart of the VDB is the policy of grass roots planning and development. In a nutshell, money is given to the villagers to be used in development schemes selected and undertaken by the villagers themselves.

Besides grain banks, VDBs also run piggeries. The VDB buys pigs out of its funds. These pigs are then given to households to be looked after. When the pigs multiply, the litter is equally divided between the VDB and the household. The VDB then distributes the piglets, thereby covering more households. It should be noted here that the households are responsible for looking after the pigs. This is indeed a novel way of increasing the income of farmers.

The VDB also runs fisheries and weaving centres and the produce are sold in the local market.

The effectiveness of VDBs varied from village to village. Some villages showed greater interest in the activities of the VDBs. Some VDBs are more successful in the more backward villages, that is, there was an inverse relationship between the success of a VDB and the level of advancement of a village. This was probably because the more advanced villages had less need for basic development schemes. However, this should not be taken as a rule. Indeed there were advanced villages such as Jakhama whose VDBs were doing extremely well. All said and done, perhaps the success of VDBs depends more on the Secretary and the members than anything else.

C. ASHOKVARDHAN, *I.A.S.*

PROFILE OF THE CONTRIBUTORS

Professor P. S. Datta*

Professor Parthasarathi Datta was the Vice Chairman/Coordinator of Land Reforms Unit, Lal Bahadur Shastri National Academy of Administration. He was also Joint Director of ICSSR, North Eastern Regional Centre, Shilong. During his career as an eminent Academician, he has been associated with many Institutions and organizations. His in-depth knowledge and keen interest on developmental issues of North-East region are supported by several publications, projects undertaken by the author. Presently, he is deeply involved in research, publications and other academic activities.

Shri Ajay Sinha*

Shri Ajay Sinha was working as a Research Associate in the Land Reforms Unit, Lal Bahadur Shastri National Academy of Administration. Later on he has also worked as Research Officer in the Village Study Unit of Lal Bahadur Shastri National Academy of Administration. He has several publication on Rural Development, Poverty and Land Reforms. Presently he is posted as Assistant Project Officer in UNICEF, India.

Shri Gorky Chakravarty*

Shri Gorky Chakravarty was a Research Associate in the Land Reforms Unit, Lal Bahadur Shastri National Academy of Administration. He has contributed significantly towards the Research activities of Land Reforms Unit. Later on he joined as a Lecturer in Economics.

---

* Implies he/she is one of the three authors, who have prepared the State paper on Assam.

Dr. C. Ashokvardhan

Dr. C. Ashokvardhan is an IAS Officer of 1980 Batch and belongs to Bihar cadre. During his career as Indian Administrative Officer, he has been posted in several important Government Departments. Prior to joining Indian Administrative Services, he was teaching in Colleges as a Lecturer in Political Science. He is the author of many books and articles pertaining to issues on Land Reforms, Police Reforms, Agriculture, Rural Development etc. At present he is the Additional Member, Board of Revenue, Government of Bihar.

Shri Kamal K. Sharma

Shri Kamal K. Sharma, belongs to the 1980 Batch of the Indian Audit and Account Service. He has worked as Deputy Accountant General, Joint Director and Director of Audit in Nagaland, Defence and Scientific Departments respectively. He was also teaching Financial Management in Lal Bahadur Shastri National Academy of Administration. He has written a number of articles for leading newspaper and journals.

1

ASSAM

AJAY KUMAR SINHA, GORKY CHAKRABORTY, CHANDANA BHATTACHARYA AND **P. S. DATTA**

1. INTRODUCTION

The Ahoms, called Assam as *mungdun chun kham* which meant a country of *golden gardens*. Assam is still known for its natural beauty. The lush green surroundings, the mountains, the valleys and the sweet flowing rivers make the State an exotic habitat for the nature loving people. The State is broadly divided into three regions, the Brahmaputra Valley, the Barak Valley and the Hill Region. The mighty river Brahmaputra divides the State into two halves, with the Northern areas and the adjoining places included in the Brahmaputra Valley whereas the Southern part is called as the Barak Valley. The hill region occupies a location in between these two. The hill population can be divided into hill tribes including Karbi, Dimasa-Kachari, Rengma Naga, Zeme Naga, Kuki, Hmar and Garo; while the plain tribes are mainly the Bodo-Kachari, Mishing, Burman, Lalung, Rabha, Deori, Kachari, Hajong and Mech. The official language of the State is Assamese which also happens to be a connecting thread between people speaking various languages and dialects (from time immemorial). The golden age of Assamese literature may be said to have begun during the Coch King Naranarayana and all great patrons of learning including Sankardeva initiated the *Vaishnav* movement in Assam that in a sense initiated the process of concretising the emergence of a composite Assamese society. It was during this period that the process of bringing the tribal within the feudal fold began. But in the Ahom dominated areas the dominant trend remained based on the semi-tribal legacy and the rulers maintained it till the British occupation. It was partly due to this clash of ideas regarding whether to assimilate the tribes into the mainstream Assamese society (and thereby into the process of cultivation), the *Vaishnavite* preacher Shankardeva was perceived as a thread to the Ahom rulers and was expelled from the Ahom territory. He took refuge in the court of Naranarayana and continued to further his mission. It is a fact that feudalism had a stunted growth in Western Assam, encompassing only the upper strata while in Eastern part the system was not even given a fair trial.

Assam is located in the heart of the country's North-Eastern region. A region, that is also known as the Land of the *Seven Sisters* (Assam, Meghalaya, Arunachal Pradesh, Manipur, Mizoram, Nagaland and Tripura). These States are linked with the rest of the country through a narrow corridor in the northern region of West Bengal. While Assam provides the corridor for the other six hill States of the North-Eastern region.

Assam occupies an area of 78,523 sq. km. which is 2.4 per cent of the total land area of India. The State may be divided into two physical divisions – plains and hills. The plain division can be further divided into two – the Brahmaputra Valley and the Barak Valley. The hill division comprises of two autonomous hill districts – Karbi Anglong and North Cachar hills (as per Sixth Schedule to Constitution of India). There are 23 districts and 45 sub-divisions in the State.

Assam is more or less a hilly area in between parallel ranges of hills. Due to the presence of hills, plains and river valleys, the general appearance of the State is very picturesque. In this State, 5 micro-regions have been delineated on the basis of topography, geology, soils, forest and climate. These regions are:

1. Western Brahmaputra Valley covering the districts of undivided Goalpara and Kamrup;

2. Central Brahmaputra Valley covering the districts of undivided Darrang and Nagaon;
3. Eastern Brahmaputra Valley covering the districts of undivided Lakhimpur, Dibrugarh and Sibsagar;
4. Cachar plain covering Cachar district; and
5. Karbi Anglong and North Cachar hills covering the districts of Karbi Anglong and North Cachar Hills.

Physiographically, Western Brahmaputra Valley is a unique region. In its northern boundary lie the folded ranges of the Himalayas and towards its south lies the senile Shillong plateau. This part of the region has dense forests, tall grasses and middle plain is intensively used for cultivation. The Brahmaputra banks and *char* lands have swampy vegetation. The region is agriculturally rich. Forest resources are also immense. In this region, industrial development, however, has been confined in Kamrup district. Guwahati city, because of its central location, has been attracting various industries including oil refinery (in the public sector of course).

Central Brahmaputra Valley covers the district of Nagaon and Darrang. Climatically, Nagaon has the lowest rainfall in the State. The deficiency of rainfall calls for irrigation for efficient agriculture. The soils of the Nagaon district is fertile. Rich sal forests abound on the southern foothills. Kaziranga National Park is located in Sibsagar district adjoining with north-eastern tract of Nagaon district. The central part of Nagaon district replenished by flood silts, support rich rice crops. The low lying bowl shaped plain also produces jute in abundant quantities. Tea is again a widespread industry in Darrang district.

Eastern Brahmaputra Valley covers the undivided districts of Sibsagar, Dibrugarh and Lakhimpur. Physiographically, the greater part of the valley is mainly a flat alluvial plain which is formed by the Brahmaputra Valley rivers and its tributaries such as the Subansiri and the Dhansiri rivers. The northern part falls under Lakhimpur district and is known as foothills plain. The Brahmaputra Valley flows through the Valley. The general climate of the area is damp and cool. The soil is mostly alluvial silt although the fringe bordering the hills contains some diluvium with grit and pebbles. Economically, this is the most important region in Assam. It has all the oil fields and some of the important coal mines of the State. As the soil is fertile, rice and sugarcane are abundantly grown in this region. Industrially, the area is fairly well developed.

Cachar plain covers the undivided Cachar district. This plain is bordered in the north by the North Cachar Hills and Jaintia hills along with Meghalaya border, in the east by the Manipur hills and in the south by the Mizo hills. The region is a sort of a heterogeneous land composed of high hills, low lands and level plains. The climate is characterised by excessive humidity and trapped by the hills on almost every side. Flood is a chronic problem. Agriculturally, the Cachar plain is a rich one. The low lying areas are used for jute growing. Though industrially the region is not so developed.

Karbi Anglong and North Cachar Hill regions covers the districts of Karbi Anglong and North Cachar Hill. Physiographically, the region is described as a mass of rugged hilly area except some plains formed by the Jamuna and the Kopili rivers that fall under Karbi Anglong district. Because of the altitude, this area is characterised by coolness, generally high humidity throughout the year and abundant rainfall. The majority of the population is Scheduled Tribes who practice shifting cultivation. Limestone is found in Karbi Anglong. Industrially, this region is underdeveloped in more than the term 'underdeveloped' can denote.

Demographic Profile

Assam has a population of 2,22,94,562, according to the 1991 census, estimated rate of growth during 1971-91 being 2.13038 per cent. The average density of population was 254 per sq. km. as against the all India average of 211 in 1981 and increased upto 284 in 1991. A notable aspect of the State's population is that till 1961, the State had a lower density of population than that of the country, but the position reversed during the subsequent two decades. Another notable feature of the state's population has been its faster population growth compared to the rest of the country. Demographic profile of all the districts of Assam is depicted in Table 1.1. Decennial growth rate (Percentage) of Assam was 30.05 (worked out from projected population) in 1971-81 and it became 35.86 in 1981-91. All India figure for the two decades was 25 and 23.50 respectively.

Table 1.1 : Rural-Urban Population by District in Assam, 1991

	State Population 1991			Percentage Growth Rate 1981-91	
District	Total	Rural	Urban	Rural	Urban
Assam	22294562	19823674	2470888	48.65	91.66
Dhubri	1325653	1164012	161641	53.60	73.40
Kokrajhar	796880	746198	50682	71.20	197.08
Bongaigaon	806472	732639	73833	62.63	84.68
Goalpara	661801	613602	48199	49.12	118.74
Barpeta	1382715	285455	97260	42.80	41.51
Kalbari	1012608	989369	23239	48.75	47.16
Kamrup	1987662	1339393	648269	40.07	158.65
Darrang	1286633	1222679	63954	52.38	98.80
Sonitpur	1418484	1314914	103570	57.51	44.71
Lakhimpur	749675	701125	48550	53.93	91.52
Dhemaji	472183	463357	8826	100.79	—
Karigaon	640379	605758	34618	42.90	—
Kagaon	1892087	1686493	205594	48.94	72.28
Golaghat	801740	753821	47919	52.24	67.77
Jorhat	868445	735920	132525	29.38	54.09
Sibsagar	895112	830301	64811	35.25	60.29
Dibrugarh	1038090	856600	181490	33.40	58.54
Tinsukia	963176	804772	158404	48.63	40.12
Karbi Anglong	655415	585129	79286	58.50	589.08
North Cachar Hill	149346	115140	4206	62.51	558.19
Karimganj	825551	765438	60113	46.04	3.69
Bhilakandi	448506	414400	34106	45.14	53.77
Cachar	1215952	1097159	118793	42.86	113.90

Source : Census of India, 1991, Series I.

According to the 1971 census, Scheduled Castes and Scheduled Tribes are 6.24 per cent and 10.99 per cent respectively in the State. The proportion of scheduled castes is slightly more in urban areas than in rural areas. The overwhelming majority of the Scheduled Tribes is found in rural areas. Naturally Scheduled Tribes constitute the majority of population in the hill districts of Karbi Anglong and North Cachar hills.

As per the 1971 census, 28.15 per cent of the total population of Assam were literate. This rose to 43.20 per cent in 1991 provisional figure. Literacy rates of males and females in 1971 census were 36.68 per cent and 18.63 per cent respectively. However, these increased to 50.62 per cent and 35.18 per cent respectively in 1991 census. The literacy rate was 25.24 per cent for rural area as against 58.29 per cent for urban areas in 1971. Corresponding figures in 1991 was found to be 39.96 per cent and 69.19 per cent respectively. If these figures are compared with All India, Assam would project better picture.

Socio-Economic Profile

Assam is predominantly a rural economy. Cultivation is the most important use of land in this State. Agriculture is the backbone of the State's economy and meets the food requirement. However, agriculture depends mostly on geographical factors and rainfall. The method of cultivation in the plain districts of Assam is more or less similar to all India pattern. Most of the hill tribes practice a system of cultivation known as *jhumming*. Tribes clean the jungle in the slopes with axes, daos and hoes and burn the cuttings. The most striking feature of the agriculture of Assam is its high productivity. It is mainly due to the unique fertility of the Brahmaputra Valley which is in fact the granary of Assam. In Assam, rice and jute are main crops which are cultivated generally during the rainy season. Tea is another major crop. Other crops are rape, mustard, sugarcane, tobacco etc. Maize is more popular in the hill districts. Sugarcane is another crop grown in every district of Assam. Sibsagar district has high production of sugarcane. Leading jute producing districts are Nagaon, Goalpara, Kamrup and Darrang. Tea is mostly produced in the undivided districts in upper Assam (Sibsagar and Dibrugarh).

Assam has rich mineral resources. The known minerals are petroleum, coal and limestone. Assam has abundant of forest resources that naturally play an important role in State's economy. There are both minor and major forest produces of the

State. Among the major forest produces, mention may be made of timber and fuel. Besides these, there are varieties of minor forest produces such as cane, thatch, bamboo, agar wood, kutha, medicinal plants, ivory, rhino horn, minor minerals like gravels etc. Prior to 1984-85, forest sector contributed significantly to the Assam's coffer.

Industrially, Assam is not so developed. Industrial development is mainly handicapped by its isolation from the rest of India and weak communication network. As a result, Assam has very few industries of significance, other than the production of tea and refining of oil. There is a bright future in agro-based and forest resource-based industries besides the enormous vast scope for plywood industry, saw mills, jute and sugar mills in Assam.

Economic engagement of the people of Assam is understandably agro-based and large percentage of population is involved in cultivation. Assam has a large labour force, of them, mostly are immigrants or migrants. Figures of proportion of main worker to total population of 1991 is presented below. According to this figure, 51.14 per cent of the people are cultivators and 12.89 per cent workers are working as agricultural labourers. However, other workers constitute nearly 34 per cent of the total main workers who are engaged in unorganised activities like fishing, plantations and other small household activities. According to the 1971 census, 55.86 per cent of the workers were cultivators and 9.92 per cent agricultural labourers. This comparative data has one striking thing to project: the people involved in cultivation dwindled over the time but number of agricultural labourers increased in last 20 years. This increase in proportion again justifies the overall increase in the labour force. The decrease in cultivation might be due to various factors like lack of irrigation facilities, inputs, migration towards cities, Government's apathy and decline in output – all of which directly or indirectly may raise questions about the policy-capacity and intervention-capacity of the Government at all levels.

Table 1.2 : Proportion of Main Workers to Total Population in Assam, 1991

(Per cent)

Workers	Total			Rural			Urban		
	Total	Male	Female	Total	Male	Female	Total	Male	Female
Main Workers	31.70	47.55	14.57	31.86	47.28	15.40	30.43	49.64	7.54
Cultivators	51.24	51.20	51.41	56.86	57.72	54.02	4.09	3.85	5.98
Agricultural Labourers	12.89	12.72	13.49	14.18	14.22	14.07	2.08	1.90	3.57
Household Ind., Manufacturing, Processing & Servicing Industries	2.51	1.91	4.66	2.29	1.66	4.36	4.30	3.59	9.90
Other Workers	33.36	34.18	30.44	25.67	26.40	27.55	89.53	90.66	80.61

Source : Census of India, 1991, Series I.

2. SOCIAL STRUCTURE

Population and Demographic Structure

There has been a tremendous increase of population in Assam during the last 4 decades. Phenomenal increase in population has also been observed in rural Assam where 88 per cent of the total population live.

Table 1.3 : Demographic Structure in Surveyed Villages

Sl. No.	Name of Villages	Year	Population			Sex Ratio	Family size (Ave.)	No. of Households
			Total	Male	Female			
1.	Heerbond Pt - II (Cachar)	1991	700	360	340	944	6	148
2.	Pangram Pt - II (Cachar)	1988	692	390	302	774	5	127
3.	Nowbaisha (Jorhat)	1988	4221	2021	2200	1088	9	520
4.	Bokelmajh Gaon (Dibrugarh)	1988	4276	2035	2241	1101	8	421

Contd. ...

Sl. No.	Name of Villages	Year	Population			Sex Ratio	Family size (Ave.)	No. of House-holds
			Total	Male	Female			
5.	Khajuabil (Darrang)	1990	1756	1236	520	420	7	246
6.	Da-Parbatia (Sonitpur)	1991	4000	2013	1987	987	8	398
7.	Nam-Deuri (Jorhat)	1991	1231	620	611	982	8	124
8.	Sadarashi (Karimganj)	1991	2497	1301	1196	919	6	425
9.	Bhakatpara (Darrang)	1991	691	362	329	911	5	135
10.	Mirigaon (Jorhat)	1992	1123	552	571	1034	8	128
11.	Sahan (Kamrup)	1988	1180	637	543	852	7	164
12.	Changmai (Dibrugarh)	1992	1100	574	526	918	6	125
13.	Madhusulmiri Pt.-II (Dhubri)	1991	3451	1800	1651	918	7	443

Source : Village Study Reports, LBSNAA, 1988-92.

Dhubri, Barpeta, Sonitpur, Nagaon, Dibrugarh and Cachar are most populous than the districts of Hailakandi, Dhemaji, North Cachar hill and Karbi Anglong. But since last decade, North Cachar hill and Karbi Anglong too have shown a high population growth rate especially in their urban areas.

Issues and Comments

Demographic data of the selected villages is presented in Table 1.3. It is difficult to project the trend of the population growth as the data for previous years are not available. However, if one tries to understand the villages as an entity, it is necessary to have information about the number of people inhabiting a village. A village like Pangram Pt. II has smaller number of people because of its geographical locations and hilly tracts. Other demographic indicators also show skewed distribution. Sex ratio of the same village is found to be 774 (1988) as against state's average of 925 (1991). According to the report, people of Pangram Pt. II have more attraction towards sons than daughter. Again there are other villages like Nowbaisha and Mirigaon which have sex ratio exceeding the state's average. Average sex ratio of the selected villages is found to be 911. If we study the trend, Assam's sex ratio declined from 908 in 1921 to 876 in 1961 which improved to 901 in 1971 and further rose to 925 is 1991.

Assam's population pattern projects heterogeneity in character. This heterogeneous character has been accentuated by large scale immigration into Assam. For historical reasons Assam experienced highest net immigration in 1911-21 and 1921-31 and again during 1951-61. The migrants may be of four categories:

(a) Labourers in the tea gardens from basically the tribal belts of Bihar, U.P., Orissa and Rajasthan;
(b) Muslim agricultural settlers from erstwhile East Bengal and subsequently East Pakistan and Bangladesh;
(c) Hindu refugees from East Pakistan; and
(d) Immigrants from other parts of the country.

The fertile land of Assam attracted large Muslim agriculturists from the adjoining province of erstwhile Bengal from the very beginning of the present century. This farmer migration led to the increase in the population of the villages. These settlers settled in all the four lower and central districts of Assam – Goalpara, Kamrup, Darrang and Nowgong. Today these same districts reportedly continue to have the highest concentration of Muslim population.

Since the partition of India, the influx of Hindu refugees from East Pakistan continued unabated to India, mainly to West Bengal, Assam and Tripura. Considerable number of these refugees belong to middle class Bengali Hindu community. This refugee population has spread over in all the districts of Assam. Cachar being on the border of Sylhet district, which went over to East Pakistan due to partition of India, has given shelter to a very large number of refugees who have come mainly from the Sylhet district.

Thus, around 85 lakhs immigrants settled permanently in Assam as per 1971 census. Such a huge immigrant population is a unique feature of the population composition of the State of

Assam which may partially explain the high growth rate of the population in the State.

Social Indicators

This section will review literacy, educational facilities and health parameters of the villages. Information of these indicators of the few selected villages is presented in Table 1.4. Status of these indicators are dealt separately.

Table 1.4 : Status of Literacy and Health in Villages covered

Sl. No.	Name of Village	Year	% of Literate	Educational Facilities			Health Facilities	
				No. of primary schools	No. of middle schools	No. of Teachers	No. of P.H.Cs	No of M.H.Cs
1.	Kharua (Nalbari)	1991	18.30	3	1	4	0	0
2.	Hearbond Pt -II (Cachar)	1992	21.43	1	1	6	0	0
3.	Jajori (Nagaon)	1988	40.00	1	0	2	3	0
4.	Pangram Pt -II (Cachar)	1988	37.00	1	3	8	1	0
5.	Kachu-arkas Pt-1 (Dhubri)	1988	28.00	1	2	9	1	1
6.	Bokelmajh Gaon (Dibrugarh)	1988	42.00	2	1	8	1	0
7.	Khajuabil (Darrang)	1990	37.00	2	1	4	-	-
8.	Nam-Deuri (Jorhat)	1991	44.70	2	1	5	1	0
9.	Jayantipur (Nalbari)	1991	35.00	2	1	10	0	0
10.	Sadarashi (Karim-ganj)	1991	40.00	2	2	-	1	0
11.	Marigaon (Jorhat)	1992	50.00	2	1	8	0	0
12.	Changmai (Dibrugarh)	1991	39.00	0	0	0	1	0

Source : Village Study Reports, LBSNAA, 1988-92.

Literacy is defined in the census as the ability to write and read in any language. According to 1991 census, rural literacy was observed to be 39.96 per cent. Male and female literacy in rural area was found to be 47.53 per cent and 31.88 per cent respectively. Compared to All India figure, Assam's literacy performance has been better. Even the rural Assam projects better literacy rate than the All India figure.

Literacy rates of the surveyed villages is indicated in Table 1.4. Villages of Jorhat indicate better literacy performance while villages in Cachar and Nalbari lagged behind in primary education where even in 1992, these villages have shown dismal performance with respect to primary education.

In 1971, the districts of Sibsagar, Cachar, Dibrugarh, Nowgong and Kamrup reported higher literacy percentages than that of the State while the N.C. Hills, Darrang, Goalpara, Mikir Hills and Lakhimpur district reported lower literacy percentage than all Assam figure. Thus, while Sibsagar district reported highest literacy (36.2), Lakhimpur district reported the lowest (16.56).

Issues and Comments

In terms of educational infrastructure, the villages are found to be more or less well equipped to impart primary and middle education. Except for Jagori in Nagaon district and Changmai in Dibrugarh district, all the surveyed villages have at least one primary school which imparts education upto class fifth standard. Interestingly, there are no separate schools for Harijans and untouchables. All the pupils, whether they belong to Scheduled Castes or Tribes attend the same school without any social discrimination. Buildings of the primary school are *Assam types* where wall is made of bricks upto 3 feet height above which is a bamboo mesh wall plastered from both sides with a thick layer of strong mortar. The average duration of school life is around 6-7 years. This is because of a high rate of dropouts. Students have to opt out from the schools mostly to help their parents in household activities. Few villages like Kuthori (Nagaon) have the privilege of housing public library which are run by local social organisation. The schools of the villages are also cultural centres where every year a number of cultural functions and sports meets are organised. Interestingly, villages of Assam do not have *Navodaya* schools for rural meritorious students.

Teacher-Pupil ratio is adverse in most of the schools. Less teachers are employed because of the shortage of fund and non-availability of competent and qualified teachers. Few villages have Adult Education Centres and ITIs.

Table 1.4 also indicates availability pattern of health infrastructure in some of the selected surveyed villages. Villages are the most neglected in terms of health infrastructure. 33 per cent of the surveyed villages do not have primary health centres (P.H.C.). The villagers generally have to travel more than 3-4 km. to reach the nearest P.H.C. or dispensaries. Maternity health centre (M.H.C.) are mostly unseen in the villages. Under the Minimum Needs Programme (M.N.P.), few sub-centres were opened in few villages but due to lack of infrastructure, these sub-centres remained closed or are striving to survive. P.H.Cs. are also not equipped with midwife and nurse and, therefore, the villagers generally rely on nearest Block hospital.

As on January 1, 1990, Assam reportedly had 111 hospitals with a 3482 bed capacity in rural areas while total number of P.H.Cs. and sub-centres functioning in Assam is 442 and population served per doctor was only 1:8550 (one of the lowest in comparison to the North-Eastern States).

Villagers generally suffer from water-borne diseases. Most such cases are seen during floods when the villagers have to depend entirely on flood waters for daily needs. Other common diseases prevalent are T.B., cholera, gastroenteritis, small pox, cancer and various types of flues. Even when there is no flood, the people use water from river or stagnant ponds inviting many a disease. Drainage facilities too are not at all upto the mark in the villages.

In villages, people also try and practice traditional methods of treatment and even till now evil spirits are supposed to be the cause of various diseases which are tried to be appeased by rituals and sacrifices.

Most of the houses in the villages are *Assam Type* houses with sloping roofs or non-RCC material to take care of excessive rains and earthquakes in this high rainfall and seismic area. Despite the above commonality, the dissimilarities between Scheduled Caste and non-Scheduled Caste houses are seen. The non-S.C. houses are roofed with asbestos sheets or corrugated iron sheets or tiles; the Scheduled Caste houses are roofed with grass or leaves or reeds or thatch wood or bamboo or mud. In the non-SC houses, the walls are made of burnt bricks and lime or cement while the SC houses have mud and straw walls. The floor of the non-SC houses are of bricks or stone or lime or even cement but the SC houses have mud flooring.

Social Stratification

Social organisation in the traditional Assamese village consisted of both castes and tribal groups. Social status of the tribal groups of people, who formed a major proportion of the Assamese population, was evaluated within the frame of Hindu hierarchical system. For these reasons, non-Hindu tribals too were considered as a part of the Hindu social structure.

Before 1826, Hinduism was widely known among the people but was not the accepted religion of the entire population. It was mostly through an evolutionary process that people began professing the Hinduism of Shakta or Vaishnavism varieties. The interaction between tribal animism and Hinduism led to the birth of a sort of a *Tantrik* form of Hinduism. *Tantrik* rituals centring around the temple Kamakshya became famous for magic as well as sacrifice and is still held in reverence by the villagers.

The *Varna* system and the related stratified order had a weak start in Assam. For one, Kshatriyas were not found in Assam while the protagonists of the *Varna* system contrived to treat Koches as Kshatriyas, the Kalitas were universally considered to be Aryan settlers and were accorded a high place in the social order. Because of a combination of reasons, caste system in Assam has been destined to be fairly flexible in comparison to rest of the country.

In the villages, the Assamese and the Bengalees are the two distinct linguistic communities with a number of other dialect-speaking groups. There are also Muslims with linguistic affinities to Assamese as well as Bengalees. The trading community of Rajasthan and the working force from Bihar, U.P. and Bengal are also found in the villages, though in a varying degree of numerical strength.

In rural Assam, there appears to have been a synthesis of the three religious traditions, the orthodox Hinduism (mainly *Saktaism*), *Vaishnavism* and tribalism. These three religious traditions have, in various ways, influenced the pattern of social stratification of rural Assam. However, tribalism in Assam underwent considerable transformation initially due to the influence of *Vaishnavism* and orthodox Hinduism and later, probably to a much lesser extent, by Christianity.

In 1961, 6.17 per cent of the total population in Assam were Scheduled Castes against all India figure of 14.69 per cent whereas 17.48 per cent of Assam's population were Scheduled Tribes against all India figure of 6.87 per cent in the same year that indicates that Assam had considerably less Scheduled Caste population and high Scheduled Tribe population. Within Assam, the Scheduled Caste population had concentrated in the plain division whereas the Scheduled Tribe population had, naturally concentrated in the Hill divisions. However, this scenario changed in the subsequent decades. In 1971, 6.24 per cent of population belonged to Scheduled Castes and 10.99 per cent belonged to Scheduled Tribes. In comparison to 1961, SC population remained almost the same whereas the Scheduled Tribes population reduced from 17.48 per cent to 10.99 per cent. Reorganisation of Assam and creation of smaller tribal States probably hold the clue to understand the reasons for decline in Assam's tribal population.

Issues and Comments

From the village study, only fragmented data were available on social stratification. Few villages like Heerbond Pt-II (Cachar district), Kharua (Nalbari district), Khajuabil and Bhaktapara

(Darrang district) and Bhelewguri (Nagaon district) have high tribal population with lesser Scheduled Caste population. Considerable percentage of Muslim population was also seen in Madhusalmeri Pt. II (Dhubri district), Heerbond Pt.II (Cachar district), Bokelmajh Gaon (Dibrugarh district) and Da-Parbatia (Sonitpur district). In fact, in Da-Parbatia village, Muslim population was observed to be 88 per cent – a very high figure in any standard.

Cultural Life

Social life in the villages generally centres around a family system which is paternal in character. There is today of course a discernible trend of switching over from joint family to single family system. *Dayabhaga system* generally holds good in the matters of inheritance and succession.

As in most other identical societies, in Assam too the pivot of the family system is marriage. A few important features of marriage in the villages, which may perhaps be generalised, are that infant marriage is unknown average age of men and women getting married is fairly high, and dowry system is not prevalent among the rural people. *Mehar* is, however, prevalent among Muslims. Monogamy is preferred.

The staple foods in the villages are rice and fish. Vegetables are scarce; tomato, brinjal, lemon are grown in the backyard. The *Tamul* is an addiction with the populace. Milk is almost absent in the diet because of poor breed of local cattle. Total prohibition of opium, *ganja* and *bhang* has been enforced in the villages (though they are not totally beyond the reach of the addicts in many parts of the State).

The social life in the village is replete with festivals. One of the important festivals which is traditionally celebrated in Assam is *Bihu. Rangali Bihu* is observed on the last day of *Chaitra* and first day of *Bohag* which is Assamese New Year's Day. The dance and music are the most important feature in this spring festival. The next in order of importance is *Bhogali Bihu* or *Magha Bihu*. It begins on last day of *Puh,* sometimes in the middle of January. And the last is *Kati Bihu* which falls on the last day of *Ahin* (October). A couple of other widely celebrated festivals are Biskarma *puja*, Kali *puja* and Durga *puja*. Muslim festivals are also celebrated in the villages with full gaiety.

One of the unique institutions around which the traditional, religious and cultural life of the villages vibrates is the *Namghar*. A legacy from Sri Sankerdev, *Namghar* is the community prayer hall and the meeting place of the villagers for observance of all the religious festivals. It keeps alive the spirit of co-operation and unity among the villagers. It also provides shelter for open theatre called the *Bhaona*.

In Assam's context one thing must be borne in mind that Assam's society is a poly-cultural society and hence the cultural traits found in Assam are very difficult to be located in any stereotype uniform culture-frame. Synthesis and accommodation are the key spirits to be remembered whenever any attempt is made to describe the cultural life in Assam.

3. AGRARIAN SCENARIO

Topography and Soil

Topography plays an important role in the evolution of any farming system. In Assam, it is found that areas with a variation in topography have hence helped evolve different farming systems. For example, in the hills, the tribal people use hill slopes through *jhumming* – a system of shifting form of cultivation. Some of the hill slopes are used for horticultural crops and forestry. In sub-mountain regions, having good drainage systems, tea gardens have flourished while low-lying areas are used with deep water for paddy, jute, pulses and mustard.

Topography of Brahmaputra Valley is by and large, characterised by alluvial plains interspersed with small hillocks in the western part of the State, particularly in the districts of Darrang, Kamrup and Goalpara. Cropping pattern of the valley appears to be generally dictated by the whims of Brahmaputra and its more than 50 tributaries. Barak Valley is characterised by rolling undulating topography with small hillocks and marshy low lands. The valley is again dependent on the behaviour patterns of river Kusaira and its tributaries flowing from and through both Mizoram in the south and North Cachar in the north.

The Brahmaputra happens to be the most important major river system in Assam and the valley consists of undivided districts of Dibrugarh, Lakhimpur, Sibsagar, Nowgong, Darrang, Kamrup and Goalpara while Barak is the major river system of the Surma or the Barak Valley consisting of the undivided Cachar district (reorganised under three districts as of now).

Soils of Assam may broadly be understood as under the following four categories :

(i) *New Alluvial Soil :* These are found in the riparian tracts. Being in the flood-prone plains of the Brahmaputra and the Barak and their tributaries, both big and small, these tracts are subject to recurrent flood, which carry annually large load of silt which gets deposited when the floods recede. These soils are sandy loamy or silty loamy in texture. These are less acidic than the older alluvial and are moderately rich in plant nutrients.

(ii) *Old Alluvial Soil :* The highlands in the plain districts of the Brahmaputra Valley which are not victims of recurrent floods, comprise of old alluvial soils. On these soils settled agriculture is practiced and varieties of crop are grown. Being older in formation they are more acidic in nature and unfit for crop that are sensitive to calcium depleted acidic conditions. These soils, however, are some of the more manageable soils of the State.

(iii) *Red Loam Soil :* Typical red loamy soils are found in the high rainfall areas of the State particularly on the hill slopes and the outskirts of the hills in the plains districts. In texture, these are more friable and loamy.

(iv) *Lateritic Soil :* The Lateritic soils constitute a small area exclusively in the hills and do not appear to be of much of agricultural significance. Being highly leached, these are poor in plant nutrients and are acidic in nature.

This type of soil is generally brick red in colour and is difficult to work on.

The main characteristics of Assam soils, in general, is acidity which has been believed to be caused by high rainfall and humidity. Richness in organic matter and consequent high content of nitrogen are other typical features. It is found that more than 75 per cent of the soils in the non-riverine tracts are acidic in nature. The percentage of neutral soils ranges from 0.6-21.5 in different districts. It is reported that more than 50 per cent of the soils of the undivided Sibsagar, Nowgong and Kamrup districts are medium in organic carbon contents. In undivided Goalpara district, more than 50 per cent of the soil are rich in phosphorus. Potash is rich in only 20 per cent of the soil in the undivided Cachar district.

The soil in the villages is generally classified in six categories for the purposes of revenue assessment. These are as follows :

1. Sailora : Cultivable Land
2. Badi : Homestead
3. Asrawa : Low lying land
4. Chara : Tilla land
5. Patit : Fallow land
6. Shreni nai : Classless

Of the above categories, Sailora and Asrawa are used for the purposes of cultivation. Government land constitutes only a minor fraction of the total land of the villages. These lands are mostly ceiling surplus lands and are used for grazing purposes.

Land-Use Pattern in the Villages

Data regarding land utilisation are classified under nine categories: forest, land put to non-agricultural uses, barren and uncultivated land, permanent pasture and other grazing lands, miscellaneous tree crop and groves, cultivable wasteland, fallow land and other than current fallow, current fallow, and net area sown. However, this classification was not adopted during village survey and more simplistic classification was formed which is presented in Table 1.5.

Table 1.5 : Land-use Pattern in Selected Surveyed Villages

(In hectares)

Sl. No.	Name of Village	Total Land	Land under Cultivation	Area under Forest	Village Grazing Reserve	Waste-land	Home-stead
1.	Kharua (Nalbari)	476.39 (100)	407.39 (85.52)	0 (0)	4.98 (1.05)	17.80 (3.74)	46.22 (9.70)
2.	Aithan Digholia (Dibrugarh)	320 (100)	260 (81.25)	0 (0)	2 (0.62)	23 (7.19)	35 (10.94)
3.	Khajuabil (Darrang)	241 (100)	105.29 (43.69)	0 (0)	54 (22.41)	61.71 (25.61)	20 (8.29)
4.	Da - Parbatia (Sonitpur)	266 (100)	183 (68.80)	48 (18.05)	11 (4.14)	0 (0)	24 (9.01)
5.	Nam-Deuri (Jorhat)	376.60 (100)	319.31 (84.85)	0 (0)	0 (0)	33.8 (8.98)	23.49 (6.24)
6.	Sadarashi (Karimganj)	398.62 (100)	289.35 (72.59)	0 (0)	0 (0)	105.21 (26.39)	4.06 (1.02)
7.	Bhakatapara (Darang)	249 (100)	157.02 (62.88)	0 (0)	2.83 (1.13)	39.66 (15.88)	50.18 (20.01)
8.	Bhelewguri (Nagaon)	361.20 (100)	258 (71.43)	0 (0)	37.74 (10.45)	0 (0)	65.46 (18.12)
9.	Mirigaon (Jorhat)	172.02 (100)	153.68 (89.34)	0 (0)	6.83 (3.97)	3.35 (1.95)	8.17 (4.74)
10.	Sahan (Kamrup)	136.01 (100)	107.15 (78.78)	0 (0)	0 (0)	10.80 (7.94)	18.06 (13.08)
11.	Hierbond – I (Cachar)	180.49 (100)	141.64 (78.48)	0 (0)	2.02 (1.12)	27.92 (15.47)	8.90 (4.93)

Note : Figures in parentheses indicate percentage.
Source : Village Study Report, 1988-92.

Issues and Comments

Analysis of Table 1.5 makes it more or less apparent that around 80 per cent of the total land are under cultivation. Comparing with all Assam figure, in 1985-86, 88.26 per cent of the total area was under cultivation. Most of the villages excluding Da-Parbatia (Sonitpur), however, reported no area under forest. Wasteland of course constituted high percentage of area in more or less all the surveyed villages while around 10-15 per cent of the village area were reportedly used for homestead.

Going back to Assam figure, 34.46 per cent of the total geographical area in the State were reportedly under crop during 1988-89. However, there has been a marginal shift in the area under crop since 1978-79. In the same year, the figure was 33.83 per cent. In regard to area not available for cultivation, Assam reported an increase (31.27%) in 1988-89 from 1978-79 (30.92 %). This percentage is only next to 'net area sown' which may be because of the fact that under this pattern of land-use, land belonging to 'Land put to non-agricultural uses', 'permanent pastures, and other grazing land', 'fallow lands' etc., belonging to two hill districts of Assam have (rightly or wrongly) been included under 'barren and uncultivable land'. In the relevant table percentage distribution of district-wise land utilisation patterns in Assam has been shown.

The uneven topography of the State besides variation in the distribution of soil alongwith commensurate climatic conditions are no doubt relevant to understand the degree of variation in the distribution of forest in the State. Among the plains districts of Assam, the undivided district of Goalpara (most of which today fall under Bodoland Autonomous Council) reported more land under forest while Nowgong reports the least area under forest while in the hill division, the districts of N.C. hills reports less area under forest than Karbi Anglong.

Land Reforms

Land reforms have an important role to play not only as a measure of social justice but also as a necessary factor in the process of economic growth. Land reform, which envisages the distribution of surplus land among the landless and security of tenure for the unprotected tenants of share-croppers provides the critical element for triggering off the process of development among rural destitute. Since the First Plan period the official perception has been that land endowment to the landless is one of the basic prerequisites for initiating a programme of economic upliftment of the landless. Assam adopted a number of land reform measures during the post-Independence period in order to abolish the institution of intermediaries, to regulate rent, to offer security of tenure and to confer ownership rights to tenants.

Owing to various defects of the land tenure systems in the country, there was a persistent demand from all corners of the country for land reforms. Several Commissions and political parties like the Indian National Congress advocated the abolition of the *zamindari* system, protection of tenants against eviction and rack-renting and the imposition of restriction on sub-letting. After Independence, the Government of Assam enacted the following legislations :

1. The Assam Adhiars Protection and Regulation Act, 1948,
2. The Assam State Acquisition of Zamindari Act, 1951,
3. The Assam Fixation of Ceiling on Land Holdings Act, 1956,
4. The Assam Non-Agricultural Urban Tenancy Act, 1956,
5. The Assam State Acquisition of Land Belonging to Religious or Charitable Institutions of Public Nature Act, 1954,
6. The Assam Consolidation of Holdings Act, 1960,
7. The Assam Gramdan Act, 1961,
8. The Assam Tenancy Act, 1971, etc.

The Assam State Acquisition of Zamindari Act, 1951 which came into force on June 15, 1954 abolished the right of proprietors and tenure-holders in the permanently settled areas of Assam (district of Goalpara, Garo Hills and Karimganj subdivision of Cachar district) to prevent absentee landlordism and rack-renting of the tillers. The Act brought a large number of tenants directly under the State Government. By another Act, i.e. the Assam State Acquisition of Land Belonging to Religious and Charitable Institutions of Public Nature Act, 1959, lands belonging to Mathas, Satras and other religious and charitable institution were acquired by the State. All rights and interests in such lands were vested in the State free from all encumbrances.

The acquisition of *zamindaris* as provided under this Act, is made in two stages – first stage relates to the acquisition of proprietary rights. In the erstwhile Goalpara district (which is now partitioned into four districts of Dhubri, Kokrajhar, Goalpara and Bongaigaon), six major *zamindaris* embracing 19 estates, were acquired and vested in the State between 1954 and 1957. The total area acquired is 6,15,425.07 hectares.

In the second stage, during the period 1954 to 1972, the land rights and interests of the intermediaries – *Jotedars*, commonly known as tenure holders were re-acquired as a result of which the tenants were placed directly under the Government.

In Karimganj (originally under Sylhet district, made a subdivision under Cachar district after partition, presently a district since 1st July, 1983), there were permanently settled areas to the tune of 2,07,003 acres approximately (323 sq. miles) covering 4732 numbers of estates.

The rights and interest of tenants in the erstwhile permanently settled areas in Goalpara and Karimganj sub-division were formerly governed by the provisions of the Goalpara Tenancy Act, 1929 (Assam Act I of 1929) and the Sylhet Tenancy Act, 1936 (Assam Act XI of 1936) respectively. By the enactment of the Assam Land Holdings (Adoption of Relationship under the Assam Land and Revenue Regulation, 1886 in the acquired permanently settled estates) Act, 1974, the Goalpara and the Sylhet Tenancy Acts have been repealed. The provisions of the Assam (Temporarily Settled Areas) Tenancy Act, 1971 have now been made applicable in the said districts. Further the provisions of the Assam Land and Revenue Regulation Act, 1886 (as amended) are extended to the acquired estates and tenures in the said districts. All these developments have resulted in the introduction of uniform pattern of revenue administration throughout Assam.

Ceiling on Land Holdings

The Assam Fixation of Ceiling on Landholding Act was passed in 1956, but brought into force in 1958. Since then it has been amended several times, the latest amendment being in 1976.

The Ceiling Law of Assam applies only to agricultural land. For urban land, the central legislation on urban ceiling has been applied in two towns of Assam, namely Gauhati and Tinsukia. Even out of agricultural land, the following classes have been exempted from the operation of the ceiling law :

(i) Government land,
(ii) Land under tea cultivation and its ancillary purposes,
(iii) Land held by a factory,
(iv) Land of a co-operative sugarcane farming society which feeds a co-operative sugar factory, and
(vi) Land vested in a *Gramdan* Gramsabha.

Ceiling in Assam applies to a family holding. A family consists of husband, wife and minor children and includes a joint family. The ceiling is now fixed at 50 bighas (6.68 hectares). In addition to these 50 bighas, an area upto 4 bighas or 0.52 hectares is also allowed. Any land above this limit is treated as excess land.

Any *benami* transfer made after November 12, 1955 is to be disregarded. Any other transfer made with a view to evading the ceiling is also disregarded.

The burden of declaring the excess land is laid on the owner. If he does not do so, the Collector determines the excess land through his own agency. He publishes a draft statement of excess land, services it on the owner giving 15 days time for filing objection, affords an opportunity of being heard, and thereafter finalises and signs the final statement. On such signing, all rights in the excess land including even the rights of tenants rest in Government. There is no appeal provided for against the Collector's order, though the State Government may call for the final statement at any time and revise his order.

Compensation is paid at the rate of 25 times the land revenue for fallow land and 50 times cultivated land. If the land is not tenanted, then the entire compensation goes to the owner. But if it is tenanted, it is apportioned between the owner and the tenants.

The acquired excess land has to be redistributed among landless, actual cultivators. But all the excess lands so acquired are not available for settlement with new persons, as in most cases involving excess lands (except those belonging to tea gardens), there are generally some tenants. Where there is a cultivating tenant, the acquired land is settled with him with the status of a landholder on re-imbursing the Government the compensation money paid by it.

Where there is no tenant, the acquired land is settled with landless cultivators (preference being given to those who are affected by flood, erosion and earthquake and agricultural farming corporation.)

The Assam Fixation of Ceiling on Landholdings Act, 1955 has been amended several times, and the original ceiling area has been brought down twice. Originally it was fixed at 20.07 hectares; in 1972 it was brought down to 10.02 hectares, and in 1976 to 6.69 hectares. The frequent revisions, to a great extent, upset the records before they could be finalised, and the progress of implementation was naturally hampered.

The uneconomic size of the great majority of landholdings, inequality in ownership and use of land, and landlessness of a considerable portion of the population are some of the serious defects of the agrarian structure in Assam. The National Sample Survey Report on Landholdings (Eighth Round) revealed that in Assam in the year 1953-54, 41.7 per cent of the households were either landless or owned less than 0.005 acre, 40.02 per cent households owned holdings between 0.01 acre and less than 5 acres, and only 0.86 per cent households owned holdings of the size 25 acres and above.

In July 1972, Government of Assam adopted a policy for settlement of land for agricultural purposes whereby it was decided that all government agricultural lands for ordinary cultivation would from then onwards not be given on individual basis, such land would be amalgamated and allotted to the Agricultural Farming Corporation formed of landless cultivators.

Ceiling Laws were expected to promote labour intensity as well as productivity in the agricultural sector so that not only gainful employment in rural areas within the agricultural sector would increase significantly but production per hectare, if not per man would also increase. But unfortunately, the objectives of the ceiling laws have been frustrated by the manner in which the land ceiling laws have been implemented. The land ceiling laws so far implemented in Assam have not been able to touch the real problems of poverty, productivity and equity due to high ceiling level, manipulation of land records, fictitious and fraudulent partitions of land and above all the poor quality of the implementation of the law.

The Ceiling Act of 1956 has enabled the Assam Government to acquire land in excess of the ceiling fixed for distribution among the landless cultivators. Altogether, 17.34 lakh bighas were acquired as ceiling surplus land and the same was distributed among 218 thousand landless families till April 1977. Government also provided financial assistance under the State sector scheme for supporting services to *adhiars* and other tenants and Central sector scheme for financial assistance to the allottees of ceiling surplus land for development and cultivation of such lands. Under the State sector scheme each allottee was given a cultivation grant of Rs. 250.00. Under the Central sector scheme a sum of Rs. 250.00 per hectare was granted as short-term input subsidy to new assignees of ceiling surplus lands. In total, a sum of Rs. 15 lakh and Rs. 29.27 lakh was sanctioned respectively under State and Central sector schemes in 1976-77. The number of families benefited was around 6,000.

Notwithstanding the above achievements, acquisition of ceiling surplus land was much below the original estimate. Although theoretically Act was enforced since 1958, its implementation was delayed (till 1961) as it was challenged in the court of law. Meanwhile *benami* transfer of land took place on a large scale. It was only in 1970 that transfers were prohibited through an amendment of the Act.

Most of whatever progress has been made with regard to acquisition and distribution of ceiling surplus lands was attained during the national emergency. The lifting of the emergency has also brought the progress in land reforms to a virtual standstill.

As has been already indicated, frequent changes in the level of the ceiling as well as in other ancillary provisions upset the records and naturally slowed down the progress of detection as well as acquisition of excess lands above the ceiling. Nevertheless, the ultimate result was not that much unsatisfactory. Till 1981, a total area of 2,33,550 hectares of surplus land has been obtained from two main sources: from tea gardens, and from individuals. The area acquired from tea gardens has been 1,60,817 hectares while that from individuals to 72,634 hectares.

Table 1.6 : Progress of Implementation of Land Ceiling Laws in Assam till 1993

		(Acres)
1.	Land estimated to be surplus	6,12,380
2.	Land declared to be surplus	6,12,380
3.	Area taken possession	5,75,827
4.	Area taken possession as a percentage of area declared surplus	94.02%
5.	Ceiling returns filed	21,894
6.	Ceiling returns disposed of	21,072
7.	Ceiling returns disposed of as a percentage of ceiling returns filed	96.25%
8.	Area distributed	4,89,460
9.	Area distributed as percentage of area taken possession	84.99%
10.	Area distributed to SC as a percentage of total area distributed	7.30%
11.	Area distributed to ST as a percentage of total distributed	9.50%

Source : A Study of the Land Systems of North Eastern Region, Vol. I, Assam, (Gauhati: Law Research Institute, 1982).

Surplus areas had been mostly under the occupation of tenants, who have to be provided the status of settlement holders. Total number of such tenant families was 1,87,151 and the total area so settled with them was 90,442 hectares. So far an area of 37,813 hectares had been settled with 70,259 landless cultivating families while 2,537 hectares was allotted to 77 public institutions. The remaining areas still remain unallotted, as some areas are locked up in various court cases while others are uncultivable due to (in most cases) costly reclamation. The ceiling level in Assam is one of the lowest in India, (6.69 hectares) irrespective of any difference in the quality of land or the size of the family.

The original Act was amended for the third time in 1975 reducing the ceiling limit to 50 bighas, but retrospective effect was given from 13th October, 1972. Upto September, 1986 total land acquired under this Act was 6,04,172 acres; out of this the Government of Assam has already distributed an area of 4,03,373 acres of land to 3,43,780 families (including 396 institutions).

Thus, on the basis of the above statistics, it is seen that only 66.76 per cent of the land acquired by the State has been distributed and the remaining portion is still involved in court cases and in revision cases. This has definitely impeded the progress of allotment of ceiling surplus land.

Again, on the basis of the figures of beneficiaries and area distributed, it turns out that average amount of land obtained by each beneficiary family has been only 0.47 hectares which is grossly inadequate to yield enough output for raising the standard of living of any family, particularly if it happens to be a poor one as the average amount of land distributed to landless families is uneconomical for cultivation. Moreover, the beneficiaries constitute a very small proportion of agricultural labourers.

Quite often, lands declared as surplus and distributed to the landless have been of an inferior quality. Besides, poverty of the allottees does not naturally give them access to supplementary inputs like credit, fertilisers, better quality of seeds etc. Thus, the very purpose of ceiling has been sabotaged from within.

As per provision of the Amendment Act, 1976, the procedure for acquisition has been simplified, the scope for filing objection reduced from 30 days to 15 days. The procedure for servicing notices has been modified making it incumbent on the objector to ascertain the date of hearing. The amending Act, 1976 empowered the Collectors to acquire the excess land by publishing the final statement as against the earlier procedure for the publication of notification by the Government in the official Gazette. As a result, more areas have been acquired under the ceiling laws. Out of total cases 21,894 of ceiling returns filed, 21,072 have already been disposed of. Only 822 cases of returns filed are pending disposal as on date. Till now the possession of 5,75,837.00 acres of declared ceiling surplus land has been taken over. The possession of balance 36,543.00 acres could not be taken due to involvement in litigation, etc. This is not exactly a mean achievement in comparison to many a State in the country.

According to a paper published by the Government of Assam while from 1987-88 to 1990-91, the target achievement was merely 16 per cent but during 1991-92, 87 per cent of the targeted surplus land was distributed.

Most dismal performance of the State Government has however been in the field of updation of land records. Even the paper released by the Government admits that during 1987-88 to 1990-91 only 60 per cent of the target could be achieved. This no doubt needs attention of the concerned departments of the Government.

Tenancy Situation

Since family is the unit of labour for agricultural operations in India (except for wage-earners), landholdings per family and the nature of these holdings affect the overall economic efficiency of farming.

According to the World Agricultural Census of 1970-71, about 60 per cent of the operational holdings in Assam were below 1 hectare and 24 per cent between 1 and 2 hectares. Thus, nearly 84 per cent of the operational holdings were below the minimum economic size of holdings. The position did not report any significant improvement during the 1976-77 World Agricultural Census. During that year 60 per cent of the operational holdings were below 1 hectare and 23 per cent between 1 and 2 hectares. Average size of operational holdings in Assam during 1975-77 was 1.37 hectares compared to all India average of 2 hectares.

Issues and Comments

Table 1.7 presents size-wise operational holdings of selected villages between 1988 and 1992. The pattern that emerges from the figures indicates concentration of most operational holdings below 5 acres. Most of the villagers have small landholdings and unlike many other States large landlords are virtually absent.

As has been already stated, in Assam, ceiling limit is 50 bighas (6.69 hectares or 16.5 acres). However, the villagers possessing 50 bighas or more are rarely seen in surveyed villages and such problems of excess landholding is not prevalent in Assam unlike in northern States. Most of the villagers are more or less marginal farmers. One of the problems these farmers face is the recurring fragmentation of their lands. There is a serious problem of fragmentation in all districts excepting the Hill district. Particularly in Karbi Anglong. The problem is more acute in Goalpara, Cachar and Kamrup districts. In the villages, landless families constitute considerable portion though generally ceiling surplus lands are distributed (according to availability) among them subject to its availability.

Table 1.7 : Operational Holding in Surveyed Villages

Name of villages	Less than 5 Acres No. of land holders	5-10 Acres No. of land holders	10-20 Acres No. of land holders	> 20 Acres No. of land holders	Land-less family	Total No. of land holders
1. Hierbond-I (Cachar)	133 (88.08)	15 (9.93)	3 (1.99)	0 (0)	–	151 (100)
2. Nam-Deuri (Jorhat)	83 (75.45)	25 (22.73)	2 (1.82)	0 (0)	–	110 (100)
3. Kharua (Nalbari)	250 (80.13)	50 (16.03)	12 (3.85)	0 (0)	–	312 (100)
4. Pangram Pt. II (Cachar)	100 (80.00)	17 (13.60)	8 (6.40)	0 (0)	26 (20.80)	125 (100)
5. Khajuabil (Darrang)	194 (97.49)	5 (2.51)	0 (0)	0 (0)	37 (S.C.-6) (18.59)	199 (100)
6. Adabari (Dhubri)	257 (93.12)	19 (6.88)	0 (0)	0 (0)	45 (16.30)	276 (100)
7. Marigaon (Jorhat)	101 (83.47)	20 (16.53)	0 (0)	0 (0)	3 (2.48)	121 (1)
8. Da-Parbatia (Sonitpur)	430 (97.51)	11 (2.49)	0 (0)	0 (0)	64 (14.51)	441 (100)
9. Changmai (Dibrugarh)	113 (99.12)	1 (0.88)	0 (0)	0 (0)	–	114 (100)

Note : 1. Figures in parenthesis indicate percentages.
2. Percentage of Landless Family is also derived from the total number of Landholders.

Source : Village Study Report, LBSNAA, 1988-92.

Tenancy is fairly common in the villages. The relationship between landlord and tenant generally takes two forms: (a) *Adhi* and (b) *Thika*. Under the *Adhi* system, the produce including the straw in divided fifty-fifty. While the landlord pays the cost of seedling, manure and pesticides, the tenant has to use his own agricultural implements, bullocks and of course labour. Under the *thika* system, the landlord gives the land on contract to the cultivators and takes a fixed amount of produce from him. The cultivator bears the entire cost of cultivation and gives on an average of 15 maunds/hectare of *sali* and *Ahu* paddy and 4 maunds/hectare of jute to the landowners. It is clear that the share of the tenants is much less than what is prescribed by the *Assam Tenancy Act* of 1971. According to Assam Tenancy Act,1971, the maximum amount of rent has been fixed as one-fifth of the produce of the major crops or three times the land revenue payable for the land holding. Under tenancy has been removed. Only two classes of tenants have been recognised; occupancy and non-occupancy tenants and both these classes have been vested with definite powers which includes, *inter alia*, protection against ejection and enhancement of rent.

As a consequence of this Act, many landowners got deprived of their lands by unrecorded tenants. Thereafter, the landholders in the villages became shaky in leasing out their lands. However, all these rights and privileges are enjoyed only by recorded tenants. For unrecorded tenants these rights for ejection at the will of the *pattadar* while security of their tenure depends upon their personal equation with the landowner. The Tenancy Act, 1971, also provides for acquisition of ownership rights by tenants.

Table 1.8 : Class of Land with Revenue Rate (in Rs./Bigha)

Class of Land	Revenue Rate (Rs./ Bigha)
Lahitali	1.75
Salitali	1.69
Bao	0.84
Bisesha-Furring	1.49
Furring	0.69
Bisesha-chai	1.75
Chai	1.69
Bhal-Bari	1.85
Bari	1.75
Jalatak	0.42

Source : Village Study Report, LBSNAA, 1988-92.

Land Tenure and Revenue System

Land tenures that prevailed in Assam during these days can be classified under several heads. Given below also indicates Class of Land with Revenue Rate as is indicated from an assignment.

(a) Revenue Free Estates

In these estates revenue waiver was given by the State for various reasons. The revenue free estates included (a) *Lakhiraj* Estate – *Lakhiraj* is derived from the Arabic words *La* and *Khiraj* meaning 'free' and 'revenue', i.e. revenue free estates. These estates were largely granted to the religious and charitable trusts and organisations. Religious endowments made in favour of temples were called as *Debottar* which were of two types *Bhogdari* and *Paikan*. Charitable endowments made in favour of religious congregations or *Satras* were called as *Dharmottar* and the personal grants made in favour of Brahmins were called as *Brahmottar* while those made in favour of Sudras were called as *Nankar*. Some of the grants were made for the temples of Hajo, Madhab, Gopeshwar etc. The revenue free character of these estates were maintained all throughout the Ahom rule. With the advent of the Britishers, David Scott levied tax on the *Lakhiraj* estates except for the *Debottar (Bhogdani* variety) estates. In 1860, Jenkins made the *bona fide Debottar* land revenue free and the *Dharmottar* and *Brahmottar* lands were allowed to pay half the amount of the revenue due. The Assam Land and Revenue Regulation of 1886 termed the holders of *Lakhiraj* estates as proprietors. They enjoyed all the benefits of permanent settled estates and were allowed not to pay revenue. These estates were heritable and transferable which were more or less spread over all the plain Districts of Brahmaputra valley.

(b) Baksha Estates

These types of estates were granted as rewards for services rendered in case of religious activities. These estates were mainly found in the district of Cachar which were however not hereditary and alienation by sale or gift of *Baksha* land was also not allowed.

(c) Fee Simple Estates

The Britishers encouraged to bring the uncultivable lands under tea cultivation and thereby granted revenue exemptions in these types of estates. The holders enjoyed same rights and privileges like the *Lakhiraj* estate holders.

(d) Special Revenue Paying Estates

This kind of estates were found in Darrang, Kamrup, Nowgaon, Sibsagar and Lakhimpur. These were half revenue paying estates. Originally, these estates were revenue free grants made by the Ahom kings for various religious and charitable purposes like the *Lakhiraj* grants which, with the advent of the Britishers got half revenue exemptions, and were renamed as the *Nisf-Khiraj* estates.

(e) Chamua Estates

These were the full revenue paying estates but enjoyed some privilege over the ordinary revenue holders. The *Chamuadar* paid the revenue directly to the Government and the assessment of revenue was done in accordance with the papers supplied by the *Chamuadar* for which he got commission to the tune of 10 per cent on his assessment.

(f) Khat

These estates were usually situated at a distance from the residence of the proprietors. These lands were either cultivated by own servants as *ryots*. The *Khat* holders had to pay full revenue rates. Different types of *Khat* holdings were found in Nowgaon, Kamrup, Lakhimpur and Sibsagar districts. The *Khatdar* paid revenue directly to the Government treasury. They received no *pattas* though those were issued to the cultivators of these estates. The *Khat* holders received 10 per cent commission collected by them from the total amount of collection.

(g) Six-Pie Lakhiraj Estates

Some temple lands in Darrang district belonging to *Auniati* Gosain and Dabhinpatia Gosain, were transferred from the Lakhimpur to the Darrang district in 1868. These lands were originally revenue free lands granted by the Ahom kings. But with passage of time, Dafla, a hill tribe of Arunachal Pradesh, used to exact from the Gosains *Posa,* at the rate of 6 pie per *bigha* on all cultivated lands. When the British took over the country, the Dafla's were provided pension from the Government and thereafter the Government started accepting the *Posa* directly from the Gosains.

(h) Ten Twenties of Sibsagar

These type of tenures were found in the Sibsagar district. Half the revenue assessed in these tenures were remitted, where the revenue exceeded Rs. 20; where the assessment exceeded Rs. 10 but did not exceed Rs. 20, half the excess over Rs. 10 was remitted. This was granted in 1844 as a relief to the old families who were reduced to comparative tenures and were not heritable in nature.

(i) Acknowledged Estates

Mali observed : "The Northern portion of Goalpara district was known as Eastern Duars consisted of five Duars – Bijni, Sidli, Ripu, Guma and Chirang. Duars, Ripu, Guma and Chirang were the absolute property of the government. The revenue system was some as in force in the temporarily settled districts of the Brahmaputra valley. Bijni and Sidli Duars had separate settlement." The holders of the Acknowledged Estates were called as proprietors.

(j) Permanently Settled Estates

In Assam Permanently Settled Estates were found in Goalpara, Sylhet (now in Bangladesh) and in the Garo Hill areas (now in Meghalaya). The Permanent Settled Estates in Goalpara district consisted of three thanas of Goalpara, Dhubri and Karaibari. These areas originally formed a part of the Permanently Settled areas of the Rangpur district (now in Bangladesh). These areas were occupied during the Mughal invasion but left with the hereditary chieftains who paid nominal tributes. After the British annexation this grant was received by the Britishers. There were altogether 19 permanently settled estates in the District of Goalpara covering an area of 1,518,982 acres.

(k) Temporarily Settled Estates

It consisted of two types of settlements – the Annual Lease and the Periodic Lease. The Periodic lease included the *Ilam* and modified *Ilam* estates of Sylhet, the *Nisf-Khiraj* estates, *Mirasdari* lease of Cachar etc.

(l) Mirasdari Estates

Mali has observed on another occasion: "During the reign of Sura Darpa Narain in Cachar, an Assamese Hindu named Bikram Rai, was sent from Dimapur to cultivate and settle in Bikrampur, a part of Cachar district. He had orders to encourage Bengali settlers from the West to settle in Cachar" (Mali: 1985). The Bengali's migrated and undertook the possession of the uncultivable land which were in abundance in this region. The waste lands were made cultivable and a group of *Mirasdars* became the major holders of land, independent of each other in this part. Revenue was first paid in kind and labour and some villages paid bamboo, timber, rice etc. to the Raja. These *ryots* were bestowed with the occupancy rights and were at the liberty to transfer or sell the plot.

(m) Annual Lease

These leases were found in the Brahmaputra valley and here the *ryots* held the land directly from the Government in lease. Land under annual lease can be classified under three heads *Bari*, *basti* or homesteads, *Rupit* or low rice land and *Faringati* or high land. The annual lease holder had however no legal status over these lands where the sole ownership laid with the Government.

The history of land revenue administration in the Assam goes back to the days of Ahom rule in Assam. There was no 'land tax' in Assam during those days. The system of taxation in force was mainly one of personal service. It was only after the advent of the British that some attempt was made to assess properly the land revenue to be paid by the cultivators. At that time Rupit land was assessed at 3 annas a bigha and subsequently it was increased to Re. 1 for basti land, 10 annas for rupit and 8 annas for other lands.

The Land and Revenue Regulation which came into force in 1886 provided for several types of estates in land. The tenures, which have been either created or acknowledged under this Regulation, fell under two main classes: those under which land was held for the cultivation of ordinary crops and those under which grants were made for the growth of tea or other crops not otherwise included within the ordinary staples of the State. Here, collection of revenue was organised under a *mauzadary* system in all the districts except the then Cachar and Goalpara districts where the *Tehsildari* system was in vogue.

The land in the villages was generally classified into ten classes according to its productivity, nature of crop and land-use and each class was assessed by a different rate of revenue.

Agricultural Practices

There are three cultivating seasons in Assam. These three seasons are winter (rabi), spring (Pre-Monsoon) and Monsoon (kharif). Farmers grow *sali* (a general name for paddy varieties) during *kharif* season. The *sali* season begins during April-May, depending upon the onset of monsoon. Generally, by the end of March, the first showers occur and the rice crop is sown in separate seed beds. Transplantation is taken up when the main plot of rice is harvested, i.e. approximately in the month of July.

Cultivation of *Ahu* (Paddy) varieties is grown during pre-monsoon which begins approximately in January. The farmers take up first ploughing in the month of January and further ploughing, if required, is taken up in the month of February while sowing begins in the month of March. No transplantation is taken up during rice sowing in *Ahu* season. Some farmers also grow mustard and wheat during *rabi* season. Vegetables are also grown by many farmers during the *rabi* season who use early maturing paddy varieties.

There have been, of late, some changes in the agricultural practice. The farmers are taking up mustard cultivation as a cash crop, during the *rabi* season as mentioned above. Earlier the farmers used to take only one crop, that of *sali* paddy (during *kharif*) but now many of them take mustard crop or grow vegetables during the *rabi* season. The limiting factor for the second crop is mainly irrigation and the suitability of soil for the *rabi* crops. Some of the farmers whose land is not suitable for mustard have started taking up *Ahu* paddy (Pre-*kharif* paddy) in addition to the *sali* paddy.

For ploughing, *Nangal* is widely used in the villages. It is a normal plough using drought power of the animals. Tractors are not used as most of the villagers do not possess the same. However, government has started providing tractors to the villagers after charging Rs. 40 per bigha. Level of modern scientific knowledge usage in agriculture is very low in the villages. The use of chemical fertilizers is negligible. Cowdung alone is used for manuring purposes. One quintal/bigha is the standard rate for field application. The cultivators still use traditional agricultural tools and implements. Mechanised farming has not begun in most of the villages. There are no electrical/diesel pumps or water lift pumps for irrigation. Traditional irrigation methods are more or less used for using water from wells and tanks. No HYV seeds are used. In a way the much talked about technology-transfer has remained only on paper in rural Assam.

Production Dynamics

The concept of commercialisation of agriculture has not yet taken its root in the villages. Average Landholdings are small with a high percentage of it are fragmentation. Therefore, agriculture is not considered economically viable and productive. Most of the villages face the wrath of flood every year rendering agriculture uneconomical. Other support systems including irrigation, use of fertilizers and pesticides, HYV seeds are minimally used in the villages. Except for tea cultivation, most of the produces are basically consumption oriented.

However, to have a glimpse of the cost of production, the average yield, the sales price and amount of each crop sold outside the village, a sample data of a village is presented in Table 1.9.

If the harvest is good the farmer earn some surplus but the problem arises when flood or other factors affects the farm resulting into heavy losses. That is to say, the farming activity does not give the farmers staying capacity. This is especially true in the case of jute.

Most of the villages do not have co-operative society, and hence, the products are sold to middlemen (*marwaries*) at the *hat*.

Table 1.9 : Agronomic Data, 1990

Crops	Sown in the month	Reaped in the month of	Average productivity (maunds per acre)	Total production	Cost of cultivation (Rs. Per acre)	Area under cultivation	Sold outside the village	Price per maund
Ahu	Feb. 15 to March 15	May 15 to June 15	Two maunds per acre	2500 maunds	Rs. 465/acre	61 hectares	200 maunds approx.	Rs. 120
Sali	Aug. 15 to Sept. 15	Nov. 15 to Jan. 15	10 maunds per acre	2700 maunds	Rs. 425/acre	68 hectares	400 maunds approx.	Rs. 130
Jute Cohitali	March 15 to April 15	Sept. to Oct.	20 maunds per acre	820 maunds	Rs. 1600/ acre	20 hectares	800 maunds approx.	Rs. 200
Devngliya	Feb. 15 to March 15	July to Aug.						
Mustard	Oct. to Nov.	Jan. 15 to Feb. 15	6 maunds per acre	200 maunds	Rs. 225 per acre	15 hectares	180 maunds approx.	Rs. 150
Dal	June 15 to July 15	October	6 maunds per acre	60 maunds	Rs. 225 per Acre	8 hectares	20 maunds approx.	Rs. 200

Source : Village Study Unit, LBSNAA,1988-92.

The agricultural wages range between Rs. 15 and Rs. 20 per day depending upon demand (though the wages are slightly higher during sowing and harvesting seasons).

Animal Husbandry

Rearing livestock has been a common practice among the villagers. Possession of livestock is commonly seen. Table 1.10 presented below shows the distribution of livestock population in the surveyed villages. On an average, every household has approximately 4 to 5 animals.

Table 1.10 : Livestocks in Surveyed Villages, 1988-92

Name of the villages	Cow	Buffalo	Hen	Goat	Fowl	Duck	Pig	Bullock	Veterinary Dispensary
1. Heerbond Pt-II (Cachar)	200	150	80	175	150	250	NA	300	0
2. Pangram Pt-II (Cachar)	NA	150	NA	120	0	0	NA	NA	1
3. Kachuarkas-I (Dhubri)	173	8	NA	108	0	0	2	94	0
4. Nowbaisha (Jorhat)	400	NA	NA	NA	0	0	0	500	0
5. Bokelmajh Gaon (Dibrugarh)	1500	NA	NA	1000	50	20	0	6	1
6. Kuthori (Nagaon)	207	160	NA	193	0	97	0	NA	0
7. Nam-Deuri (Jorhat)	690	NA	NA	212	1219	160	247	387	1
8. Sadarashi (Karimganj)	218	95	184	110	NA	226	0	89	1
9. Bhakatapara (Darrang)	61	4	NA	NA	NA	NA	0	141	1
10. Bhelewguri (Nagaon)	600	40	NA	NA	NA	NA	NA	500	0

Note : N.A. stands for Not Available.
Source : Village Study Reports, LBSNAA,1988-92.

Though most of the households possess cows, milk is not very popular and the yield per cow is quite low. There are no improved breeds (like *jersey*). Bullocks are used for ploughing purposes. Almost 90 per cent of the villages lacked breeding centres. However, around 50 per cent of the villages have the veterinary facilities, which is not a bad scenario keeping in mind the general backwardness in rural Assam.

Few villagers rear pigs. Pig is more prevalent among Mishing tribes. They are the heavy eaters of pork. Goats are reared for meat purposes. Poultry is very popular among the villagers. In most of the villages, the people are engaged in pisciculture in the ponds since fish is the most common food relished by the Assamese. Those who cannot afford pond they buy fish from the local market. Common animal diseases are said to be tetanus, gas formation, clift feet (sabooka beemar) etc.

Table 1.11 : Livestock Status in Assam, 1982

Cattle			Buffalo	Sheep	Goats	Horses/ Pones	Pig	Duck	Fowl
Total	Cross-breed	Local Varieties							
2,88,739	75,66,378	66,04,693	5,57,883	45,987	17,28,846	15,791	5,78,166	2,88,739	75,66,378

Source : Livestock Census of India, 1982.

It is estimated that in India the value of products from livestock is about 50 per cent of the national value of the livestock. In Assam, there is no estimate as such, though it is naturally anticipated to be much lower than the national level. For example, the average milk output per day from local cows is less than 1 litre as against about 5 literes per day from the improved breed which constitutes only a small proportion of the total cattle production in Assam. Milk production in Assam had increased only by about 70,000 tonnes, eggs production by about 52.60 million and meat production by about 6,000 tonnes during 1974-79.

Cattle/pig rearing has been a non-commercial tradition though now many educated middle class have taken up cattle breeding and milk projects and pigs as poultry rearing on commercial lines. Government has taken up as plans on a cluster basis for distribution of milch cows, fodder cultivation programmes, distribution of fodder minikits, assistance for construction of cattle shed etc. Development of piggery and poultry have been two other main planks of the Animal Husbandry plan for the State. Integrated projects and composite farms are being encouraged and appear to be an assured avenue for fund deployment.

4. ECONOMIC ACTIVITIES

Economic Conditions and Occupational Structure

The rural economic surveys show that between 75 and 85 per cent of rural population in Assam are dependent on agriculture. According to 1991 census, 51.24 per cent of the people are engaged in cultivation while 12.89 per cent are agricultural labourers. 56.86 per cent of the rural people are engaged in cultivation and 14.18 per cent are working as agricultural labourers. Therefore, around 65 per cent of the people are dependent on agricultural activities. Though accurate figures for livestock, fishing and forestry are not available separately there remains ample scope to believe that considerable percentage of the rural people depend on them.

The proportion of persons dependent on agriculture and allied activities varies considerably according to the geographical location. Percentage of workers is the highest in North Cachar Hills, Dhemaji, Karbi Anglong, Lakhimpur and Golaghat districts (see Table 1.12). In the plains, the highest proportion of workers is found in Darrang and Lakhimpur districts. Lowest percentage of workers is found in Karimganj districts. As regards male and female workers, the proportion of workers among men is much higher than women. In the hill districts, where shifting cultivation appears to be the rule, women participate in cultivation in much greater number than their counterparts in the plains districts.

After agriculture, the next highest proportion of workers is engaged in livestock, forestry, fishing, hunting, plantation, orchards and allied activities. In Table 1.12, this category of workers is however included in Agriculture and Allied activities.

There is a considerable number of agricultural population in upper Assam and Cachar who are tea garden labourers. Tea cultivation in Assam occupies about 1657 sq. km. with a labour force 5.5 lakh (1971) working daily. As the labour was not available locally, it was imported from the different parts of

India. Apart from that the colonial interest found it more beneficial to engage *innocent* outsiders towards maximisation of their profits from their ventures in tea.

Table 1.12 : Economic Classification by District, 1991

(Percentage)

District	Total workers	Agricultural workers	Mining and Allied activities	Mfg. (Non-Household and quarry)	Household Industries	Construction etc.	Service
Barpeta	30.02	76.31	0.02	2.43	1.21	1.64	18.39
Bongaigaon	35.10	74.48	0.56	2.29	0.80	1.52	20.34
Cachar	31.85	69.04	0.40	3.37	0.55	2.02	24.63
Darrang	40.19	83.95	0.01	1.56	0.68	0.89	12.90
Dhemaji	44.97	85.65	0.01	1.06	0.26	0.85	12.17
Dhubri	29.45	75.85	0.02	2.86	1.10	1.90	18.27
Dibrugarh	39.52	68.64	2.11	4.44	0.41	1.40	23.00
Goalpara	33.68	75.16	0.04	1.76	1.49	1.63	19.93
Goalghat	40.98	80.92	0.16	2.36	0.55	1.03	14.97
Hailakandi	31.49	77.20	0.08	3.15	0.86	1.06	17.64
Jorhat	38.35	68.94	0.55	3.31	1.06	1.90	24.24
Kamrup	32.59	45.44	0.21	6.40	2.40	3.15	42.41
Karbi Anglong	42.78	84.96	0.13	1.86	0.22	1.42	11.50
Karimganj	28.90	68.87	0.12	3.28	1.87	2.31	23.56
Kokrajhar	35.54	84.02	0.01	1.32	0.55	1.08	13.02
Lakhimpur	42.86	80.48	0.06	1.74	0.32	1.20	16.21
Marigaon	34.88	82.21	0.03	3.34	0.51	0.81	13.11
Nagaon	35.46	74.30	0.12	3.69	0.62	1.32	19.95
Nalbari	33.13	71.63	0.03	2.65	1.94	1.85	21.90
North Cachar Hills	32.05	62.80	1.53	2.38	0.24	3.63	29.42
Sibsagar	41.93	75.39	3.39	2.09	0.45	1.00	17.67
Sonitpur	40.23	77.80	0.02	2.43	0.52	1.02	18.21
Tinsukia	40.68	71.95	1.88	6.09	0.30	1.56	18.23
All Assam	36.09	73.50	0.49	3.11	0.88	1.57	20.45
India	37.46	66.92	0.61	7.65	2.38	1.94	20.50

Source : CMIE, November 1993.

Issues and Comments

Village-wise analysis of economic and occupational structure is not being done here because of paucity of data. However, the trend shows that around 85-90 per cent of the villagers are engaged in agriculture and allied activities. Majority of the villagers who do not have their own lands, work as tenant. In some of the villages, a high percentage of the people are engaged in pisciculture, livestock, poultry and piggery.

Wages in the villages are relatively high as compared to other States. Minimum wage, set by Assam government, is Rs. 30 per day. However, it varies from Rs. 25 to Rs. 40 from village to village. During ploughing season, an agricultural labourer gets around Rs. 30 per day. Wages of men and women also vary except during rice transplantation. A villager, clearing the mustard crop gets around Rs. 30 per bigha.

Village Industries

The tea, coal and petroleum are the so-called major industries (of various scales) in Assam. Tea industry employs a large labour force. The principal manufacturing industries in Assam are plywood, cement and match factories while all other industries may be classed as basically small scale and cottage industries.

Village industries mostly comprises of small and cottage industries. In Assam, Assam Saw Mills and Timber Company (the first plywood factory in India) was established in 1918. The factories in the villages generally use *Semul* trees which are plenty in the State to manufacture plywood. Hollock, holling and mango trees are also used for making plywoods. These plywoods have great demand in tea industry. Most of the plywood industries are located in the Upper Assam – districts of Dibrugarh, Sibsagar and Jorhat. The main products of the plywood factories are commercial plywoods, tea chests, black boards, flush doors etc.

Few villages have match industry. People use timber since this is abundantly found around the villages. However, cottage match industry has not flourished widely in the villages though the potential is very high. Marketing network and input-oriented deficiencies are mainly responsible for this.

Most of the Assamese women know how to weave and in most of the villages cotton and silk handloom industries are widely prevalent. In rural areas, women still depend on home-made clothes than mill-made yarns. Most of the handloom clothes are used for family needs. There are three varieties of silk worms (e.g. *endi, muga* and *pat*) commonly reared in the villages. North Kamrup and Nowgong districts are important centres of manufacture of silk fabrics. Tribes in the villages too are known to produce fine quality cotton cloths.

Husking of rice is universal in the rural areas of Assam. Every rural family has got an important tool called *dehenki* to husk paddy by pounding it with the foot. About two-fifth of the entire production of husked rice in the Assam comes from the *dehenki* processed rice.

Sarthebari and Hajo in Kamrup district, Titabar in Sibsagar district and Raha in Nowgong district are important centres for the manufacture of hand-made brass, copper or bell-metal wares.

Barpeta in Kamrup district manufactures attractive icons and other ivory products. A variety of fine mats known as *Sita Pati* is produced in Karimganj. Nalbari area in Kamrup district is the important centre for the manufacture of *jhapi,* a kind of hat, produced from bamboos and palm tree leaves.

Bamboo works, blacksmithy, *ghani* (or vegetable oil extraction), *gur* (coarse sugar) manufacturing, pottery, soap manufacturing, tailoring, bee-keeping, umbrella manufacturing and carpentry are other small occupations of the villagers.

Issues and Comments

However, in most of the surveyed villages, rural industries were found at the very primitive stage. Traditionally, weaving of *Mekhla chadara* has been a common custom practiced by Mishing society. *Mekhla chadara* is a traditional handicraft and involves weaving of cotton and development of beautiful designs in a wide range of clothes. The other items produced are *riha, churia, cheleng, borkapor, gamosa* etc. The implements used, besides looms are *ugla, mako,* spinning wheel etc. Generally, throw shuttles loom, loin loom, and ply shuttles loom are used for weaving. The first one is found in every Assamese household while the second is common among the hill tribes. The Bengali weavers mostly use pit looms. The ply shuttle loom is of recent origin and is an improved type of traditional loom. Interestingly most of the raw materials are imported from outside the State. The average income of a weaver is generally around Rs. 25 a day.

Sericulture has an important place in the rural economy of the State. The sericulture industry reached its peak during Ahom rule. The villagers produce three principal varieties of silk: *pat, endi* and *muga*. The first variety is the finest and of course the costliest. *Endi* is of a little coarse variety and is generally used by the common people. The third variety, *muga,* is stouter and more durable than *pat. Pat* is expensive because worms producing this type of silk are very delicate and a large number of them die before they spin. Secondly, the supply of mulberry leaves is also limited.

Pottery is a very ancient industry and is still in vogue. The raw materials required for the industry are the glutinous clay and the tools and implements used are wheel, the mould, the mallet and polisher. The articles made are cooking pots, water jars, vessels for boiling rice, large vessels, lamps etc. There are some artisans who specialise in making the images of Durga, Kali, Saraswati etc.

Bamboo and cane works are most universally practiced industry among every section of the people. Its products have wide range of uses and as such are commonly found in every household. It very often provides a subsidiary occupation to the cultivators and full-time occupation to the highly skilled artisans who produces fine decorative items, furnitures, mats, etc. on commercial scale. The essential implements are *dao* and knife. Plucking baskets made of cane are required in large number by the tea gardens and hence quite a large number of people are engaged in producing the same.

Credit and Savings

Data on rural credit and savings were however most scanty. The lending activities of the bank in the villages are primarily confined to IRDP schemes or loans to small businessmen. Only few villagers received loans for improvement of land. Traditionally, moneylending was done in the villages by *kabulis* and *mahajans*. In this sector, most loans are either crop loans or consumption loans. On an average, for crop loans, an amount of Rs. 100 borrowed at the beginning of the season is repayable at the time of harvest in the form of one maund (40 kg) of paddy. This is equivalent to approximately Rs. 145. This effectively translates to an interest rate of about 15 per cent a month.

Similarly in the case of consumption loans, interest rates are high ranging from 6 per cent to 10 per cent a month. These loans are generally given without any collateral or security. The most common cause for such loans are religious or social or in some cases for revenue payment.

In the case of default of loan, generally the tiller gives up tilling the land and the rights of cultivation pass on to the lender, who can get the land cultivated till the loan is repaid by the original tiller. However, this mortgage is not recorded in the land records that further complicates the hazy picture about who actually has how much land and in what capacity.

Nevertheless, few families reportedly have saving in the banks. Some people have started investing money in the National Savings Certificate, Indira Vikas Patra etc. Most of the villages do not have co-operative or Gramin bank. Savings are used for purchasing lands and bullocks. The co-operative movement in Assam began with the passing of the Co-operative Societies Act of 1904. However, the movement could not maintain the momentum mainly because of paucity of working people and lack of people's faith. In 1948, Assam Co-operative Appex Bank was set up to provide credit to co-operative societies. But as stated earlier, co-operative banks has not taken roots in the villages.

SWOT Analysis of Villages covered

A stage has come to evaluate holistically the strengths and the weaknesses of the surveyed villages which would help in framing policy prescriptions for the planners while plans for the districts are being prepared. A village is a microcosm of a State and reflects overall socio-cultural traditions of the people. Nevertheless, a village survives because of certain inherent strong traditions which binds the people together. These strengths are also accompanied by certain weaknesses (inherent in the system itself) which influences the social conditions of the people. An attempt is being made to highlight the strengths, weaknesses, opportunities and threats existing in the villages. The basis for this attempt is of course the observations and findings of the Officer Trainees during their survey of the respective villages.

Strengths

(1) The strength of the villages lies in their people and resources. Most of the land in Brahmaputra Valley is very fertile. Fertility of land is so strong that multiple cropping may easily be made possible.

(2) Unlike the States in the mainland Assam is predominantly free from caste-based equations. Caste system which is so strong in the north is not so rigid in the North-East region. The villagers are peace loving people and incidences of communal riots on caste is virtually absent (though linguistic communalism alongwith occasional religious communalism are not totally absent).

(3) Forest resources are remarkably in abundance in Assam.

(4) Small farmers and agricultural labourers are not exploited by the big landholders since such category virtually does not exist there. Wages are also high as compared to the other States.

(5) Tenancy rules and regulations appear to be quite strictly followed and the landless families generally are able to get ceiling surplus land. People living below poverty line is also less, if of course the available data is of any real value.

Weaknesses

1. Most of the holdings are fragmented and this causes reductions in total cropping area and crop intensity. This also increases the categories of area under fallow land and land not used for cultivation.
2. Because of low awareness level, Government programmes are not been able to be appreciated by the villagers.
3. Heavy dependence exists on primary activities. Very few secondary and tertiary sector jobs are available. Therefore, the people either migrate or depend on agriculture.
4. Another weakness is the poor communication system. A lot has to be done to improve the status of roads, transport and communication.
5. Because of heavy migration and immigration, original settlers become gradually deprived of their own lands. Most of the locals are either marginal farmers or they work as agricultural labourers.
6. Health-care infrastructure is lacking in most of the villages. Maternity health centres do not exist in most of the villages.
7. Most of the villages lack modern Irrigation facilities.
8. Around 50 per cent of the surveyed villages are not fully electrified.

Opportunities

1. Improvement in yield level of crops is possible by reducing fragmentation and introducing latest farming technology, irrigation, chemical fertilizers, pesticides etc.
2. As most of the villages have natural ponds, pisciculture can be easily strengthened and improved and unemployed youths can be encouraged and trained. IRDP can engineer this programme in a more meaningful way.
3. Duck farming has high potential in some of the villages.

4. Cottage and handicraft industry has real scope because of natural resources and the people's interest in it. This industry can be commercialised by forming co-operative society which would buy products and sell outside the village at a higher price than what the people are getting from the middlemen.
5. Underground water resources can be used for irrigation purposes.
6. Cultivation of bamboos can be promoted for commercial purposes. Agro-based industries have high prospect which may even become backbone of the rural economy.

Threats

1. Alarmingly rising communal tendency, unheard of earlier, in recent years.
2. Tendency of migration of youths to town in search of jobs.
3. Perpetual flood that the villages face almost every year.
4. A system of cultivation, known as *jhumming,* practiced by the tribals in the hill districts, is understood to be depleting forest resources and causes soil erosion.
5. Because of heavy immigration to the villages, most of the lands are being transferred from the locals to the alien people. As a result permanent settlers are feeling discontented and frustrated.
6. Growing unemployment in the villages are creating a situation leading to unrest, idleness, tension and adverse feelings towards government.
7. In some of the villages, people are getting addicted to drugs and alcoholism. Border villages are more susceptible to this.
8. Growing deforestation in Assam is causing ecological imbalances and natural resource depletion.

Case Study of the Poorest Person

Profile of a poorest person is hard to sketch. Most of the village study reports did not cover this aspect at all. However, one report has presented a case of the poorest person which is presented verbatim.

"Mr X is the poorest man in the village. He is 65 years old. There is nobody else in the family. His wife died long back. He had 5 children but only one of them survived. This last child also died 10 years ago during the floods at the age of 16. Since then Mr X has been all alone fending for himself. He does not have any land. He was working as labourer in town for quite some time. For the past 5 years, he has been in the village. He is too old to work as a labourer now. He gets up quite late in the morning. He spends his day sitting near a pond trying to catch fish. He is getting an old age pension of Rs.100 per month. This money he uses for buying rice, salt and oil. He has to do his own cooking. However even this paltry sum of Rs. 100 does not come in regularly and he usually gets money for two or three months at a time. This further adds to his woes. He cooks once or twice in a day. During floods, he moves out to one of the relief camps and survives on relief provided by district administration as long as relief camps last." (*Source* : Socio-economic Survey of Village Hierbond - I, Alok Khare, 1992 Batch.)

5. GOVERNMENT INTERVENTIONS

Before embarking on the scope of government interventions in the villages, a brief review of the development programmes already implemented in the villages is being done. In Table 1.13, performance of development programmes initiated in the villages through government interventions is attempted to be captured.

Employment Generation and Poverty Alleviation

Under rural development sector a number of poverty alleviation programme, i.e. IRDP, TRYSEM, NREP, RLEGP were implemented during the Seventh Plan. The old programmes of NREP and RLEGP were merged with JRY in the year 1989-90.

Table 1.13 : Government Interventions in Surveyed Villages

Sl. No.	Name of Village	IRDP	TRYSEM	MRNP	RLEGP	JRY	MMP	PMRY	DWCRA
1.	Nowbaisha (Jorhat)	189 families	5 Girls	3 schemes	3 schemes	6	–	–	–
2.	Bokelmajh Gaon (Jorhat)	93 beneficiaries	4 persons	1 scheme	–	1	–	–	–
3.	Jagori (Nagaon)	29 beneficiaries	–	–	–	–	–	–	–
4.	Batamari (Sonitpur)	32 families	2 girls	1 scheme	–	1	–	–	–
5.	Kachaarkhas (Nagaon)	–	–	1 scheme	–	1	–	–	–
6.	Kuthori (Nagaon)	–	–	1 scheme	–	1	2 persons	–	1
7.	Adabari Pt. I (Dhubri)	27 beneficiaries	–	–	–	–	–	–	–
8.	Sadarashi (Karimganj)	13 beneficiaries	–	2	1	3 schemes	2 persons	–	–
9.	Marigaon (Jorhat)	8 beneficiaries	–	–	–	–	–	–	–
10.	Charaikhola (Kokrajhar)	14 beneficiaries	–	–	–	–	6 persons	–	–
11.	Bhaktapara (Darrang)	20 beneficiaries	20 women	–	1	1 scheme	–	–	–

Note : Figures indicates number of beneficiaries.
Source : Village Study Reports, 1988-92.

Village study reports show that most of the villages have been benefited from IRDP. Under the IRDP, loans and subsidies have been given for purchase of bullocks, cows, bullock carts, boats, fishing nets, stitching machines, weaving looms, hand driven *thelas* etc. The IRDP functionaries work in co-operation with DRDA and in few villages DRDA has started giving assistance for setting up poultry farms and fisheries. Under IRDP, loans are provided by the nearest co-operative banks. According to the Draft Eighth Five Year Plan and annual report, 1992-93 of Government of Assam, during the Seventh Five Year Plan, 3,10,492 beneficiaries were assisted against the target of 3,34,711 – recording 92.7 per cent achievement of whom 23,380 were Scheduled Castes and 69,859 were Scheduled Tribes. During the Annual Plan, 1990-91, 50,345 beneficiaries were assisted against the target of 43,216 beneficiaries which is about 116.49 per cent of the target involving Rs. 1029.00 lakhs.

TRYSEM schemes in the villages have been initiated from 1986-87. Under this scheme, villagers were given training in knitting and tailoring. However, this scheme is multifarious in nature and trains youth for self-employment. Nature of training depends on the need and the skill of the people. In villages, few beneficiaries were trained in cane making and bamboo furnitures. Trainees were also imparted IRDP loans to establish his/her own business.

As is known, NREP and RLEGP have been merged with Jawahar Rozgar Yojana, this programme has helped the villagers build up community assets and reasonable rural infrastructure in past few years. The major activities undertaken under RLEGP/NREP have been construction of school building, irrigational channels, erosion protection structures, rural sanitation latrines, waiting sheds, dwelling houses, community building etc. According to the Draft Eighth Five Year Plan, 1992-97 of Assam, 122.61 lakhs mandays against the physical target of 105.58 lakhs were generated. During the Annual Plan, 1990-91, an amount of Rs. 1063.62 was utilised and the number of mandays generated was 126.02 lakhs against the target of 122.75 lakhs which is 103 per cent of the target.

Programmes under forestry was also initiated in some of the villages. The programme comprised of commercial plantation of quick growing species, social forestry, production of selected forest produce, preservation of wildlife etc. Under Minimum Need Programmes, the landless villagers were given ceiling surplus land for cultivation.

Education

In the Seventh Five Year Plan, 1985-90, the main thrust were (i) to provide schooling facilities to all the children in the age-group 6-13 years within walkable distance, (ii) 100 per cent of enrolment of children in the age group 6-10 years and 75 per cent in the age group 11-13 years, (iii) to provide minimum essential facilities to the schools, and (iv) improvement of quality in education imparted to the children. It was, therefore, proposed to open 3,000 new primary schools and 2,000 new middle schools during the Seventh Five Year Plan period. But till the end of 1989-90, only 1175 primary and 677 middle schools could be opened. The remaining schools could not be opened due to basically constraints of fund. A State is in which law and order machinery eats up the lion's share of the budget, in a stated or unstated way, this appears but to be only natural !

Health and Family Welfare

In order to achieve the goal of 'Health for All' by 2000 AD, Assam requires following health centres and Sub-Centres :

1. Sub-Centre - 5133
2. PHC - 855
3. CHC - 214

As against these, at the end of the Seventh Plan, the position was as below :

1. Sub-Centre - 3998
2. PHC - 202
3. CHC - 45

During 1990-91, 43 PHC and 16 CHC have been established. The target for 1991-92 was to establish 45 PHCs and 9 CHCs. The other activities, which were carried through, were development of medical services in districts and sub-division, school health services, programme for Health Education, control of communicable diseases like Malaria, Filaria and Leprosy.

Water Supply

The State Government have been giving priority to the problem of Rural Water Supply since the Fifth Five Year Plan, since the time when rural water supply was made part of the Minimum Needs Programme (MNP) of the State plan. To supplement State Government efforts, Government of India also launched the accelerated Rural Water Supply programme from 1975-76. In 1990-91, 250 villages in Assam were fully covered under this programme. In 1986, National Drinking Water Mission was launched to impart a sense of urgency to the rural water supply programme and to ensure delivery within a stipulated time frame. Cachar and Darrang districts were selected as Mini-Mission district. Providing potable water to weaker sections of the society like Tribal and Scheduled Caste people has been given due importance. It was estimated that about 60 lakh rural population of the plain districts will be left without the facility of potable water at the beginning of the Eighth Plan. Maybe evaluation of the Eighth Plan in 1997 will provide us even a more sad picture !

Agriculture and Allied Activities

The primary objective of the Seventh Five Year Plan and the Annual Plans of 1990-91 and 1991-92 was self-sufficiency in production of rice and reduction of deficit of other foodgrains with added stress on *rabi* crops during the flood free period. Augmentation in the production of oil seed, commercial crop and horticultural crops were also the thrust areas. In the year 1990-91, record production of almost all crops took place due to mainly suitable weather condition, less damage by flood and the high use of fertilizers. However, scope for increasing agriculture productivity still remains by improving HYV seeds, irrigation facilities and introducing latest farming technology.

The major schemes implemented under Animal Husbandry are cattle and buffalo development, frozen semen production, poultry development, fodder and pig development. Under TSP at the end of Seventh Five Year Plan, 20 veterinary dispensaries were established with respect to raising the economic status of the tribal people. Under family-oriented schemes 5,830 beneficiaries were covered. 7,910 poultry including ducks, were distributed to the beneficiaries.

The main thrust during the span of Seventh Five Year Plan was reportedly on enhancement of milk production *vis-a-vis* economic uplift of rural dairy farmers. Achievement in respect of milk production was recorded at 670 million litres per year, i.e. a growth of 2.4 per cent.

The State possesses high potential for fishery resources and the demand for fish is also very high. The demand is established at around 2,70,000 tonnes of fish per annum taking 11 kg as per capita consumption while the present production is about 76,000 MT. During Seventh Plan and during the Annual Plan 1990-91, the thrust was on increased production of quality fish seeds, fish production, creation of additional water areas and socio-economic improvement of the weaker sections of the society.

Rural Electrification

At the end of 1990-91, 19,642 census villages, out of 21,995 populated census villages, had been electrified leaving a balance of 2,353 villages. The power situation in terms of generation and availability, is that at the end of 1990-91, the per capita consumption of power in the State was 50 KWH as against all India average of 170 KWH. The existing installed generating capacity of Assam is 514 MW, out of which 230 MW are available for utilisation. Special attention is to be given to maximising capacity utilisation and renovation and modernisation of power plants.

6. IN LIEU OF A CONCLUSION

Highlights

Part 1 discussed about Assam's Natural division and Demographic Structure. The State of Assam may be divided into two natural divisions, viz. the plains and the hills. The plains division consists of the Brahmaputra and the Barak valley. The hills division consists of two autonomous districts of Karbi Anglong and N.C. Hills (both of which are covered under the provisions of the Sixth Schedule to the Constitution of India. The two hills districts cover an area of 15,222 sq. km. and accounts for about 19.4 per cent and the plains division cover an area of 63,301 sq. km. and accounts for about 81.96 per cent of the total land surface of the State of which about 89 per cent is the Brahmaputra valley and 11 per cent is in the Barak valley.

In Part 2 discussed Social indicators. There has been quite a substantial growth of population in Assam. The rate of growth of population in Assam during 1901 to 1951 was below 20 per cent per decade which became around 35 per cent every decade during 1951 to 1971. The projected growth of population in Assam during 1971-81 was 36.05 per cent. Against all this, the all India average after 1951 has been around 22 per cent every decade. In 1981-91, percentage growth rate in rural area was 48.65 and in urban area it was 91.66. The rapid growth of population in Assam has been caused by three probable factors: natural increase, immigration from Bangladesh and Nepal and immigration from other States in the country.

Population of Assam consists of many heterogeneous elements. Assam has about 6.24 per cent SCs and 10.99 per cent STs. The *Namasudras* and *Kaibartas* are the major S.C. while the major plains tribes are Bodos, Kacharees, Sonowals and Dimasas. There are different groups of people professing different religions. Hindu constituted 72.50 per cent of the population while Muslims and Christians constituted 24.56 and

2.61 per cent respectively (1971 Census). Different tribes have their own social institutions. These institutions vary from tribe to tribe. Caste system amongst the Hindus, as reported already, is less than in other parts of India.

In Part 3, Agrarian Scenario has been discussed. Assam is predominantly an agrarian State. About 70-80 per cent of the rural population is dependent on agriculture. Agricultural practices and patterns are dependent on the physiographic pattern of the State and the cultural background of the people. Hill tribals of the Karbi Anglong and N.C. Hills are accustomed to shifting cultivation. The main crops produced are rice, maize, wheat, oil seeds, sugarcane etc. Traditionally, Assam has been producing one of the finest quality of tea. Rice is the principal crop. Cultivation of jute as commercial crop has been introduced in Assam. The size of landholding in Assam is very small. Land ceiling limit is 50 bighas. There is a high degree of fragmentation of land holding which is untenable and non-productive. The system of land tenure is ryotwari. This system gives permanent, heritable and transferable rights to the owner of the land. Brahmaputra Valley has very high fertile land but due to lack of irrigation facilities, fertilizers and latest farming technology, agricultural productivity has severely affected.

Economic activities of the villages are discussed in Chapter 4. A typical characteristics of the Assam economy is overdependence on agriculture as the principal and main source of income. Other allied activities are fishing, forestry and livestock which too constitutes a chunk of population. Handicraft also play an important role in the economy. This sector provides a subsidiary occupation to a large number of persons. The important handicrafts are cane and bamboo, brass metal, sital pati, wood carving, kuhilla keth, solapith, ivory work, pottery etc. Assam has a glorious tradition of handloom weaving. It occupies an important place in the life of the rural people. Handloom products provide a vital second line of economic defence to many, while it remains the only economic base for an equally large number, if not more, of people in rural Assam.

In Part 5 looked at the implementation of various government programmes in the villages and also reviewed scope and steps taken under Seventh Five Year Plan in the State.

Limitations and Suggestions

The present study is based on the findings of the village study reports surveyed during 1988-92 by young Officer Trainees and not by professional researchers. Naturally this study suffers from various limitations which may be confessed to be as follows :

(i) Data provided in the village study reports were inconsistent and inadequate. Because of wide gap in the data base, a comprehensive study of village in Assam could not be attempted at.

(ii) Village study reports were not comprehensive and exhaustive. Some reports covered socio-economic aspects of the village but left out other sectoral analysis like Economic Activities and Agrarian Reforms. As a result the data culled out from these reports were fragmented and incomplete, though in itself, each report contained several insights.

(iii) Household Schedule Questionnaire, used by the Officer Trainees, were not used for the purpose of analysis in most of the reports. Hence the very basic objective of collecting data through questionnaire has not been fulfilled. It appears that the questionnaire has just been supplemented along with the reports.

(iv) Some reports were very descriptive and not based on empirical study. That also created another type of problem.

(v) Serious attention could not be given to the issues like land revenue, SWOT analysis, profiles of the poorest persons, Government Interventions in most of the assignments. And to that extent, this attempt too has to inherit those basic inadequacies, despite best of our intentions.

(vi) Regional profile could not be taken up in the study not only because of weak data base of the villages but also due to the fact that the training location for the Officer Trainee is decided by the State Government, which has its own compulsion to opt for districts in some particular regions within the State at the cost of others. Academy has no control whatsoever in deciding the training location.

(vii) Data in most of the reports have not generally been supported by citing sources and references. Therefore, village data tabulated in the study, may be used judiciously.

APPENDIX-I

WHAT AILS ASSAM ?

Need for Soul-Searching

(Reproduced from P.S. Datta, *India's North-East : A Study in Transition*, Delhi : VIKAS, 1992, pp. 140-146.)

Assam is burning today. Autonomy demands of the Bodos, Karbi-Dimasas and the religious and linguistic minority dominated areas of Cachar-Karimganj and the Scheduled Tribes status demand of the Koch-Rajbongshis, tea-tribals, Muttak-Morans (and also may be the Ahoms, who ruled Assam till 1826) are together causing this bonfire in Assam today. To cap it all the United Liberation Front of Assam (ULFA) is providing that magical extra constitutional touch to this already surcharged situation. Assam in 1990s is altogether a different picture than that of Assam during 1979-85 and for many it is a big puzzle.

For any unaware Indian, this is all as if a development from nowhere. Till the other day, for the average Indian, the ethnic tangle in Assam was known to have only two actors – the Assamese and the Bengalis. At least for about the last half a century the real or imaginary maladies of Assam have been made to be believed to be solely because of the 'expansionist designs of the Bengaleese' and it was very conveniently forgotten that India's much celebrated 'tryst with destiny' robbed a vast majority of them of their homeland. This unhealthy, but a sufficiently populist and monistic pathology suggested only a naturally monistic therapy by implying the clipping of the civil rights aspirations of the Bengaleese and legitimising the same by well-orchestrated campaign of half truth. The academicians, the mediamen and the politicians – for none in fact existed any other dimension of Assam's ethnic tangle and the rest of India believed it too.

But the much-trumpeted Memorandum of Settlement in 1985 between the Government of India on the one hand and the

AASU-AAGSP combine on the other, opened up a Pandora's Box and newer forces came to be known to the countrymen for the first time spearheading movements against a very much 'Assamese' Government (and not against the Bengaleese) demanding redressal of the various conditions that had culminated in oppression, deprivation, subordination and marginalisation (supposedly meted out to them) by the Assamese in general and the ruling caste Hindu Assamese elite in particular. From where and why does all this talk about preservation and protection of interest and identity of a number of population groups, who were made to be known as Assamese during all these years, arise? Are they not Assamese, then? To appreciate the situation properly it is imperative that history must be understood in the fullness of its past, present and future.

Identity-Consciousness or identity-assertion among different ethnic groups in Assam is nothing new. Many such cases may even be traced much before the days of Indian Statutory Commission (Simon Commission) in 1930. It is a fact that the hillmen always reported higher degree of consciousness than their counterparts in the plains but that does not mean that the plainsmen of Mongoloid origin lacked identity-consciousness. In the modern sense of the term, with emergence of a 'middle class' through expansion of modern education and entry to jobs under colonial administration, the seeds of identity-consciousness were sown. This is in the 'modern' sense because a distinct identity and self-perception about that distinct identity were not new at least to the hillmen. This holds good to a large extent for the plainsmen of Mongoloid origin as well.

For the hillmen it was more manifest as neither the Ahom rulers nor the Britishers disturbed the basis of their traditional economic-political-cultural arrangements. This was not exactly so for the plainsmen though they too had their own traditional arrangements sufficient enough to provide the material push towards an identity-consciousness. Hence even if there was no expansion of 'modern' education or no emergence of a 'modern middle class' at least the hillmen would have continued to have their identity consciousness and tried to maintain their traditions and customs. But this emerging 'middle class' could provide them a definite direction by articulating their aspirations in tune with the changed rational-legal framework. An advanced section of this 'middle class' also definitely drew inspiration from the long drawn freedom struggle. Equipped with modern education and a sense of history this 'middle class' was destined to occupy the position of leadership in their otherwise tradition-bound and more or less stagnant societies.

Though the colonial administration was never expected to provide a people-oriented education system, yet since the introduction of the modern education the number of literate and educated people started increasing not only in the core Assamese indigenous societies of Assam but also (may be at a lesser rate) in the non-Assamese indigenous societies of Assam. The number of government employees also kept on increasing over the years. With the spread of Christianity, expansion of education and increased scope for jobs in government establishments the tradition-bound smaller societies, later on named 'tribes', became pregnant of an untraditional segment – the 'middle class'. And this very class of people played a pioneering role in unfolding, consolidating and then spreading an identity-consciousness among the members of their own societies. It was they who brought newer dreams to their people. It was they who very often tried to rise above the traps of insularity so inherent in tradition-bound smaller societies.

Many among this first batch of pathfinders, in their early stage of consolidation identified themselves with the larger Assamese society. Some of them even distanced themselves from their respective ethnic-roots. But with the increase in their volume (in the Assamese as well as their own societies), members of this 'middle class' stood exposed to a hitherto unknown competition as employment opportunities or avenues for advancement in various economic spheres were not expanding at an identical pace. As a result they now found the road to further prosperity full of hurdles which was not so in the earlier phase. On the other hand, social discriminations, the superiority complex of the caste-Hindu Assamese society and the caste-based social equations gradually started pushing them away from the larger Assamese society. Gradually the unresolved economic apprehensions started getting a political direction. The atmosphere of neglect and indifference expedited the process further.

The hurt sentiments of the 'middle class' realised that without political power no malady could be remedied and thus bargaining for political power sharing started. But no effective mechanism was evolved which could satisfy the legitimate aspirations of this 'tribal middle class'. Instead a deliberate attempt at projecting them as mere show-pieces in different political organisations and fora without giving them any real power further damaged the situation. They were never taken into confidence and the governing caste-Hindu Assamese elite in fact never seriously thought of sharing power with them. This stubborn situation was potential enough to provide motivation for them to start thinking in terms of their own political boundary. Their leadership was already established in all spheres of their respective societies. Hence it was not very difficult a task for them to arouse the latent identity-consciousness among their own people and direct it towards the aspiration of self-determination.

Due to specific historical and administrative traditions the self-determination aspiration in the hills has been from the very beginning political in nature. The Nagas, the Mizos, the Khasi-Jaintia-Garos, the Karbi-Dimasas all of them began their assertions with a more or less definite political idiom. On the other hand, plainsmen belonging to a number of smaller ethnic groups of Mongoloid origin – who later on came to be known as "plain's tribals" – had to begin their assertions mainly with an apparent non-political focus-safeguarding cultural identity, preservation of language, choice of a script, instruction through mother tongue, continuation of English as medium of instruction in higher education, etc. And after completing a varying period on probation, each of them graduated to the next higher stage and all the above demands culminated in political demand – a separate political identity.

On this question, however, all the groups of Mongoloid origin in the plains could not proceed at an identical speed. There were variations in the degree of assertion among them.

Some demanded Scheduled Tribe status, some demanded federal structure while some other demanded autonomous State. But whatever might have been the level of aspiration or degree of assertion, the 'middle class' and the student-youth force were able to mobilise the people of their respective societies and what began as a sense of deprivation among a few now spread as a sense of deprivation of the whole society. The major preconditions of a movement – collective mobilisation and orientation towards change – thus fulfilled, the important question of 'sustenance' was ironically left to be taken care of by the rigidity of the core Assamese society and also the Indian polity.

Identity-consciousness among these smaller groups was the result of not only their pride in their tradition but it also acted as a defence mechanism against the designs of legitimising a system of deprivation which they thought was victimising them to a point of no return. However, identity-consciousness alone was not sufficient to protect them from the alleged onslaught of a political economy of which they were compelled to be partners. Necessarily there arose the need for identity-assertion as well to provide them some elbow room within the existing system. Thus the consciousness of a few became the consciousness of the larger society and identity assertion developed into a demand for self-determination.

There has been another stream of aspiration too in Assam – the aspiration of the religious and linguistic minorities. Basically they do not have any self-determination aspiration. They cannot probably have it either. Their demand has been the extension of the natural human rights enjoyed or supposed to be enjoyed by Indian citizens anywhere in the country. This demand includes the right to education in the mother tongue, ban on discrimination in employment, end to forceful eviction and harassment in the name of foreigner, etc.

Some amongst us feel that the rickety pace of development during the last few decades since independence has failed to open up avenues for further assimilation in poly-ethnic Assam. They think if a continuous process of all embracing development was available in Assam, avenues for the much needed assimilation would not have been closed. On the other hand, if a modernised agriculture could have been introduced in Assam replacing the backward feudal remnants then too probably a renewed process of assimilation would have begun.

But this argument suffers from a serious lacunae. Our experience since independence is that in the name of development a process of dependent development has been initiated. Our system has miserably failed to usher in justice oriented growth and as a result in the name of development, paradoxically, the volume of poverty increased rather than decreased. More and more people and groups of people were marginalised with every passing year and with every passing plan period. Under the circumstances then, probably 'development' does not hold the clue to solve the ethnic tangle in Assam. We of course do not advocate rejection of development. Development has to continue but at least development styles and instrumentalities have to be changed. Pending a final decision on the existing political economy, we can safely say that there is no natural possibility of the acquired political direction of ethnic assertion in Assam dying out. Rather, this will be sharpened by each passing day.

Identity-consciousness and identity-assertion that have emerged in the 'tribal' societies of Assam and the human rights aspiration of the religious and linguistic minorities do not depend on anyone's liking or disliking. It seems it was historically destined to emerge. No one today can wish these assertions away. To search for a foreign hand behind them too will be an exercise in futility.

It is quite possible that the maladies of Assam today are in fact all rooted in certain wrong perspectives and premises of the core Assamese society itself. We are yet to have a definition of Assamese which is stable over time and place and people. With the changing circumstances the definition too changes. On some people an Assamese identity is imposed while some others are allured to accept an Assamese identity. At another point of time the allured neo-Assamese are identified as non-Assamese and hence non-Indian.

Recently another trend has been observed in Assam. A significant section has been naming the 'tribals of Assam' as 'Assamese tribals'. It is indeed very difficult to establish the sociological justification for this terminology. In Assam today there are two main categories of 'tribals' – Hills and Plains. Each of these has its own name, language, culture and tradition. To call them 'Assamese tribals' is probably nothing but a clandestine attempt at imposing an Assamese identity on them. On the other hand, the ill-fated millions who once had to disown their ethnic-roots in search for 'security' and accept Assamese identity in the past are now being pushed away from their adopted society. In fact the real or imaginary fears of the core Assamese society and its ambitions have been alleged to be victimising the other ethnic groups of Assam since long.

Independent of a political solution there is today a serious need for initiating an incisive attempt at fretting out the elements of self-contradiction in the core Assamese society. It is indeed an unavoidable responsibility for all the right thinking members of our society to find answer to the question as to why the friends and neighbours for centuries are raising accusing fingers and asking for social and political separation and why even the most genuine aspiration of the Assamese society makes them apprehensive.

It is no doubt a painful task. But no one else can travel the road for us. It is our society and we alone will have to carry the cross.

APPENDIX-II

LIST OF OFFICER TRAINEES WHOSE ASSIGNMENTS WERE AVAILABLE AND USED

Sl. No.	Name of the Officer Trainees	Batch
1.	Mishra, R.M.	1986
2.	Cooper, Ravi	1987
3.	Chaturvedi, D.	1987
4.	Jhingran, D.	1987
5.	Kharkongor, P.	1987
6.	Kumar, S.	1987
7.	Samant, N.S.	1987
8.	Barua, J.	1988
9.	Jauhari, M.C.	1988
10.	Kumar, N.	1988
11.	Radha, S.	1988
12.	Rao, M.S.	1988
13.	Srivastava, P.K.	1988
14.	Abbasi, S.	1990
15.	Khare, S.K.	1990
16.	Kumar, Anil	1990
17.	Kumar, K.N.	1990
18.	Narzary, H.	1990
19.	Prasad, R.S.	1990
20.	Prasad R.S.	1990
21.	Singh, Maninder	1990
22.	Suchiang, R.V.	1990
23.	Kumar, Pramod	1991
24.	Vijayendra	1991
25.	Bhutani, A.K.	1992
26.	Khare, Alok	1992
27.	Samal, B.	1992

REFERENCES

Agnihotri, S.K., *Rural Development Through Land Reforms* (Assam Study), Delhi: Periodicals Experts, 1986.

Allen, B.C., *Assam District Gazetteers: Kamrupa*, Allahabad: Pioneer, 1905, Vol. 4.

Allen, B.C., *Census of Assam* 1901, Delhi: Manas, 1984, Vol. 2.

Bahadur, K.P., *Caste, Tribes and Culture of India,* Assam, Delhi: Ess Ess Publications, 1977.

Baishya, Prabin, *Small and Cottage Industries*; Study in Assam, Delhi; Manas, 1989.

Barooah, Jeuti, *Single Women in Assamese Hindu Society,* New Delhi: Gyan Publication, 1993.

Barua, Indira, *Social Relations in an Ahom Village*, New Delhi: Sterling Publication, 1978.

Barua, K.L., *Early History of Kamrupa from the Earliest Times to the End of Sixteenth Century*, Shillong: Author, 1993.

Barua, P.C., *Planning and Development of Assam*, New Delhi: Mittal, 1992.

Barua, S.L. (with special reference to Non-tribal societies), New Delhi: Omsons, 1992.

Bhadra, Ranajit K., Caste and Class Status of Women in Assam: Social Stratification in Assam, Delhi: *Hindustan*, 1991.

Bhattacharjee, Chandana, *Ethnicity and Autonomy Movement: Case of Bodo-Kacharis of Assam,* New Delhi: Vikas, 1995.

Bhuyan, B.C. (ed.), *Tribal Women*, New Delhi: Omsons, 1993.

Bora, Ajit Kumar, *Pattern of Land Utilization in Assam*, Delhi: Manas, 1986.

Bordoloi, B.N., *Dimasa Kacharis of Assam*, Guwahati: Tribal Research Institute, 1984.

Bose, Manjula (ed.), *Land Reforms in Eastern India*, Calcutta, Jadavpur University, 1981.

Chaudhuri, Tushar Kanti, *Demographic Trends in Assam* (1921-1971), Delhi: B.R. Publishing, 1982.

Chauhan, S.K., *Caste, Status and Power: Social Stratification in Assam*, New Delhi: Classical, 1980.

Choudhury, P.C., *History of Civilization of the People of Assam to the Twelfth Century AD*, Guwahati : Department of Historical and Antiquarian Studies in Assam, 1959.

Danda, Dipali. G., *Among the Dimasas of Assam: An Ethnography Study*, New Delhi: Sterling, 1978.

Das, B.M., *Peoples of Assam*, Delhi: Gian, 1987.

Das, Bhakta, *Glimpse of the Scheduled Castes and their Socio-Economic Development in Assam*, New Delhi: Omsons, 1986.

Dasgupta, Keya, "Plantation Economy and Labour Tenure System in Brahmaputra Valley, 1839-1914", *EPW*, Vol. 18, No. 29, July 16, 1983.

Das, J.N., *A Study of the Land Systems of the North Eastern Region,* Gauhati: Law Research Institute, 1959.

Das, Lakshahira, *Development of Secondary Education in Assam,* New Delhi: Omsons, 1990.

Das, Man Mohan, *Peasant Agriculture in Assam: Structural Analysis*, New Delhi: Inter-India, 1984.

Dutta, N.C., 'Land Reforms in Assam' in Manjula Bose (ed.) *Land Reforms in Eastern India,* Calcuttta: Jadavpur University, 1978.

Datta, P.S. (ed.), *Ethnic Movements in Poly-Cultural Assam*, New Delhi: Vikas, 1990.

Datta, P.S., *Autonomy Movements in Assam*; Documents, New Delhi: Omsons, 1993.

Datta, P.S., *North-East and the Indian State*: Paradoxes of the Periphery, New Delhi: Vikas, 1995.

Datta, P.S. (ed.), "Ethnic Connotation in Assam Politics", Mussoorie: LBS NAA, 1994.

Deb, Ranabijoy, *Small Scale Industry in India: A Case Study from Assam,* New Delhi: Mittal, 1993.

Dev, Bimal J. and Lahiri, Dilip K., *Cosmogony of Caste and Social Mobility in Assam*, Delhi: Mittal, 1984.

Dutta, Narenda Chandra, *Land Problems and Land Reforms in Assam*, Delhi: S. Chand, 1968.

Endle, Sidney, *Kacharis*, Delhi: Low Price Publishers, 1990.

Gagoi, Padmeshwar, *Tia-Ahom: Religion and Customs*, Gauhati: Publication Board, 1976.

Gait, Sir Edward Albert, *History of Assam,* 3rd ed., Calcutta: Thacker, Spink, 1963.

Goswami, P.C., *Economic Development of Assam,* 2nd ed., New Delhi: Kalyani, 1988.

Goswami, Shrutidev, *Aspects of Revenue Administration in Assam : 1826-1874,* Delhi: Mittal, 1987.

Guha, Amalendu, *Planter Raj to Swaraj: Freedom Struggle and Electoral Politics in Assam, 1826-1947,* Delhi: Indian Council of Historical Research, 1972.

Guha, Amalendu, "Assamese Agrarian Society in the late Nineteenth Century: Roots, Structures and Trends", *IESHR*, Vol. 17, No. 1, March 1980.

Hunter, W.W., *Statistical Account of Assam*, Delhi: B.R. Publishing, 1982, Vol. 1.

Hussain, Monirul, *The Assam Movement: Class, Ideology and Identity*, New Delhi: Manak, 1993.

Kakati, Banihanta, *Assamese: Its Formation and Development*, ed. by Golackchandra Goswami, 3rd ed., Guwahati: Lawyers Book, 1972.

Kar, M., *Muslims in Assam Politics,* New Delhi: Omsons, 1990.

Mali, D.D., *Economic Problems and Planning in Assam,* New Delhi: Omsons, 1989.

Mali, D.D., *Revenue Administration in Assam*, New Delhi: Omsons, 1985.

Minutes of Evidence Taken Before the Rural Commission upon Decentralization in Eastern Bengal and Assam, London: His Majesty's Stationery Office, 1908, Vol. 5-7.

Mukherjee, Aditya, "Agrarian Conditions in Assam, 1880-1890: A Case Study of Five Districts of the Brahmaputra Valley", *IESHR*, Vol. 16, No. 2, June 1979.

Murty, T.S., *Assam : The Difficult Years,* Study of Political Developments in 1979-83, New Delhi: Himalayan Books, 1983.

National Council of Applied Economic Research, *Techno-Economic Survey of Assam,* New Delhi: NCAER, 1962.

Paul, Madan C., *Dimensions of Tribal Movements in India: Study of Undayachal in Assam Valley,* New Delhi: Inter-India, 1989 (Tribal Studies of India series: T 135).

Phukan, Umananda, *Ex-tea Garden Labour Population in Assam: Socio-Economic Study*, Delhi: B.R. Publishing, 1984.

Phukan, Umananda, *Agricultural Development in Assam* (1950-1985), New Delhi: Mittal, 1990.

Rafiabadi, H.N., *Assam from Agitation to Accord*, New Delhi: Genuine and Media, 1988.

Rao, Venkata V., *Hundred Years of Local Self Government in Assam*, 3rd ed., Pathshala : Bani Prakash, 1967.

Saikia, A.S., *Assam : Village Survey Monographs;* Katanipara, Guwahati : Director of Census Operations (Census of India 1961).

Saikia, P.D., *Indian Rural Women; Study on Role and Status of Rural Women in Assam*, Delhi: Mittal, 1986.

Sarma, P.K., *Forest Resources and their Utilisation in India: A Study of Assam*, New Delhi: Mittal, 1991.

Sasananada, S., *History of Buddhism in Assam*, New Delhi: Bahri, 1986.

Sharma-Thakur, G.C., *Lalungs,* Guwahati: Tribal Institute, 1985.

Tribes of Assam, New Delhi: National Book Trust of India, 1969.

Tungkhungia Buranji or *A History of Assam* 1680-1826 A.D., London: Oxford University, 1933.

Vasu, Nagendranath, *Social History of Kamrupa,* Delhi: Northern Books, 1990, Vol. 3.

Reports

1. A Study of Land Systems of North Eastern Region: Assam, Vol. I, Guwahati : Law Research Institute, 1982.
2. Agro-climatic Regional Training in Eastern Himalayan Regions: Profile and Strategy, Jorhat: Assam Agricultural University, 1991.
3. The Assam Land Revenue Regulation, 1986, Guwahati : Government of Assam, 1990.
4. Understanding Ethnic Unrest in Indian Peripheries, A Syndicate Report Prepared by the 1993 batch of I.A.S. Officer Trainees in LBS NAA, Mussoorie.

2

ASSAM

C. ASHOKVARDHAN

This chapter represents basically a condensation of the socio-economic survey reports prepared by successive batches of IAS probationers allotted to the Assam cadre. The reports begin with an introduction of the village, its geographic setting riverine tracks, historical perspective and a demographic profile. The probationers have also endeavoured to identify sociological characteristics of a typical Assamese village describing family, clan and cultural systems. The studies focus attention on agronomy and agricultural practices, since agriculture is the mainstay of the rural economy. Factors responsible for low yield in agriculture as well as in animal husbandry are diagnosed by in-depth analyses. Labour and employment correlates in terms of seasonality of employment and migration have been duly examined.

The studies further dwel upon cottage and small-scale industries, which thrive on locally produced and available raw material. While such vocations provide meaningful engagement of skilled and semi-skilled labour, especially in lean seasons, there are no shades of a sustained economy. The returns are low.

We find schools in the villages under study but dropout rates are fairly high, quality and competitive education is wanting. Female children work at home, hence their education is casualty. Education does not have a vocational tinge. Same is true to health, sanitation and family welfare infrastructure. There are no maternity and health care services, no immunization programme, no provisions of treatment even for minor illness. There is a conspicuous absence of Integrated Child Development Service in the study area.

Social development process is directed at equipping the rural population with social and educational skills coupled with nutritional and health amenities necessary to eventually increase their economic efficiency.

It is found that all these programmes are totally absent. The priorities of the programmes have to be identified on the basis of actual needs, starting with a dispensary or primary health centre, Integrated Child Development care, and potable drinking water facilities and a mobile banking facility or co-operative credit societies. Some kind of socio-economic consciousness and awakening regarding the inadequacy of the existing standard of living and the absence of social infrastructure is necessary. One distressing revelation is the insignificant part played by the cooperative movement which has not been able to provide any significant rural credit. It is necessary to strengthen and revive the cooperative societies in the village and the state as a whole.

There are very few anti-poverty schemes and order development schemes being taken up in the village, both under IRDP and JRY. Besides there are no wells being taken up under the Million Wells Scheme, no houses built under Indira Awaas Yojana. There are no social forestry works on government and community land, no evidence of soil and water conservation works, minor irrigation, flood protection and other viable scheme. Under IRDP, credit should be available on personal security, on personal earnings on a crop etc. In order to encourage realisation of dues, the local Panchayat should be empowered to realise arrears without expensive legal proceedings in court. To guard against the use of credit for unproductive purposes, provision of credit could be made in kind, like supplying of manure, seeds, barbed wires, agricultural implements, building material and even livestock. This would require a close association between the agriculture department and the farmers. If credit can be made cheap and easy and if the utilisation of credit for productive purpose can be ensured, a great improvement of rural economy will be ensured. Apart from the economic benefits, the cooperatives promote a better link between the rural community and the administration, so that such societies can act as a focus for many local activities and stimulate and demand for health services, education, agricultural training and rural amenities. If people become conscious of their responsibility and requirements, much of the ignorance and inaction will disappear and the pace of economic development will accelerate.

The study area has a great potential for underground water resources. This can be easily utilised for irrigation purposes during the dry season. Concurrently with this, the whole village should be electrified so that electric-pumping machine can be used for lifting of water.

There is also some proportion of wasteland in the study area. This can be brought under plough by reclamation. The process of reclamation can be accelerated by providing tractors and people should take up cultivation immediately after reclamation, otherwise the land may become a jungle again in a year or two.

The main thrust of the development strategy in the village should also be to develop cottage industry in order to maximise employment. The cottage industry that could be set up are weaving, rice milling, bamboo work, pottery and handicrafts. Steps should also be taken to promote sericulture and community handloom. This can be done by making yarn available at cheaper rates, supplying of shuttle looms, and arranging for marketing of the finished products. This will generate additional income and at the same time will provide employment to the villagers.

All this will need sincere efforts of the people, and the government's involvement in the village economy through its development programme. Steps have been taken by the Government of Assam to strengthen and empower the Panchayat Institutions.

Land reform measures have been implemented in the study universe. The surplus land has been allotted to the tenants themselves. Most of the excess land acquired from holders of large holdings are under cultivation of the tenants. Therefore, the excess land acquired from their owners are settled with the cultivating tenants themselves. Allotment certificates have been given but the pattas have not been issued. The area of the land allotted is very less and the allottees sometimes work on other fields, on a sharecropping basis. The owner/pattadar do not bear the cost of any inputs like seeds, fertilizers, implements, cost of harvesting etc. The owner takes about 50 per cent of the produce. Some of the allottees have taken land on lease besides cultivating on their own land. The lease is only for one year. This is a ploy employed by all pattadars to deter the lessees from occupying the land for good. Right of occupancy normally accrues on three years of occupancy. In this way the leases keep rotating from one field to another every year.

The fixation of 50 per cent shares for the landlord has been done without considering the productive efforts employed by the tenants to grow the crops. There are fields where the tenants has to employ more labour and capital to bring the land under cultivation. Most of the landowners who let their land to share croppers are residents of the village and belong to high caste Hindus.

Social Structure

Social structure implies the whole network of enduring groups and interpersonal relations in a society. Again, agrarian social structure could be conceived as social arrangements through which work is organised and the conditions under which it divides them. Differentiation of society into discrete group where each group is bound by a sense of unity, duty, obligation and rights provide individuals with a framework of action.

In the Assames society, the concept of *atmiya* (kin) denotes a large number of persons who are related to each other by birth and marriage (descent and affinity). Social group which are based on common agnatic descent are categorised in the village society as *pariyal* (family), *bhagi* (agnates) and *bangsa* (lineage) according to the genealogical distance from a common ancestor. The cultural connotation is that blood relationship becomes weaker as genealogical distance between kins increases and ceases to exist outside the limits of *bangsa*. This distinction is clearly seen during the period of pollution (*asouchi*) after death and birth. The pollution observances are more elaborate in the case of close agnates of the deceased and become less and less important as the genealogical distance increases.

In the village agricultural work is ideally organised on the basis of *pariyal* labour. But in actual day-to-day life the *ghar* or household is the effective unit of production. The members of a *pariyal* usually trace descent from a common ancestor in the second ascending generation (e.g., a grandfather as far as present heads of households are concerned). The term is also used to refer to more distant kin of the same *bangsa*. In the majority of the cases, a family or *pariyal* is divided into more than one household. In most cases the household members (*gharar manuh*) constitute the unit of production. Authority for management of household affairs (including agriculture) and ownership of land lie with the head who is usually the oldest male member of the household. Tradition imposes a rigid division of labour based on age and sex. The women, for instance, are not allowed to plough or drive a cart. The charu of hearth unit too assumes the role of a production unit following separation of landed property belonging to a household.

The other agnatic social units (namely, *pariyal* and *bangsa*) also have supportive functions for the peasants. A cultivator often invokes the agnatic kin ties in different stages of his agricultural operations. At the surface level, it is visible as reciprocal exchange of draught animal, seeds and manpower. But the essence of the functions of these agnatic descent groups can be understood if we perceive the Assamese conception of *bipad* (situations of crisis). The danger or threat to the normal rhythm of life and the actual occurrence of an accident or calamity are all crisis situations. *Bipad* may take many forms – illness, death, financial crisis, quarrels and friction, attack and injury by others, loss of animals, draught and so on. At sometimes when *ghar* members cannot contain the situation effectively, the more expensive kinship ties are invoked. In case of agrarian disputes centring around land and crops, an influential and powerful *bangsa* is very helpful in consolidating one's position. On the other hand, potential disputants often do not dare to come into direct conflict with a person who belongs to a prominent *bangsa*.

The affinal kin or *mitir* is category which has no direct connection with the agrarian social structure. But at the time of *biapad* and on certain other occasion this intimate relationship is effectively used by the people.

An interesting feature of home life is that a family lives in a cluster of houses, constructed on four sides of one or two courtyards. The *chora ghar* (reception house), *bara ghar* (living house), *gohalu ghar* (cow-shed), *bhoral ghar* (granary) and *nam ghar* (prayer hall), make a house unit complete. Most people, however, construct fewer houses, very few families have *nam ghar*. By and large people depend on the common village *nam ghar*. The Muslims go to a mosque.

There are no social restrictions on S.C. families in village Baker Majh Gaon (Dibrugarh). They are engaged in fishing apart from cultivation. One of the notable features in village Jayantipur (Nalbari) is the absence of untouchability. Caste and social stratification are free from rigidities and dogmatic overtones. There is social communication between the members of different castes. The children of all castes study together in the same school, drink from the same well, attend community festivals and ceremonies. Caste endogamy is however maintained. There is tendency to assume the name of higher caste. This is evident in some families who have avoided using their surname. Some have even adopted other surnames. This is particularly noticeable in the members of the lower caste community. The system of bonded labour is totally absent. The few well-to-do families employed workers at the minimum wage rate applicable in the state. There is sizeable number of Muslims in some villages. Their forefathers had migrated to these villages between 1926-38 when the Assam Government was dominated by Muslim League leaders who encouraged the new settlers. With their superior knowledge of cultivation, the Muslims were employed to cultivate the fields of the Assamese landlords. The migrant Muslims quickly adapted to the Assamese way of life and are now completely imbibed with the Assamese culture, speaking their language and adopting the Assamese habits. These migrants have not created any serious socio-political and economic problems for the indigenous population of the village. They live in complete harmony with the rest of the people. There was never any communal tension among the different communities.

Bihu is the main festival. Even the Muslims celebrate the non-religious festival connected with agriculture. The first Bihu is known as Rangoli Bihu. It heralds the new year and the farmers get ready for tilling the soil with the onset of rainy season. It is observed by music, dancing the feasting. The second Bihu is observed after the planting of the wet crop is over. On this occasion there is no dancing and feasting. It is held when food scarcity prevails. The third Bihu is known as Bhogali Bihu. This is observed after harvesting in the form of community feast and dancing.

Society is not so complicated and infested with pernicious ideas like caste and communal hatred. Social values with regard to the institution of marriage are fairly strong. Inter-caste and tribal-non-tribal marriages are not prohibited. Dowry system is absent.

Agriculture and Animal Husbandry

The economy is predominantly agricultural. In agriculture, the primitive plough and harrow drawn by bullocks, sickle, hoe and rake are still the main implements of cultivation. The yield is therefore very low. Bao rice is grown in these areas. The land remains submerged for most part of the year. It is sown during March-April and harvested in November-December. The average size of land-holdings is about 8-10 bighas. The average yield is 30-40 maunds. There is hardly any surplus grain for sale. Therefore, agriculture is mainly of the subsistence type. There are no inputs in the form of fertilisers, pesticides, high yield variety seeds etc. and mostly cultivators depend on the rain water. A few cultivators have borrowed loan from the AIDC to buy a Diesel pump set. No cash crops like mustard, jute, sugarcane, oil seeds etc. are grown. The farmers continue to grow only the traditional crops, i.e. paddy.

There are a few fishery ponds in the village. The fingerlings are bought from the market and reared in the ponds. Even the fishmeal is bought from the market. The rearing of fish is not scientific. The embankments are not well packed which may bring about leakage. The embankments are, therefore, prone to soil erosion. Every household has one or two cows which are of local breed and are weak. Since the village agriculture depends on animal power, the cows are mainly used for ploughing. The yield of milk is very poor. Each cow barely produces 2-3 litres of milk per day. There are no subsidiary or non-farm activities like poultry, piggery and horticulture. The evolution of new breed of cattle with higher milk yield is very essential. This could be done through artificial insemination. There is one derelict veterinary sub-centre, the officials of which are never available. Another problem in rearing cattle is the scarcity of fodder and grazing fields.

In *Hatkola Gaon (Dibrugarh)* the area under irrigation is nill. There are no pump sets, tube wells used for the purpose of irrigation. There is virtually no irrigation in the village. The agriculture is rain dependent. One irrigation canal has been constructed but no pump set or channels exist for drawing water. The canal is choked with weed and sand. After the canal has been constructed only once water has been released.

In *Reng-Beng* village Paddy is the main crop. The other crops are pulses and horticultural crops. Almost every household is having Arecanut trees, which are mostly used for domestic consumption of *tamul*. As there is no irrigation facility most of the crops are single crops. *Ahu* (Khari) and *Sali* (Rabi) are the two seasons. As all the cultivators are small and marginal farmers the produce is mostly used for domestic consumption. The inputs required for agriculture, i.e. fertilisers, pesticides and seeds are available in the nearest Kathiatoli village.

The whole net sown area (22.86 ha) is under rained cultivation. As the land is upland area (classified as B-faring land in the record of rights), there is no conventional irrigation system in the village. However there are 9 low-lying spots in the village, which are filled with water during rainy season (called as *Nalas*). These water sources are used for irrigating the adjacent field especially for seedling cultivation of paddy.

In *Naharani Grant village (Sonitpur)* agriculture is the main occupation of the people. Most of them are small and marginal farmers and agricultural labourers. Paddy is the main crop and it is grown in the low-lying areas. Only one crop of paddy is grown in a year, i.e. sail crop. In some areas vegetables are also grown for self-consumption.

Since most of the cropped area is ceiling surplus land, the operational holdings are very small. Therefore, they are not so viable. The soil is quite fertile. Fertilisers are hardly used. There is no system of irrigation. Agriculture here is totally rainfed. Productivity is below average. Subsistence form of agriculture is practiced.

Double or multiple cropping is unfamiliar to the villagers of *Naharani Grant***.** Upon questioning, the villager expressed their difficulty regarding infrastructural facilities. They don't have many implements and often they even have to borrow ploughs, hoes etc. They sow self-grown seeds, though a few families grow PUSA and JOYA variety of seeds. In the survey, 3 out of 30 families were found to use fertilisers and only two families were using HYV seeds. There are very few institutional facilities for the supply of inputs for agriculture and veterinary cover, such as seeds, fertilisers, pesticides, insecticides, medicines etc. The block supplies seeds and fertilisers at subsidised rates upon linking up with certain schemes under the department of agriculture. Most of the bank loans are taken to invest in agriculture, land etc. The villagers sell a part of their produce in the Rangapara market.

The principal crop is rice. For this, not much input is required as it is solely rain dependent. Seeds are self-grown. Fertilisers and pesticides are not used. Yield per acre is low and is about 780 to 800 kgs per acre. This crop brings in an income of Rs. 4000-4500 at the rate of Rs. 5 a kilo. This meagre income is not enough to gain supplementary income. Almost all the families have a garden in their homestead land where they grow fruit trees such as mango, jack-fruit and citrus trees. Coconut and arecanut trees are also grown widely and they bring in a sizeable income.

For supplementary income, almost every family keeps livestock, such as draught and milch cattle, goats, fowls, pigs etc. Fishery is also taken up as a source of income. There are four small ponds in the village. The fingerlings were supplied by the block. Livestock is generally used for ploughing and for meat. The main products are milk, meat, eggs etc. These are consumed by the household itself or sold in the Rangapara market.

There is a lot of scope for the development of livestock and horticulture. The Government through the veterinary and the horticulture departments must provide the necessary backward linkages such as good breed of animals, good quality seeds, fertilisers, medicines etc. For the forward linkages, it is heartening to note that a new daily market complex is being constructed by the DRDA Sonitpur under the EAS just a few hundred metre away of the produce especially since there is no proper means of communication to the present market except by foot, cycle or *thela*. Petty sellers should be able to benefit much from this.

There is a small rivulet running by the village, called the Dipota river. If a check dam could be constructed here, this would be beneficial to the entire village. With such irrigation, two crops could be possible every year. IA project under watershed development could be taken up here because, even though this area receives about 200 cm of rainfall per year, most of it is only during the rainy season, i.e. between June to August and the water is generally lost as runoff. Water conservation would enable Rabi crops to be grown.

In village *Baihata (Kamrup),* there are around 200 working oxen and around 250 cows. There is no buffalo.

According to villagers, the present condition of the cattle is normal, but seeing the cattle, one can say that they are not in good condition. The cattle have enough to eat, but they are not looked after properly. There ·is no VGR (villager grazing reserve) in the village. Own fields are used for grazing. The average milk yield per cow is around 1 litre. Goats are not milched. The number of goats in the village is around 500.

The survey result of the 40-survyed households is as follows:

	No. of cattle	No. of Households
	0	8
	1	6
	2	7
	3	12
	4	2
	5	3
	6	-
	7	1
	8	1
Total	94	40

A local disease *Chabaka* is very common among working oxen during cultivation season. In this heels (Nails) of the oxen get woundy. This is treated with traditional method. Potash is also used. Government Veterinary Departments also prescribed medicines.

Every fourth house in the village is having a pond for fishery. They use the fish for domestic consumption. There are few community ponds in which fish is grown.

At present there are 4 fishery cooperatives existing in the village. Among these the 'Baihata Navajyoti' Fishery Cooperative is Government Registered Cooperative Society. The Government has allotted 6 B-2 K-5 L (2.13 acres) of land in the name of Navajyoti Fishery Cooperative. This fishery cooperative has also received a sum of Rs. 45000 as grant-in-aid from the Fishery Department, Government of Assam in the year 1993-94. 35 households, with a share of Rs. 10 per member of this society. The product of these ponds are sold in the open market in the nearby town and the profit is shared among the members of the society. These types of societies are very helpful for the poor people of village.

There is no poultry farm in the village but some households have chicken for eggs and meat.

Almost every household possesses coconut and betel-nut trees in the house stead land. Everyone in Assam takes *Tamul-pan* (Betel-nut). Hence they consume a lot of *Tamul-pan*. They sell it in open market. By this way they are financially benefited. Whenever some family needs money for house, one of the family members can take one or two *tokari* (basket) of *Tamul pan* to market and sell it there.

Bamboo plantation too is found in abundance in the village. So the people can repair their own house from their own plantation and also sell the excess goods. In this way, they somehow lead their day-to-day lives.

In NIZ *Lohoal* village (*Dibrugarh*) agriculture is the backbone of the economy and meets the food requirement. Agriculture depends totally on the rainfall and other geographical factors. Paddy is the only crop grown by the farmers. It is supplemented by the vegetables. The concept of the commercialization of agriculture has not yet taken its roots in this village. Average landholding is small with a high degree of fragmentation. This village faces the wrath of the flood very frequently. Other support systems including irrigation, fertilizers, pesticides and HYV seeds are not used in this village. Most of the production is consumption oriented and very few farmers have a sizeable surplus of agricultural production.

Productivity is low as compared to the other parts of the district. This is due to the soil here. Average yield varies between 500-600 kgs paddy per acre. There is no concept of irrigation and double crops in this village and crop is affected badly at least once in four years. During such time when flood shows its bad face, villagers heavily depend on the district administration and government for the relief measures. Various inputs are available locally, particularly seeds, but actually they are imported from the government side. There is no initiative for the distribution of the fertilizers. Till date, in this village no scientific inputs have been used to increase the agricultural productivity and here lies the ray of hope for enhancing the production of paddy in this particular village.

Gaolia (Cooperative) Bank is functional in this village and United Bank of India is also operational in this village. There are no moneylenders in this village but during the time of crisis well to do people lend money to the villagers. No need to say that the interest rate is very exorbitant. Hardly any credit is given by the banks for agricultural purposes. Now-a-days farmers have started applying for the loan for the purchase of the power-tiller. Those of the farmers who have the surplus production, sell it in the local market.

Bullocks are used for the tilling purpose. Some families have got cows. As such, there is no tradition of mixed farming or animal husbandry in this village. Traditionally Assamese people do not use milk. Now they have started using powder milk. Livestock development is the other prospective area which can change the economic condition of the villagers.

This village has got one fishery pond which is privately owned. During the monsoon villagers get fish in the water-logged areas. Fishing is a main pastime during such period. Villagers depend on the local fish market for their need for fish. *Tamul* (Betelnut), pineapple, banana and mango are other horticultural crops of the village. Poultry is very common in this village.

The whole of the area in the Nagakota Grant village (Sibsagar) is under crop cultivation. Double, multiple and mixed farming is almost unknown to the villagers. The reasons being unawareness, illiteracy, destitute existence, lack of credit and infrastructual facilities. There are no institutional facilities for supply of inputs for agriculture and veterinary, e.g. seeds, fertilizers, pesticides, insecticides, medicines, HYV seeds etc. For supply of credit, villagers are to rely upon the money lenders from far off town who keep visiting the area on and off, villagers find it easy to borrow money from such person than indulging into the complex formalities for bank loan. As far as marketing arrangements for agricultural produce are concerned, Borhat, 3 kms from the village is the only market known to villagers. Borhat is a small business town with a railway station, police station, hospital, a small market and school with around 3000 population. Even today, barter exchange is practiced but mainly for chicken, salt and alcohol. Villagers generally sell their agricultural produce without understanding the market economics and but other essential commodities for domestic use such as spices, salt sugar, *gur,* clothes etc. As far as economy of principal crop, namely paddy is concerned, not much input is required as there is no irrigation, seeds are not bought from the market, fertilizers and pesticides etc. are not used. Productivity is low and is around 6-7 maunds/bigha. Paddy (rice) is sold for Rs. 120 per maund, which implies an annual family income of around Rs. 4000-4500. This meagre income is not sufficient to support a family and therefore, for supplementary income these villagers have to work as agricultural labourers in neighbouring tea garden for six months in a year.

Almost every household has to depend upon livestock for supplementary income. Livestock is undernourished and medical facilities are insufficient. The tribals do not drink milk and instead livestock is used mainly for meat (self-consumption and also selling in the market) and for ploughing. The fodder is collected either from nearby jungles or from paddy husk. Generally, cattle are freed in open for grazing and sometimes husk is also bought from the market. Pig meat is very common and is a delicacy in tribal households and it sells at a very high price in the market during festivals. Apart from piggery, poultry is also done on a small scale. There exists enormous potential for livestock development and piggery can become one of the prime occupations of the people in this area. Sufficient demand exists for the piggery products in the nearby areas including Naga villages providing forward linkages. For backward linkages government needs to open breeding farms and supply mix breed varieties of pigs to the farmers and supporting veterinary facilities. Horticulture is limited to self-consumption and has pineapple and arecanut. Waterlogged areas can be utilised for the development of fishery. Infrastructural support for backward-forward linkages by the government can help bring many Below Poverty Line (BPL) families above the poverty line.

Almost all the cropped area is under single crop cultivation. Rainy season begins from May and ends by October. This falls under excessive rainfall (around 2000mm per year) area and 90 per cent of the rain is received during rainy season. Paddy is mainly grown during this season from July-August to

November-December (*sali* paddy) and during rest of the period fields lie fallow. There are no government irrigation projects and no private means of irrigation exist. In fact, despite being excessive rainfall this is the reason for no second crop. Drought occurs because of the water runs down through the small rivulets and tributaries very fast to Brahmaputra. Government of India has launched a watershed development project under National Watershed Development Project at the foot of Naga hills which is very close to this village. Because of high speed of the water gushing down the slope, it has resulted in a lot of soil erosion from the area incurring physical and financial losses. No significant step has been taken by the government so far in this regard.

RURAL INDUSTRIES

The rural artisans of the village *Da-Parbatia* (*Sonitpur*) are richly endowed with multifarious skills like weaving, silk-spinning, wood-works, bamboo and cane-work, boat-making, net making, painting, stone sculpture etc.

In the traditional Assamese society, the knowledge of weaving is a must for every single female member of the household. Because of this tradition, every household in the village is having at least one loom. The womenfolk in the village is quite adept in weaving. Women usually weave *gosain kapar* pieces of woven cloth placed at alter with various motifs, flowers and creepers. The common cotton and silk yarns are procured from the local market. The looms are built by the local carpenters. Till very recently, there was no one to exploit the vast potential of weaving skill. But with the formation of a 15-member mahila samiti under DWCRA scheme, a positive step has been taken in this direction. The weaving skills of the women can be greatly improved upon if they are given training in their youth under TRYSEM scheme and are provided with loans for the purchase of modern looms under IRDP scheme.

Few others are engaged in other tasks like silk spinning (12 households), wood works (14 households), bamboo and cane works (36 households), boat making (7 households), net making

(27 households), painting (16 households) and stone sculpture (4 households). But because of a lack of proper marketing outlet, the artifacts are sold at throwaway prices resulting in meagre income. The craft of making artistic mat (*kath*) and plaitted fans (*bicani*) with finely split cancsticks is the speciality of the village.

Hardly any rural industry exists in the Nagakota Grant Village (Sibsagar) except cane furniture making since bamboo is grown in plenty.

In *Nam Deuri* (*Jorhat*) women of Deuri community are expert weavers. Most of their dresses are prepared at their family looms. The Deuri women have realised the benefits of fly-shuttle looms over traditional looms.

Production of endi and silk yarn is another cottage industry of the village. Rearing endi worm or mulberry silk worm is an exclusive part-time job of women. Women know how to spin the yarns and usually they do the spinning themselves in leisure time. The clothes they weave are meant only for the family and not for sale.

In village *Bokelmajh* (*Dibrugarh*) weaving is the most important cottage industry that flourished in the district from ancient times. Apart from coloured and beautifully designed cotton garments, the local weavers could produce fine silk cloth some of which were ornamented. After the advent of the British, the weaving industry faced a keen competition from the mill made goods which started dominating the markets even in the remote areas. Still the weaving industry did not lose its popularity and even today it is practised in almost every household in the village.

Weaving is done in the village by womenfolk. The implements used include loom, *ugha, chereki,* spinning wheel and *neothani*. Clothes required for day to day use are produced by every family. These include Mekhela, Chadar, Riha Churia, Cheleng and Barkapore, all made of yarns of coarse quality. Cloth is not produced on a commercial scale. The 'Bihnam' a loving present to youngsters and a respectful gift to the elders is always produced in the household loom. This traditional gift from the women weavers of each family forms an important part of the social life of the village people.

Sericulture has an important place in the rural economy of the state. The sericulture industry reached its peak period during Ahom rule due to royal patronage. Silk industry also had its period of crisis like weaving during British regime when even far-flung areas were flooded with mill made artificial silk cloth. But the industry has stood the test of time having survived and risen from ravages. The villagers produce three principal varieties of silk called pat, endi and muga. The first variety is the finest and costliest. Endi is of coarse quality and is generally used by the common people. The third variety muga is stouter and more durable than pat. Pat is expensive because worms producing this type of silk are very delicate and a large number of them die before they spin. Secondly, the supply of mulberry leaves is limited. Thirdly, the rearing of this worm in the past carried a stigma of impurity and as such its rearing was confined only to the members of 'Jugi' community.

Pottery is a very ancient industry and has not lost much of its past glory and is now confined only to making common earthenware. The raw materials required for the industry are the glutinous clay and the tools and implements used are wheel, the mould, the mallet and polisher. The articles made are cooking pots, water jars, vessel for boiling rice, large vessels, lamps, etc. There are some artisans who specialise in making the images of Durga, Kali, Saraswati etc.

Bamboo-work is perhaps the most universally practiced industry by all sections of the people. Its product may be termed as pure handicraft products in which even elementary mechanical device is not used. Its products have wide range of uses and as such are commonly found in every household. It provides a subsidiary occupation to the cultivators and full-time occupation to the highly skilled artisans who produce fine decorative item, furniture, mats etc. on commercial scale. This industry is mostly concentrated in the rural areas because of availability of bamboos and very high demand of bamboo products, e.g. mats, baskets, fishing contraption etc. in every household use and only a small percentage is sold in the markets. The Japis which are ornamented and embroidered with different designs were indication of the dignity and social status of those who used them in the past.

The making of cane products is also a growing industry. The manufacture of cane furniture requires a high degree of skill. This is a very big industry in the *Batamari* Village and is practiced as a subsidiary activity. Plucking baskets made of cane are required in large number by the tea gardens. Taking advantage of the inability of small firms to cater to such large demands, some big firms have monopolised the manufacture of plucking baskets. The petty artisans generally confine themselves to individual needs like furniture and miscellaneous articles like boxes, cradles, murrahs, waste paper basket, bottle carriers etc.

CREDIT STRUCTURE

The credit scenario in *Charaikhola* and *Baraghar* is not very promising. Private moneylending in the village dose not exist in the sense that there is nobody who can be termed a moneylender who lends money on interest. However, credit is always available if one has some land, for in that case one is given some money and the land is made *Bandhak*. A Santhal who had four acres of land was only tilling 2 acres since the other 2 had been made *bandhak*. The loan was for Rs. 2000 which he had taken partly to meet personal expenditure and partly to hire bullocks to plough his field. The land would be in the possession and use of the person who had given the loan for four years after when the land would be returned and the lending since the loan money would have been more than recouped in the first year itself. There is also another variation of the above which is much harsher. Here a loan is given for a certain amount and the land is returned only after the loan is repaid.

The co-operatives in Assam are on the whole in a bad shape and this is also true of the co-operative society functioning in *Charaikhola*. The State Bank of India had refused to give any money to a co-operative because of a directive from their Headquarter. The reason for this was of course that the loan outstanding among the co-operatives had reached a staggering amount. Similarly, the Salakati G.P.S.S. (under which Charaikhola falls) has not issued any agricultural loan during the last five years and its defaulting loan in 1990-92 stood at 1.25 lakhs. The question then naturally arises what will happen to those people who do not have any land to mortgage?

40 households in 1983 and 63 households in 1990 were having deficit family budgets in *Nom-Deuri Jagraon* in Jorhat district. Usually the landless, small and marginal households are running deficit budgets. Because of their small landholding they are not self-sufficient in paddy. As a result they have either to purchase rice from the market or borrow paddy from co-villagers at the time of need. This kind of paddy borrowing from co-villagers has to be repaid in kind just after harvesting of paddy. But the borrowers have to incur some loss as some of the co-villagers demand more paddy than the borrowed quantity keeping in view the higher price at the time of actual borrowing and lower prices in the post harvest period.

The rural credit structure consists of bank facilities available at Took town where branches of nationalised banks offer credit facilities under the priority sector to villagers for starting sustainable income generating schemes. The level of literacy and awareness being quite high in the village, a number of enterprising people, approach banks for obtaining loans for starting their projects.

In addition the institution of traditional moneylenders also exists in the village. They provide loans to the villagers for consumption purposes although rates of interest are high. But there is no oppression or land alienation etc. resulting from this vicious circle. These moneylenders do this activity on part-time basis while they are basically farmers themselves.

Working of rural credit institutions can be termed as pathetic as it has not yet gained the confidence of the villagers. Most of the populace being illiterate finds bank procedures difficult, cumbersome and impersonal. Moneylenders are still popular as the procedure is simple no matter how unjust and suppressive. Very few families have opened accounts either in bank or post office in *Borhat*, and these families have at least one educated adult member in the family. There is also no cooperative as such dealing in public lending. Private lending by moneylenders is so common that almost every tribal has either borrowed money from them or at least knows about them. Interestingly these moneylenders do not belong to the same village. They are outsider *marwaris* and visit the area quite frequently. Most of the artisans too depend heavily upon the moneylenders at the time of buying of bamboo from the market. Obtaining credit from bank is too cumbersome and moreover it is not made available in time. In effect bank credit institution has almost failed in achieving its objectives. Arranging working capital for such small cottage industries is the most difficult part of the whole business and this is where these artisans are mercilessly exploited by the traditional moneylenders and still retain their position in the society as messiah for rural poor.

OCCUPATION, INCOME AND EMPLOYER-EMPLOYEE RELATIONSHIP

Agriculture is the main occupation of the villagers along with other allied activities such as piggery and poultry. Piggery is done only by tea-tribe families and never by an indigenous Assamese family. Apart from agriculture, this kind of activity fetches a family around Rs. 2000 a year as supplementary income on an average. Out of 30 surveyed households, 14 are found to be agricultural labourers including tea garden labourers, one construction worker and one Government employee in ASEB. While calculating average annual income of various activity groups, it is presumed that construction labourers and tea garden labourers get the employment only for 6 months in a year and agricultural labourers get during agriculture season only. It is evident that Tea Garden labourers, agricultural labourers and construction workers come under very low income group. Government employees make the highest income group.

All tea tribals live a very poor life because of the way they have been living as labourers, due to continuous neglect by the higher sections of the society as well as due to unhealthy habit of drinking alcohol. This is one of the main reasons for their poverty. So far as the indigenous Assamese population is concerned, they have relatively larger plots of land and Muslims among them have taken to other trades like petty business, shop keeping etc. Most of the indigenous Assamese belong to Ahom community which has been recognised as among Other Backward Classes (OBC). The reason for the poverty among the poor sections is due to their social customs, e.g. expenditure on marriage, neglect of the cottage industries and lack of guidance and motivation for the optimum use of their available resources and manpower.

Income can be directly related to the literacy levels and educational qualifications in selected activities. General category people have highest income but the literacy rate among them comes below that of OBCs, it may be because of very small sample size of general category households. Scheduled Castes though have a higher income than OBC's but their literacy rate is far below that of OBC. This is because of the social hierarchical difference and a general disinclination towards education among Scheduled Castes. Among Tea tribes literacy rate is dismally low along with the annual income. Eating habits and living standards are perceptibly different among different income groups.

Most of the tea tribes and ex-tea tribes labourers, apart from their own agriculture, occasionally work on casual basis in the tea gardens. They are given Rs. 25 per day maximum towards their daily wages. At the most such labourers, who are not permanently employed in the tea garden, can get employment only for maximum four to five months is a year during plucking season when extra labour is required by the tea garden. Apart from daily wages, these part-time labourers are also entitled to enjoy other perks and fertilisers such as medical facility available in the garden and drinking water etc. There is no security of service, wage increases at regular intervals with government intervention through legislations. There are no inflation related or productivity or profit related wage increases except bonus to only permanent labourers. Hours of work are fixed by legislation and there is a provision for extra-work payments. Conditions of work at work place, i.e. tea garden are reasonable and no leave benefits to casual labourers. There is a visible tendency amongst the villagers for government jobs. They always prefer it to opening of shops or going for small petty business.

Periodic tensions and conflicts among employers and employees keep taking place from time to time. Employees, i.e. labourers have a very strong (Chah Mazdoor Sangha) Union and they always demand more wages, more perks and facilities. On the other hand the management blames them for being irregular, non-committed, less productive and for being more demanding. Labourers go on strike and most often the district administration has to move in the resolve the conflicts. Strikes, *dharnas*, violence and closure of tea gardens are the regular features in this area. Moreover, although a number of legislations have been passed by the government of Assam to regularise the terms of contract, working hours, wage and perks to tea garden labourers, non-adherence to same by the garden management for their vested interests and over demanding nature of tea labourers cause irritations and periodic tensions between the employers and employees. Further, there is no incidence of bonded labour recorded or unrecorded in the villages.

In *Mirigaon (Jorhat)* the agricultural labourers are not paid amounts even near the Minimum Wages Act and there is disparity in men's and women's wages with men being paid more.

There is no incidence of bonded labour. Some of the persons work as labourers in the agricultural fields and got paid in the form of a small amount of cash and a share of produce.

The implementation of the Minimum Wages Act is strictly done by the Tea estate because of very strong labour unions of tea garden labourers and active interest in their welfare shown by the govt.

This problem of unemployment is quite acute in *De Parbatia* (*Sonitpur*). Most of the people are of course agriculturists. The general trend, as stated by the villagers is that due to the fragmentation of landholdings, the amount of people depending on agricultural and non-agricultural labour has increased tremendously particularly during the two decades. According to the villagers there will not be more than 35 families on Charikhola (Kokrajhar) and another 25 families in Baragarh (Kokrajhar) who would be dependent on agriculture alone for their livelihood, i.e. who are purely cultivators. Most of the people find it very difficult to get work in the lean season just before the harvest and at that time labourers are willing to work for even as little as two kilogram of rice for a day's labour. In this connection, it is the Rajbonshis and the Samthals and Bodas who are the worst hit. The labour market in the area particularly in the non-agricultural sector has been captured by the Biharis, and the Bangladeshi Muslims, and hence perforce the Rajbonshis and Bodas stick largely to agriculture labour.

The minimum wages set by the Assam Government recently are Rs. 30.00 per day though in reality the rates very between Rs. 40.00 to Rs. 50.00. In the village, however, the maximum rate paid for plugging comes to Rs. 25.00 to 30.00 per day. Most people had not heard of the Minimum Wages Act.

The only loans which have been forthcoming for the villagers of *Charaikhola* and *Baraghar* is from the DRDA. Between the year 1989-90 to 1991-92 loans to 20 families, as per the records of the DRDA had been issued under the IRDP scheme, basically for assets creation. Most of loans have gone to better off sections of villagers.

EDUCATION & LITERACY

In *Charakhola* (*Kokrajhar*) there is one Government L.P. School and M.C. School. The L.P. School has four women teachers out of a total of five teachers and in the MC School, there is one lad teacher out of a total of five. The schools were housed in *pucca* building and appeared to be reasonably well attended. Apart from these two schools there also exist some private schools. The I.P. Schools has a total of 4 teachers and high school 3 teachers. The schools are housed in thatched huts and really do not teach very much.

As regards the education and literacy, amongst all the communities the Santhals appeared the most indifferent to the idea of education. Most of the Santhals were themeselves illiterate and has not sent their children to the village school either. The Nepalese appeared to be most aware of the importance of education and this probably was due to the fact that a large number of them were employed in Grade III and Grade IV jobs. The better of Rajbonshis were sending most of their children to the LP and ME schools and some of their children were also attending Kokrajhar College. The Muslims on the other hand were a mixed bag. Two families has sent their children to Kokrajhar college to study and they did not even own much land and were basically skilled labourers. Yet the general opinion prevailing amongst them was that education was of no use for them since they would not get any government job, hence it was more viable to let the children work with them and be more productive. In fact the tendency there was to involve the child in some form of skilled labour. Obviously, the level of education and economic condition of a family were closely inter-related, i.e. the level of dropouts among the small and marginal farmers category was much higher than amongst the better off families. As regards women there was no inherent basis which prevented them from getting education and the number of boys and girls attending the government schools was almost the same.

At the moment all families begin by sending their children to school at over 5 years, though a few boys are sent below 5 years as well.

School enrolment was highest in Class V (85 students) and fell off in classes VI (68 students). The percentage of girls dropping out was much higher and this was almost always because of their marriage for the relatively smaller percentage of male dropouts, the reasons were sudden poverty (loss of the earning member) or disinterest in formal education. While the school has its vacation in June/July and December/January, the attendance of the students follows the seasons so that it is the lowest during the harvesting seasons (starting from May and starting from November) and the transplanting season (July-August). The other potent non-academic influence on the school (at least during 1991) seems to have been political: the staying away of students during SBSU-PTCA clashes, holidays for important village level political meetings, special meetings at the behest of the ULFA when Operation Rhino commenced.

HEALTH CARE

The health care not work in *Charaikhola* and *Baraghar* (*Kokrajhar*) did not exit. There was no Primary Health Centre or Sub-Centre in the village and if there was any health problem, the villagers have to go Kokrajhar for treatment. The major diseases in the village were malaria, which was endemic throughout the year although it abated during the winter and of course cholera, in the rainy season. The problems of cholera and malaria becomes particularly severe during the rainy season. Although health camps are held in the district during this period yet the people of Charaikhola had no health camp.

On inquiring, from the Chief Medical and Health Officer, he said that the basic problem with regard to epidemics was lack of clean drinking water facilities as well as the lack of awareness amongst the people in this regard. He stated that when Kokrajhar town itself did not have a proper water supply system it was unrealistic to expect that clean drinking water facilities could be made available to the villagers. When these epidemics break out regularly each year the scale is so massive that there is no way that the health care network can cope with this, given the existing level of infrastructure. As regards malaria the medicines supplied by the Health Department is quinine and people of this area have become resistant to quinine and hence the doctors themselves advise the patients to buy their medicines from outside.

There was an *Anganwadi* and integrated child development scheme running in the village. However, the supply of food was erratic and further the distance to the *anganwadi* was much. There was not much awareness amongst the villagers regarding the benefit of innoculation for their children. And they seem rather vague about exactly what this entitled.

In *Baihata* (*Kamrup*), the public health department had made facilities for drinking water in the Baihata village but it remained closed for the last 3 years. Because of this the people are very much hampered. The villagers take bath and wash their clothes at a hand-tubewell.

There is no proper drainage facilities in the village. Approx. 30 households have proper sanitation facilities, other go to the open field.

There is one PHC centre and one maternity and child welfare centre at *Kamalpur* village. There is one midwife and one nurse at M&CW Centre. One doctor is there in PHC. Vaccines and medicines are available at PHC and M&CW centre.

The health infrastructure is not up to the mark. There is a 30 bed hospital at *Girishganj,* about 2/3 kms from the village. Apart from this there is a Primary Health Centre with trained nurses and midwifes.

Most of the people have to rely on the nearby Kushiara river or stagnant ponds in front of their houses. It is a common sight to see people bathing, cleaning and washing clothes in the same tank or pond. This appears to be quite insanitary especially when there is no change of water till the onset of monsoon.

Drainage facilities are also not well laid out. Though there are some drains running through the village they generally hold stagnant water.

RURAL DEVELOPMENT SCHEMES

No JRY work has been undertaken in *Nargaon* (*Kamrup*) in past few years. Under the Employment Assurance Scheme (EAS) in 1993-94 the primary school building was built at a cost of around 1 lakh rupees. But no local person found employment. The work was done by a contractor who brought labourers from outside. There are a number of people in the village who would like to work in JRY etc. schemes in the village as they do not own sufficient area of land and do not get regular work on wages. Though the JRY or EAS guidelines forbid contractor it is a universal reality.

In spite of poor recovery and misutilisation of funds, IRDP has made impact in improving the condition of the beneficiaries. But the schemes have not had any effect on the general condition of villagers as a whole.

In *Batamari* (*Sonitpur*) 32 families have been selected from IRDP loans for cattle, dairy, grocery, fishery etc. Two girls are getting training in the TRYSEM centre. The villagers were highly critical of the procedure of the selection of beneficiaries and the corruption prevalent among the block officials.

In *Baihata* (*Kamrup*) the benefit/scheme provided to beneficiaries under IRDP are according to the wish of the beneficiaries. But the implementing authority did not care to provide backward or forward linkages for the schemes/assets. There is no link between activities/assets of different beneficiaries. No plan or thought was given to the marketing aspects before procuring the assets. No discussion took place between the beneficiaries and Government functionaries on marketing aspect. Loan for thread shop, business, grocery were provided without giving any arrangement for raw material for it.

There is a large scope for fishery development in the village. There are already four fish co-operatives in the village. Out of these, one is Government registered. Nearly all the households are having fishpond in their homestead land. If good market arrangements are made by higher authorities and loans are provided for fishery development, these poor families of the village could be benefited more.

There is no priority list made by the BDO. The priority list of the poorest of the poor should be made by the BDO for the village so that needy people get the benefit first.

The scheme chosen for a beneficiary should be chosen after giving a thought to the viability of the scheme. The scheme from which a beneficiary cannot meet the daily expenses of his food, should not be chosen. Backward and forward linkages should be provided by the authorities for a given scheme. There should be some linkages between the assets/schemes provided to the different beneficiaries. Overall the scheme/asset should be viable to the local village.

A scheme/asset provided to a beneficiary would definitely make an impact on the poverty of the beneficiary, if it is selected properly. In the village *Baihata* fishery development scheme is the most viable scheme. Beneficiaries could be brought above the poverty line if proper plan or thought is given to the marketing aspects.

The beneficiaries, who were provided with Rickshaw and Pan-shops, are very much benefited by IRDP. IRDP assets have completely changed their quality of life. These IRDP assets are the only means of their income. These types of viable schemes help the poor to come above the poverty line.

SUMMING UP

The villages under study have a lot of potential for economic growth which has not been realised yet. To begin with, the modernization of agriculture with the introduction of irrigation, double cropping, shift towards cash-crops and horticulture, improved seeds, fertilizer, pesticides and mechanisation wherever possible, could be the first step. Next in line would be the development of allied activities which have been traditionally undertaken in the villages, like fisheries, daiyring and poultry. Rearing of good breed of cows and buffaloes and undertaking poultry on more economic scales do present exciting possibilities in enhancing the overall living standards of the people.

The traditional Industry, can also be revived with little efforts. A series of fruit processing industries can also do a lot of good to the region by inducing the growth of horticulture for which the climate is ideally suited.

But for all this, the first ingredient has to be the will of the people. Only after this, the administrative efforts in this direction will bear fruits.

It has been observed that most of the government officials at the block and lower levels remain absents from duty. There is a lack of cooperation and coordination among various departments. The most significant factor leading to this state of affairs seems to be the absence of one single point at the block levels, which could control and thereby ensure the smooth functioning of various departments in connection with the development of the area. Planning at the village and Block level by involving people in its design and disseminating in formation to the villagers regarding various schemes and investments being made in the area can help in checking various leakages and also in the execution of works on ground and not only on the paper.

3

MANIPUR AND TRIPURA

C. ASHOKVARDHAN

GENERAL

Objectives of the Study

The study is intended to capture the changing socio-economic scenario in Manipur and Tripura as seen through the eyes of the IAS Probationers, over a given time-frame. The State Paper is purported to be a base paper coming mainly out of the data, information and results of the socio-economic studies carried out, in actual, live situations in certain selected villages of Manipur and Tripura.

The North-Eastern region comprising the Seven Sister States of Arunachal Pradesh, Assam, Manipur, Meghalaya, Mizoram, Nagaland and Tripura is endowed with vast natural resources and has enormous potential for development. But because of several constraints, development has not taken place as expected. It is because of this that the proverbial expression 'poverty in the midst of plenty' appears to fit appropriately to this region. North-East India has an extensive area of 2.55 lakh sq. km. comprising about 7.7 per cent of the country's area. The North-East is endowed with an infinite variety of resources including petroleum on the one hand and rare flora and fauna on the other. More than half a dozen rivers besides the mighty Brahmaputra and its tributaries, make the soil of this region most fertile, besides providing this region with one of the largest reservoirs of hydel potential. But the nature which has been so bounteous to this region has, at the same time, created hurdles in its development. The geographical structure of this region, criss-crossed by numerous lines of hills, and endless streams of rivers made the communication to and within this region immensely difficult. Almost 70 per cent of the North-East is covered by mountains and plateaus, comprising the whole of Arunachal Pradesh, Nagaland and Mizoram, part of Manipur, excluding its small basin, part of Tripura excluding its western margin bordering Bangladesh and two districts of Assam. The constraints of tribal development are thus compounded by those of hill area development. The geographical isolation coupled with a series of socio-political and historical disadvantages dragged this region out of the caravan of progress.

It is the purpose of this study to identify various parameters of socio-economic development with respect to Manipur and Tripura against the backdrop of myriad constraints.

Methodology

The State paper is by and large based on the village studies conducted by the IAS Probationers allocated to the Manipur and Tripura cadres. Their studies, in turn, were based on random interview and observation methods *vis-a-vis* the residents of the concerned villages and interactions with public representatives and functionaries. There is, of course, an element of subjectivity and ad-hocism in the selection of focal themes. Focii vary from village to village and from probationer to probationer. Hence it is not possible to subject the available information to statistical tabulation and analysis.

In the nature of things, the probationers' presentation had to be supplemented by related literature and information that the author took resort to at the LBSNAA, Mussoorie, the Secretariat at Imphal and Agartala and in the libraries of the North-East Council and the North Eastern Hill University in Shillong (Meghalaya). The author had an occasion to cover all the seven States in the North-East working as a Member of the Government of India Committee on the Revitalisation of Land Revenue Administration in India. This provided an opportunity to personally observe the processes of development in the region and develop deep, personal insights with regard to constraints and prospects.

Acknowledgement

Manipur

The State paper portion relating to Manipur is based primarily on the socio-economic studies of selected villages, carried out by the following IAS Probationers :

Sl. No.	Probationer	Batch	Village	District
1.	Rohit Kumar Singh	1985	Lower KomKeirap	Churachandpur
2.	Barun Mitra	1987	Thanlon	-do-
3.	BVR Subramanyam	1987	Nungsai-Chiru	Senapati
4.	Binod Kispotta	1987	Kamla Thabi and Heigru-Tampak	Chandel
5.	M.H. Khan	1988	Hundung	Ukhrul
6.	S.K. Dev Verman	1988	Chandel-Christian	Chandel
7.	Rajesh Kumar	1988	Parbung, Lungthulien and Senvon	Churachandpur
8.	J.C. Ramthanga	1989	Vanchengphai	Tamenglong
9.	Lungmuana Lakher	1989	Tolloi	Ukhrul
10.	Moses Chalai	1990	Moltuk	Chandel
11.	Sudhir Garg	1990	Mata and Mata Mualtan	Churachandpur
12.	Paulunthang Vaiphei	1991	Tungjoy	Senapati
13.	Rajesh Kumar Singh	1991	Shirui	Ukhrul
14.	Viraj Varma	1991	Tangpijol	Churachandpur
15.	Vumlunmang Vualnam	1992	Khekman	Thoubal
16.	Vineet Joshi	1992	Hundung	Ukhrul
17.	Sriram Taranikanti	1992	Dungjang	Churachandpur

Tripura

The portion relating to Tripura is based primarily on the socio-economic studies of selected villages, carried out by the following IAS Probationers:

Sl. No.	Probationer	Batch	Village	District
1.	GSG Ayyangar	1987	Matai	South Tripura
2.	Lalit Kumar Gupta	1987	Chenchuria	West Tripura
3.	Rakesh Sarwal	1988	Kachucharra	North Tripura
4.	Rajiv Yadav	1989	Kanchan Bari	North Tripura
5.	Lok Ranjan	1989	Holakhet	South Tripura
6.	R.C.M. Reddy	1989	Borkathal	West Tripura
7.	Kumar Alok	1990	Durgapur	North Tripura
8.	S.K. Rakesh	1990	Lebacharra	South Tripura
9.	Ashok Kumar	1991	Pakhirbada	North Tripura
10.	Manish Kumar	1991	Holakhet	South Tripura
11.	Tajinder Singh	1991	Purba Barjala	West Tripura
12.	Varun Kumar Sahu	1992	Sonaimuri	North Tripura
13.	Shashi Ranjan Kumar	1992	Trishabari	West Tripura
14.	–	–	Birchandra Manu	South Tripura
15.	Rakesh Ranjan	1992	Srirampur	North Tripura

INTRODUCTION : A NORTH-EAST PERSPECTIVE

The North Eastern Council formed in 1971, functioning since 1972 as an advisory body and playing the role of a supra-planning authority since 1973-74 over the seven NE States (there is no economical zonal system and no such other regional organisation in the country) is reported to have been putting forward problems, proposals, schemes and suggestions in respect of the North-Eastern Region to the concerned Ministries and organisations of the Central Government.[1] But from its multifarious activities like funding of improved *chulhas*, biogas plants, improved seed farms, live stock farms etc. it seems that there is no clear demarcation of its sphere of activities as a result of which there may be overlapping and duplication of State level schemes and projects. In this context and particularly in the background of limited funds allotted in the plans, the NEC may concentrate on investment in infrastructural development projects as it has already undertaken for funding power generation, roads construction and improvement, railway, airport and inland water development projects which are of crucial importance for intra-regional and economic development.[2]

Agriculture

Paradoxically, even though the region is endowed with high rainfall and high soil fertility status, agricultural productivity and level of agricultural technology is low when compared to other regions of the country. There are many institutional factors responsible for the slow growth of agriculture and slow adoption of agricultural innovations. For various historical and geographical reasons the tribal communities in the region have been practicing primitive agriculture *(jhumming)* with communal ownership of land. Of late, because of the inherent contradictions in the communal ownership of land, privatisation is gradually emerging, but the pace is rather slow.

Under the traditional system of land allotment, foot hill portion is allotted to one farmer, the middle and top portion to other farmers disregarding the natural principles of watershed management. Researches conducted at the ICAR Research Complex for N.E.H. Region have proved the superiority of model land-use, agri-horti-silvi-pastoral (3-tier system) system, wherein bottom one-third portion is utilised for annual crops, middle one-third portion for horticultural crops and top one-third for forestry. Economic evaluation under model land-use system revealed that gross income, net income, family labour income and farm business income increased by 161, 284, 90 and 100 per cent respectively over those obtained under shifting cultivation. The prevailing system of allotment of land does not allow the adoption of model land use-cum-3 tier technology.

Studies conducted at the ICAR Research Complex for NEH Region on watershed based farming revealed the feasibility of retaining over 90 per cent of the annual rainfall even in steep hill slopes which in turn helps in recharge of groundwater and streams besides minimising the risk of soil erosion. These results suggest that it is possible to arrest the soil erosion and environmental degradation and help in better soil, water conservation and water harvesting provided a well thought out land reform and land-use policy is implemented by the State Governments in the region.

All these imply assessing land resources by measuring land through cadastral surveys, delineation of shifting cultivation zones, scientific land-use policy, evolving suitable strategy for the transfer of technology, strengthening the infrastructure for better input supply and better marketing facilities. Considering the peculiar ownership structure of land involving socio-cultural ramification and the high level of cooperative spirit prevailing in the tribal communities, cooperative approach seems to be pragmatic in realising the full benefits of improved agricultural technology through the application of watershed management and model land-use system in agriculture. It is high time that the State Governments and voluntary agencies tried this cooperative approach on pilot basis in different places to explore its feasibility and adoption on wider scale in the region.[3]

With the known production technology in hand and sound research base, demonstration, training and extension efforts, the gloomy picture of the agriculture of this region can be changed.

The media can also play a very meaningful role to highlight the various aspects of shifting cultivation and the measures that can be taken to control it. It can bring into sharp focus the changes in the outlook of the farming community in the hilly areas of the North-Eastern Region. Shifting cultivation is an anachronism and it will never fit into any scheme of things to modernise agriculture.[4]

Considering criticality and regional priority, six pilot projects on shifting cultivation with focus on soil and water conservation were initiated, two each in Mizoram, Manipur and Tripura in the Fifth NEC Plan. Under the programme, 5,300 *jhumia* families were settled in 11,300 ha. affected area. The project with further ramifications in terms of coverage of additional catchment and watershed area as well as beneficiaries was continued during the Sixth Plan in 10 Macro watersheds, namely Siang (Arunachal Pradesh), Range (Assam), Dedrum (Meghalaya), Iril (Manipur), Dhakswari, Palak, Chanpur (Mizoram), Mangiew (Nagaland), Howhra, Manu (Tripura). These programmes had achieved desired demonstration effects in terms of efficient soil and water management and practicing diversified agricultural activities, predominantly by the shifting cultivators.

The various thrust areas of development in agriculture during the Seventh NEC Plan were those of the establishment of a Regional Centre of bio-fertilizers, input testing laboratories, Training-cum-Demonstration Centres of mushroom production, breeders and Foundation Seed Farms for cereals, pulses, oilseeds, cotton etc., pilot project on dryland agriculture, demonstration of water harvesting technology etc. The thrust on watershed management programmes, however, continued by way of taking up 9 additional pilot projects located at Popumpoma (Arunachal Pradesh), Hiri-Hiri (Assam), Shingo Tsuong and Dikhu (Nagaland), Teirei (Mizoram), Umtongphar (Meghalaya), Luangleima (Manipur), Rangacherra and Maharanicherra (Tripura). These projects were continued in the Eighth Plan period. For providing regional facility for training on ecological conservation and scientific use of land and water resources, two regional centres, namely, Soil Conservation

Training Centre and North-Eastern Regional Institute of Water and Land Management were established at Byrnihat and Tezpur respectively during the Seventh Plan period. These programmes have helped in building up of adequate infrastructure.[5]

Constraints in Achieving Higher Productivity

Though the NE Region is agro-climatically suitable in growing a wide variety of field crops, vegetables, horticultural crops, plantation crops, spices, tea, rubber, coffee etc., a large number of limiting factors come in the way of achieving higher productivity. The dominant factors that have so far affected overall growth and development of agriculture in the North-East include: erratic distribution and long spell of rainfall followed by alternate cycles of flood and drought, extensive *jhum* cultivation, continuity with traditional agro-techniques, low land: man ratio, lack of mechanisation, lack of availability and improper delivery system of critical agricultural inputs like seeds, fertilizers, plant protection chemicals etc. This apart, inefficient soil and water conservation, lack of extension support, agro-services and inadequate training and skilled manpower also contribute to lower agricultural productivity.[6]

Strategy to Increase Productivity in the Plains

Out of 4.00 million ha. cropped area, nearly 3.10 million ha. falls in the plain areas, mainly in the States of Assam, Manipur and Tripura and foothills and valleys of other NE States. These areas also represent zone of concentration for intensive agricultural activities involving cultivation of high yielding varieties of rice, wheat, maize etc. covering nearly 1.20 million ha. Out of this, a gross irrigated area of 8.00 million ha., with assured irrigation facilities, provides opportunities for multiple cropping for achieving higher productivity through higher cropping intensity. Contrary to this, the non-irrigated areas suffer from such serious constraints as inadequate supplemental irrigation during *rabi* and summer seasons, restrictive use of animal power, power tillers and light agricultural implements etc. rendering the farmers incapacitated to cultivate the second or the third crop in succession after the first *kharif* crop. With a view to overcome these problems faced in the plains areas as also to streamline measures for enhancing agricultural productivity through multiple cropping, certain strategies are suggested for adoption. These are:

(i) Exploration and exploitation of additional potential ground water resources for expansion and optimisation of minor irrigation facilities to areas that are hitherto not covered by traditional irrigation network.

(ii) Development of short duration, high yielding fertilizer responsive and non-lodging rice cultivation suitable for inundated and flood-affected areas during the first monsoon period.

(iii) The irrigated area may have to be brought under triple cropping system by way of providing high doses of fertilizers, manures and required quantities of irrigation water in the critical growth phases of crops.

(iv) For non-irrigated areas, light and repeated tillage operations in the post-harvest *kharif* season, using mould-board plough or light power tillers, followed by organic amendments or green manuring would help maintain better fertility and residual moisture regime so that a second crop or a crop mix may be practiced to achieve higher productivity.[7]

Introduction, adoption and intensification of suitable crop varieties are not the straight answer to the staggering problems of low yields for the region. High yielding varieties apart, the high yield performance is seemingly possible from a synergistic interaction and response through judicious and balanced application of chemical fertilizers and organic/bio-organic manures in conjunction with providing optimal level of moisture regime.

Table 3.1 summarises the supply plan of fertilizer nutrients (NPK) for the North-East States during *kharif* (1991) and *rabi*

(1991-92) against the foodgrains production target set out for 1991-92 (Table 3.2).

Table 3.1 : Supply Plan of Fertilizer Nutrients (NPK) for North-East States

Name of the States	Consumption of Fertilizer Kg/ha	(In '000 tonnes of NPK content Nutrient Supply)		
		Kharif	*Rabi*	*Total*
Arunachal Pradesh	1.20	0.40	0.15	0.55
Assam	10.50	27.48	22.21	49.69
Manipur	71.90	8.73	3.09	11.82
Meghalaya	12.60	1.82	2.97	4.79
Mizoram	13.60	0.89	0.38	1.27
Nagaland	4.50	1.33	0.54	1.87
Tripura	19.70	9.10	6.96	6.06
Total	134.00	49.75	36.3	104.81

Table 3.2 : Foodgrain Production in North-East States

(in. '000 tonnes)

Name of the States	Rice	Wheat	Coarse Cereals	Cereals	Pulses	Foodgrains		
						Kharif	Rabi	Total
Arunachal Pradesh	155	8	74	237	6	232	11	242
Assam	3370	122	22	3514	81	3242	353	3595
Manipur	485	10	33	528	19	518	29	547
Mizoram	70	14	13	78	10	76	21	97
Nagaland	164	-	25	189	2	190	1	191
Tripura	535	8	3	546	7	431	122	555
Total	4929	178	196	5274	129	4862	550	5413

It would be evident from the foregoing Tables 2.1 and 2.2 that barring Manipur, the consumption of fertilizers by all other NE States is below the National Average (i.e. 65 kg/ha).

Farming in the Hill Areas

The mode of farming in the hill areas is entirely different from the one in the plains. The ICAR Research Complex for the North Eastern Hill Region is doing commendable R & D as well as extension work for the development and utilisation of technologies appropriate to the hill areas of the North-East, but the pace of progress towards adaptation of these technologies is rather discouraging.

The pernicious effect of the age-old shifting cultivation has been well recognised and much talked about. Some efforts have also been made for the settlement of the *jhumias* to organised terraced cultivation. But the fact is that *jhumming* is still the preferred mode of agricultural practice with the tribal people and this is still their major economic activity. It may be wise to accept the fact that there ought to be some sound reasons for the survival of the *jhumming* system upto the present time. However, the problem has become acute due to the compulsion of the shortening of the *jhum* cycle from about 10 years to a bare 3 years now. While making all efforts for the settlement of the *jhumias* to organised cultivation through persuasive efforts, it will be appropriate to make simultaneous efforts towards evolution of suitable technologies for the modification of the *jhumming* system itself. This demands orientation of R & D efforts for quick building up and maintenance of the fertility of the soil so that the tribal farmers may find some means of earning enough basically through their traditional economic system, even at the reduced period of *jhum* cycling.[8]

Development of Commercial Plantations

Tea

Taking advantage of tea cultivation programme in the non-traditional areas initiated by the Tea Board, several other States of the NE Region are now poised to take up Tea Cultivation Programmes aiming at participation of tribals, otherwise engaged in *jhum* cultivation. Sporadic tea cultivation programmes undertaken by local tribals on trial basis have helped identification of agro-climatically suitable areas for tea cultivation. This comprises Tirap, Changlong, Lohit, Along and East Siang districts of Arunachal Pradesh, East Khasi and Garo Hills of Meghalaya, Churachandpur district of Manipur, Mokukchung, Zunhehoto and Mon districts of Nagaland, Lunglei and Chimtuipui districts of Mizoram and Central and South-Western belts of Tripura. For making a major impact in such a venture a greater initiative is required to be taken by the Tea Board, State level plantation and rehabilitation corporations, Markfed etc. to gear up the programme for larger benefit of the region.[9]

Rubber

It has been established well through successive exploratory surveys and trials since 1963 that extensive areas situated in the NE States are suited for economic cultivation of rubber. The North Eastern zone lies well outside the traditional rubber growing belt, but the agro-climatic conditions prevailing here are nevertheless unique in as much as near tropical features are experienced in most parts owing to low elevations, exposure to monsoons and other moderating influences. Encouraged by the results obtained from trial plantations undertaken in Assam and Tripura, commercial scale plantations were started in those States. In Meghalaya and Mizoram, the State Soil Conservation Department and in Nagaland and Manipur, the State Forest Department are undertaking rubber plantations.

A project for Accelerated Development of Rubber Plantations in NE Region during the six years from 1984-85 to 1989-90 was approved by the Government of India. The target of planting during the period was 24,000 ha. against which 23,155 ha. was planted.

Seven Regional offices of the Rubber Board have been progressively opened for the North-East at Guwahati, Silchar,

Diphu, Tura, Agartala and Udaipur. The Board has also set up 8 Regional Nurseries in Assam, Meghalaya and Tripura.

The extent of rubber plantations raised in the North-Eastern Region till 1989-90 is as follows: [10]

Tripura	16,120 ha.
Assam	8,630 ha.
Meghalaya	3,530 ha.
Nagaland	1,095 ha.
Mizoram	875 ha.
Manipur	1,015 ha.
Arunachal Pradesh	40 ha.
	31,305 ha.

Coffee

On the basis of techno-feasibility reports of the Coffee Board, NEC supported the establishment of a sizeable number of Coffee nurseries during the Sixth and Seventh NEC Plan periods in the NE States. These Coffee nurseries were located at Namdang (Arunachal Pradesh), Chutianala, Karbianglong (Assam), Churachandpur (Manipur), Marngar (Meghalaya), Wokha (Nagaland), Teliamara (Tripura), Simtlangpui, Lunglei (Mizoram). These nurseries had since catered to the needs of conducting adaptive trials for adoption by progressive planters.[11]

Need for Mushroom Cultivation

Low cost mushroom production technology developed and currently being practiced for the cultivation of mushroom throughout the North-East needs a lot more upgradation and modernisation. These improvements are specifically needed in respect of bulk pasteurization/sterilisation of compost preparations, standardising parameters for the production of quality compost, fortification of compost formulation, upgradation and scaling up of shelf and tray growth systems for cropping and spawn regeneration etc.[12]

Water Resources : Potential and Utilisation

Major part of irrigation potential remains unutilised in the North-Eastern States. As a result very small portion of the cultivable area is under irrigation. This has resulted in low production. As a result, large quantities of foodgrains have to be imported from the outside. The main cause of this problem is the ill management of water resources, lack of coordination among the States and political interference in the management programmes.[13]

Tables 3.3 and 3.4 provide information on the irrigation potential and its utilisation under major and medium projects respectively for different States of North Eastern India. The created potential in major and medium irrigation varies from zero to 29.63 per cent of the ultimate potential in different States, the highest being in Manipur. The utilisation of created potential in Assam and Manipur is 56.44 and 60.00 per cent, respectively.

Table 3.3 : Benefits from Major and Medium Irrigation Schemes

('000 ha. gross)

State	Irrigation benefits upto 1985					Target of additional benefit during the Seventh Plan	
	Ultimate Irrigation Potential	Potential	% of Ultimate Potential	Utilisation	% of Potential	Potential	Utilisation
Assam	970.00	101.00	10.41	57.00	56.44	110.00	115.00
Arunachal Pradesh	—	—	—	—	—	—	—
Mizoram	—	—	—	—	—	—	—
Manipur	135.00	40.00	29.63	24.00	60.00	25.00	30.00
Meghalaya	20.00	—	—	—	—	—	—
Nagaland	10.00	—	—	—	—	—	—
Tripura	100.00	—	—	—	—	15.00	8.00

Source : Central Water Commission, New Delhi.

In minor irrigation, Nagaland is the State which has developed 63.75 per cent of the ultimate potential. This is followed by Tripura (50.43%), Manipur (37.14%), Meghalaya (35%) and Assam (23%). From Tables 3.3 and 3.4 it is evident that the created irrigation potential is very low compared to the optimal irrigation potential. This shows the extent of water left unutilised.

Table 3.4 : Benefits from Major and Medium Irrigation Schemes

('000 ha. gross)

State	Irrigation benefits upto 1985						Target of additional benefit during the Seventh Plan
	Ultimate Utilisation Irrigation Potential	Potential	% of Ultimate Potential	Utilisation	% of Potential	Potential	
Assam	1700.00	391.00	23.00	349.00	89.26	150.00	105.00
Arunachal Pradesh	-	40.20	-	34.20	85.07	14.70	009.00
Mizoram	-	6.44	-	5.84	90.68	7.00	4.00
Manipur	105.00	39.00	37.14	34.00	87.18	14.50	0.30
Meghalaya	100.00	35.00	35.00	32.00	91.43	14.50	11.50
Nagaland	80.00	51.00	63.75	47.00	92.16	12.00	7.30
Tripura	115.00	58.00	50.43	50.00	86.21	20.00	12.00

Source : Central Water Commission, New Delhi.

Although irrigation from surface water is done in Assam valley, Manipur and other States through the Brahmaputra, Barak and other rivers, there is good groundwater potential in these States. The exploitation done so far is negligible. Details are given in Table 3.5.

It could be seen from Table 3.5 that the ground water potential is mostly available in Assam, Meghalaya and Tripura. Manipur and Nagaland have got very little potential, while Mizoram and Arunachal Pradesh have no potential.

Table 3.5 : Irrigation Potential from Ground Water

State	Level upto 1984-85						Target for VII Plan (NEC)
	Ultimate Utilisation Potential	Potential	% of Ultimate Potential	Utilisation	% of Potential	Potential	
Assam	700.00	83.00	11.86	66.00	79.52	75.00	52.00
Arunachal Pradesh	—	—	—	—	—	0.50	0.30
Mizoram	—	—	—	—	Neg	—	Neg.
Manipur	5.00	0.10	2.00	0.10	100.00	0.50	0.50
Meghalaya	35.00	8.70	58.00	8.70	100.00	2.00	1.50
Nagaland	5.00	0.10	2.00	Neg.	-	0.50	0.30
Tripura	15.00	11.70	78.00	8.80	75.21	5.00	3.00

Source : Central Water Commission, New Delhi.

Horticulture

The North-Eastern Region is potentially rich in natural resources. This region with wide ranging topography, climate and rainfall offers considerable scope for the development of agro-based industries. This area is ideal for growing varied assortment of tropical and temperate fruits and vegetables. Delicious apple, pear, pineapple and other fruits are sold in plain areas at high prices. Since these fruits can be successfully grown at higher altitudes it is necessary to develop the horticultural activity for the economic development of the hill people.[14]

In the horticultural sector, 23 pioneering projects were supported by the NEC during its Sixth and Seventh Plan periods. Through these programmes of innovative and pilot nature, NEC's efforts have been directed towards the development of temperate fruit nurseries, establishment of regional vegetable seed farms, Foundation Potato Seed Farm, Orchard-cum-Nurseries for citrus, spices, tea, coffee etc., development of minor forest products, identification and cultivation of medicinal and tuber crops, promotion of floriculture, establishment of a Regional Fruit Processing Plant etc.

To promote and effectively coordinate marketing of surplus agri-horticultural produce the North Eastern Agricultural Marketing Corporation was set up by the NEC during the Sixth NEC Plan.

Sericulture

Sericulture, despite favourable hydrographic condition and intimate traditional link with the life-style and culture of the people, could not make a dent in the commercial sense until recently for lack of planning and financial support that this sector deserves.

NEC has accordingly financed 37 sericulture projects in the Fifth Plan and 39 projects during the Sixth Plan involving the cultivation of feed plants and production of mulberry, eri and oak tassar silk. During the Seventh NEC Plan several schemes on reeling, weaving etc. have also been implemented in all the NE States. The various State-run Sericulture Units numbering 700, employ about 3,000 workers in Sericulture Industries in the region. This exemplifies magnitude of employment potential in the sector. During the Seventh NEC Plan increased emphasis has been laid on mulberry culture and with the introduction of bovine rearing tools in the region it is expected that sufficient quantities of cocoons would be available for commercial exploitation.[15]

The State-wise position of the financing of sericulture schemes are summarised in Table 3.6.

Table 3.6 : State-wise Financing of Sericulture Scheme

Name of the States	Fifth Plan		Sixth Plan	
	No. of Schemes	Allocation (Rs. in lakhs)	No. of Schemes	Allocation (Rs. lakhs)
Arunachal Pradesh	4	17.23	6	49.52
Assam	7	46.63	9	51.78
Manipur	5	41.47	3	57.79
Meghalaya	7	43.90	6	30.88
Mizoram	5	16.81	5	50.00
Nagaland	5	15.43	4	35.92
Tripura	4	18.89	6	31.33
Total	37	200.46	39	307.22

A sizeable number of Reeling, Spinning and Weaving units were established in the North-Eastern region with the financial assistance to the tune of Rs.116.20 lakhs extended by the NEC during the Seventh NEC Plan. Comparative State-wise position is reflected on Table 3.7.

Table 3.7 : Comparative State-wise Position

Name of the State	Units	No.	Allocation (Rs. in lakhs)
Assam	Reeling and Twisting	1	20.635
Manipur	Weaving	1	12.794
Meghalaya	Reeling and Twisting	1	20.635
Mizoram	Spinning and Weaving	1	13.341
Nagaland	Reeling and Twisting	1	28.95
Tripura	Reeling	1	12.43
		6	116.20

There are various cooperative societies in sericulture and Assam probably has the maximum of them followed by Manipur. In other States much needs to be done on this front. However, in Assam and Manipur, most of these societies are working for reelers and weavers. It is essential that rearers' cooperative societies are also formed.[16]

Animal Husbandry and Fishery

Animal husbandry has been a traditionally indispensable activity of the rural people of the North-East; particularly the tribals. There is also much scope for the introduction of improved breed of dairy animals, sheep, poultry etc. But lack of organised efforts towards the breeding and rearing of animals with requisite care for nutritional needs has kept this activity almost at static levels. Although in terms of number, the average livestock and poultry birds population in this region is much above the all-India average. The yield of milk and eggs is much below. The average yield of milk per cow is only about half a litre against the all India average of 3-4 litres. This situation speaks volumes about the urgent need for nutrition and health care of the animals, the requisite technology for which is readily available, but needs to be adopted and utilised.

From some experiments conducted in the farmers' ponds in West Tripura district in Tripura, it was observed that fish production can be enhanced manifold than the present level of production, by just adopting proper management practices. Nearly 2,500 kg. of fish/ha/250 days was achieved in a pond which was earlier producing 200 to 300 kg/ha/year.[17] Considering the fact that the production was achieved in the farmers' ponds and that if it could be extended to all the presently available impounded water areas, nearly 12,000 tonnes of fish per annum can be harvested. But this process would take a few years to yield the expected results and by then, there would be another increase in the population also expecting fish supply. Therefore, the strategy adopted would be:

(i) increasing the cultivable water areas either by the reclamation of beels/jheels or by excavation of new ponds;

(ii) utilising dead rivers and Gumeti reservoir for fish culture;

(iii) increasing the fish production by adopting proper scientific management techniques.

Tripura has very little scope for horizontal expansion of its fishery resources except in the available beels and additional mini-barrage, if created. Further increase in fish production in Tripura is mainly possible through vertical expansion in agriculture, scientific management of reservoirs and optimum exploitation of riverine resource after its systematic survey.[18]

Manipur has vast potential for fisheries development in various sectors like beels/lakes, paddy-cum-fish culture and ponds. The State has not only adequate resources to meet its own needs but also to take care of a substantial part of fish needs of the other States of the region. However, to attain this task a careful planning and judicious exploitation of resources are needed. The main thrust of fisheries development in this State should be on proper exploitation of captive fisheries resources and development of culture system. In the culture system, priority should be assigned to the creation of fishery States, followed by paddy-cum-fish culture. It can be expected that by 2000 AD, 10,000 ha. will be under paddy-cum-fish culture in Manipur, yielding an average production of 600 kg./ha.[19]

The Assam Agricultural University has already taken an initiative in establishing a College of Fishery with financial help from the NEC.

Industry

Table 3.8 shows the variety of deposited minerals and other products in the North Eastern region.

Nevertheless, the region remains industrially and economically backward. This fact is reflected in its total number of industrial units. Only 2 per cent of the country's medium and large scale industries and about 1.5 per cent of small scale industries have been set up in the entire region. Table 3.9 presents a State-wise break-up in this regard.

Table 3.8 : Varieties of Minerals in North-East States

Sl. No.	Description	Total NER	Total All India
Minerals (Estimated Reserve)			
1.	Crude Oil	145 (Million tonnes)	757 (M.T.)
2.	Coal	864 (Million tonnes)	1,92,359 (M.T.)
3.	Lime stone	5,404 (Million tonnes)	69,354 (M.T.)
4.	Dolomite	426 (Million tonnes)	4,608 (M.T.)
5.	Fullers earth	17 (Million tonnes)	—
6.	Fire clay	2 (Million tonnes)	—
7.	Base Metal	0.11 (Million tonnes)	—
8.	Natural Gas	135 (Billion Cubic metres)	686 (billion cubic metres)
Others			
9.	Annual Prdn. of Tea	38,400 (kg.)	7,14,000 (kg)
10.	Forest Area	119.6 (lakh hectares)	725 (lakh hectares)

Source : CMIE, Bombay, Sept., 1991 and *Eco. Times* (Tea Annual), 1991.

Table 3.9 : State-wise Break-up of SSI units in NER *vis-a-vis* some other States

Sl.No.	State	1971	1981	1985	1988	1990
1.	Assam	809	4152	6543	10910	12120
2.	Manipur	8	2422	2794	4680	5374
3.	Meghalaya	—	233	571	—	—
4.	Nagaland	—	345	395	—	—
5.	Tripura	174	1188	1715	3966	—
6.	Mizoram	—	298	684	—	—
7.	Arunachal Pradesh	—	189	262	—	—
8.	Haryana	8250	23492	44204	82600	—
9.	Tamil Nadu	22,899	36003	59756	—	—
10.	Maharashtra	25696	39414	40944	—	—
11.	West Bengal	19423	106972	120692	162745	—
	All India	239128	526035	849074	15.92 lakh	18.27 lakh

Source : National Institute of Small Industry Extension Training.

Lack of infrastructural facilities, dearth of entrepreneurship, high manufacturing cost, absence of training facilities, lack of techno-economic information and lack of coordination may be stated to be the main reasons for the slow growth and high sickness of the SSI sector in the region. The author of an article cites a recent instance of an entrepreneur in Manipur who, after installing all machines, had to wait for one full year for power connection and another six months for the sanction of working capital from a nationalised bank.[20]

The North-East region being vast in area and less in population, there should be no difficulty in locating most suitable sites anywhere for setting up agro-based industries. However, for the proper utilisation of the perishables it is preferable that processing units are located in the growing region itself. In exploring the possibilities of setting up viable industrial units in the region, significant efforts were made by the Central Food Technological Research Institute, Mysore, in collection of basic information on physical background, climate, temperature, rainfall, communication and power, demographic characteristics, agriculture and horticulture, livestock, poultry and fisheries production and marketing and existing food based industries. Based on the available resources and potential, suggestions were made for suitable food-based industries in different areas. Though considerable ground work has been done to identify potential food-based projects, not much progress is perceptible in the implementation phase.[21]

Due to the geographical limitations and weak infrastructure, Manipur has all along been industrially backward. The acute scarcity of power and limited distribution network, the long surface distances over which essential raw materials for finished products have to be transported, the absence of adequate initiative and support of the banking sector have all hindered the growth of an industrial climate. The lack of entrepreneurship and technical skills among the local people has been another key factor.

Handloom is the most important cottage industry in Manipur. Most of the women folk in the State are expert weavers and weave a variety of products which have an excellent market both within and outside the State.[22]

Except the existence of several saw mills and cane and bamboo product making units, there is hardly any other forest based industry in small sector in this region, despite the fact that almost half of the total geographical area of the North-East is covered by forests. Huge amount of saw dust from plywood factories and saw mills is creating disposal problem and it can be easily utilised for making fuel briquettes for which appropriate technology is available. Khasi pine available in Meghalaya, Arunachal Pradesh, Manipur and Nagaland has been proved to be superior to any other pine species in the country in many respects. It is high time that small scale entrepreneurs come forward for processing pine resin with available appropriate technologies for the manufacture of turpentine oil for which there is great demand in North-East itself. Production of cinnamon leaf oil and isolation of eugenol could also be taken up on a small scale. Agrwood oil industry, the oldest and the most lucrative forest based essential oil industry in the North-East is in dire need of organised efforts for modernisation with appropriate technology.

Among minor forest products, mention may be made of huge quantity of wild fruits which may be used for the extraction of non-edible oils that have huge demand in soap and other industries in the region. Some forests in the North-East are rich in tannin bearing plants. In view of the world shortage of vegetable tannins and ample domestic demand it is worthwhile to make use of appropriate technologies for tannin extraction. Manufacture of cups and plates from wild leaves and arecanut sheaths is another area needing attention for using available appropriate technology. Technology is also available for making hand-made papers for files and boards from banana fibres and wild banana plants, plentifully available in the North Eastern hills.

Rubber is an important plantation crop in the North-East, but utilisation of available appropriate technologies for the precipitation of rubber latex and pressing them into sheets is yet to be made in this region. Small scale industries for the preparation of common rubber goods like bicycle tyres, rubber bands, balloons etc. have got ample scope for development in the North-East.[23]

The trend of growth of SSI in the NE region during 1985-86 can be seen in Table 3.10.

Table 3.10 : Trend in Development of SSI (1981-1986) in N.E. Region

Year	1981	1982	1983	1984	1985	1986
Assam	4152	4230	4878	5773	6543	7362
Arunachal Pradesh	189	210	262	246	262	248
Manipur	3422	3595	4140	2594	2794	4220
Meghalaya	233	308	435	469	571	643
Mizoram	298	423	539	628	684	1191
Nagaland	345	353	361	374	395	429
Tripura	1188	1489	1715	1400	1715	2392

Source : Development Commissioner, Small Scale Industries, New Delhi.

Industries set up by the NEC sponsored entrepreneurs could be classified under certain heads. Approximate distribution under each head covering only higher range of percentages are as follows:[24]

(i)	Textile, handloom, handicraft, wool, leather products	31%
(ii)	Agro-based, food products, wood based	23%
(iii)	General engineering, automobile, electrical, electronics	10%
(iv)	Serving	12%
(v)	Printing, stationery, book-binding etc.	6%

Table 3.11 : Distribution of Handlooms in North-East India

State looms	Working looms	Idle looms	Total
Arunachal Pradesh	45,060	456	45516
Assam	1298731	110437	1409168
Manipur	266915	3346	270261
Meghalaya	7783	418	8201
Mizoram	14388	9406	23794
Nagaland	71636	5867	77503
Tripura	116659	2413	119072
Total	1821172	132343	1953515

Source : Census of Handlooms in India 1987-88, Development Commissioner for Handlooms, Ministry of Textiles, Government of India, pp. 60-62.

Table 3.12 : Productivity per Loom in NE States

States	Production of cloth per loom per day (in metres)
Arunachal Pradesh	1.26
Assam	0.63
Manipur	1.86
Meghalaya	1.58
Mizoram	0.22
Nagaland	1.21
Tripura	2.30
All States	1.29

Source : Census of Handlooms in India 1987-88, Development Commissioner for Handlooms, Ministry of Textiles, Government of India, pp. 147-149.

Marketing of handloom products is of immense significance because of the scattered nature of production in the cottage industry. Competition in the textile industry has been mounting. Effective marketing by catering to specific market niches, customer satisfaction, price competitiveness, product quality and customer awareness holds the key to a bright tomorrow for the handloom industry.[25] Tables 3.11 and 3.12 depict the distribution of handlooms in the North-East and productivity per loom respectively.

Rural Development

The North-East represents a highly rural society. More than 90 per cent of the population lives in villages and more than 80 per cent of the working force and population derives its living mainly from agriculture and allied activities, like animal husbandry, forestry and fishing. The stagnancy in the rural agricultural economy is the result of relative stagnation in the field of agricultural production. The two basic requirements of the improvement of agriculture in the region is the improvement of per hectare yield and fuller utilisation of land through multiple cropping.

In the existing rural development programmes particularly in IRDP – the priorities have been laid on :

(a) Agricultural growth, through optimisation of production possibilities of the project area, development of land and other measures in the area;
(b) Land reforms – to ensure rights over the land of the actual tillers;
(c) Rural industries – to plan for rural industries in compact rural areas on the basis of local growth centres;
(d) Improvement of social services, through education, nutrition, health and family welfare; and
(e) Development of human resources, to improve efficiency for maximising production and minimising cost per unit of land, capital and labour.

All the above programmes involve various disciplines and Government departments. Hence coordinated approach is necessary.

Rural employment programmes do not give sustained employment to all those who need it, especially during the lean season.

Rural people have become more and more dependent on the Government for such employment oriented avenues.

Nobody has seriously bothered to see whether the beneficiaries have started and continued with their ventures or whether they have diverted the financial assistance to some other activities.

There is no proper monitoring and concurrent evaluation of the schemes. This has an adverse effect on the quality and speed of work.

Role of Cooperatives

The NE Region offers excellent opportunities for the development of agriculture and agro-based industries on account of unique bio-diversity and natural resource availability. However, the cooperative movement in the region is rather weak due to lack of general awareness.

Specific programmes have been taken up in the region to create infrastructural facilities for buffer stocking and movement of agricultural inputs, storing of marketable surplus of agri-horticultural produce and processing facilities for value-added products. Besides this special assistance has been provided in poultry, piggery, fishery, dairy and handloom sector under the weaker section programme for self-employment and income generation.

The financial liberalisation policies adopted in the above mentioned activities had made possible a three times greater investment in agriculture and allied activities in 1989 as compared to the base year 1984, as could be seen from Tables 3.13 and 3.14.

Table 3.13 : Financial Liberalisation

(Rs. in lakhs)

Name of the States	Financial Assistance upto 1983-84	Upto 1988-89
Arunachal Pradesh	24.180	24.180
Assam	1495.610	4363.014
Manipur	95.884	620.313
Meghalaya	152.225	348.041
Mizoram	—	48.210
Nagaland	45.330	278.047
Tripura	177.997	630.762
Total	1991.226	6312.567

Table 3.14 : Financial Liberalisation

(*Rs. in lakhs*)

Name of the States	1984-85	1985-86	1986-87	1987-88	1988-98
Arunachal Pradesh	—	—	—	0.33	0.32
Assam	45.01	38.08	57.00	49.80	60.00
Manipur	0.81	0.25	0.34	0.89	1.62
Meghalaya	0.14	0.006	0.09	0.38	1.20
Mizoram	—	—	—	—	—
Nagaland	NA	NA	NA	NA	NA
Tripura	1.57	2.63	2.45	1.99	3.55
Total	47.53	40.976	61.54	53.39	66.69

The economy of the NE region is predominantly agrarian as more than 70 per cent of the population derive their livelihood from agriculture. For facilitating conversion of agriculture and allied products into consumable and value added products, a total of 59 processing units have since been supported in the cooperative sector in the NE region upto 1989. The State-wise position is given in Table 3.15.

Table 3.15 : Economy of North-East Region

Particulars	A.P.	Assam	Manipur	Meghalaya	Mizoram	Nagaland	Tripura
1. Cold Storage	—	1	—	—	—	1	1
2. Rice Mills	—	31	—	—	—	1	—
3. Oil Mills	—	8	—	1	—	—	—
4. Vanaspati Unit	—	1	—	—	—	—	—
5. Vegetable Oil Refinery	—	1	—	—	—	—	—
6. Oxygen Compressor Unit	—	1	—	—	—	—	—
7. Rice Bran Unit	—	1	—	—	—	—	—
8. F&V Processing Unit	—	2	1	—	—	—	—
9. Bakery Unit	—	—	2	—	—	—	—
10. Sugar Mills	—	2	—	—	—	—	—
11. Spinning Mills	—	3	—	—	—	—	—
12. Cotton Ginning Mills	—	—	1	—	—	—	—
Total	—	51	4	1	—	2	1

Table 3.15 reveals a completely disproportionate investment pattern on the agro-processing units in the region. Out of 59 units set up in the cooperative sector, 51 have been set up in Assam alone. For further growth and development a much greater attention will have to be focused in developing other NE States with greater allocation of funds to set up need based agro-processing units with a view to providing greater employment opportunities and generate income from expanded marketing of the processed end products.[26]

MANIPUR

Nestling deep within a lush green corner of the North-East is the wondrously beautiful Little Shangrila called Manipur. Manipur literally means a "jewelled land". An oval shaped virgin valley surrounded by blue green hills, rich in art and tradition, has inspired descriptions such as the "Switzerland of the East" with cascading rapids, tripping rivers, carpets of flowers, exotic blooms and lazy lakes. The valley is surrounded by hills on the east, west, and the north. The valley covers nearly 10 per cent of the geographical area of the State, and is drained by the Manipur river. On both sides of this river are located a number of shallow lakes; the Loktak lake being the most prominent of these. The State has a geographical area of 22,327 sq. km. of which 19,981 sq. km. are hilly regions surrounding the central valley area of 2,346 sq. km. More than 65 per cent of the total population of the State is concentrated in their small valley region and the rest are in the hills.

The State comprises 8 districts, namely, Imphal, Thoubal, Bishnupur (which are valley districts) and Ukhrul, Senapati, Chandel, Tamenglong and Churachandpur (which are hill districts).

According to the Constitution of India, there are 29 recognised Scheduled Tribes in Manipur. The tribes of Manipur inhabit the five Hill Districts of the State, viz., Ukhrul, Chandel, Churachandpur, Tamenglong and Senapati. The majority of the people of the North Eastern States are of Tibeto-Mongoloid stock and the people of Manipur are no exception. The hills of

Manipur are inhabited by the Nagas and Kukis. The valley is mainly inhabited by the Meiteis, who are comparatively more advanced than the other communities of Manipur.

The tribes are, by and large, well-organised social groups having their own well-defined policy framework, well-established customs, administrative structure and distinct modes of life. A Naga village is governed by the headman or Khulakpa, with the help of the councillors. The post of headman is hereditary in most cases, and the village councillors are either elected or selected. The Kukis in Manipur are a dominant tribe spreading their authority over a wide range of hill areas surrounding the valley of Imphal during the hey-day of the Maharaja of Manipur and subsequently in the British period. The Kuki chiefs were in supreme command over their respective domains in the hills. Despite changes in the matters of administration coupled with the negation of the authority of the Kuki chiefs, the traditional system of village administration continues to exist.

Agriculture and Allied Activities

The main occupation of the people in the villages of Manipur is agriculture. In the hill pockets it is cultivation of rice by means of shifting cultivation. They practice *jhumming* in areas around the village. There is no fixed area for cultivation as the sites are shifted year after year. The distance of the *jhum* land can be anything between 2 km. to 10 km.

The Government of Manipur has put forward several schemes and programmes for controlling *jhum* cultivation. The most important is the central scheme called the Shifting Cultivation Control Scheme with 100 per cent Central assistance. However there has been, as comes out of the report from village Vanchengphai in Tamenglong district, no impact of the Government schemes on the villagers is perceptible till now.

As is evident from the Khemkan report (Thoubal district), seeds mainly come from the previous year's stock. Fertilisers and pesticides are purchased from the Thoubal bazaar. Tractors are taken on hire basis. No supply of HYV seeds is reported from Dongjang in Churachandpur, nor there is any use of fertilisers, pesticides and tractors in this village. 7 households in Dongjang use bullocks, which are borrowed at the rate of Rs.500 per acre. Similarly, no scientific technology is employed in Thanlon (Churachandpur district). The only inputs are personal seeds and human labour. In Tangpijol (Churachandpur), the seed varieties are all traditional ones having low yield which goes down in subsequent years. The use of fertilisers, small implements, power tillers, buying of water for irrigation, hiring of labour is totally absent. In Parbung Lungthulien and Senvon (Churachandpur district), there has not been any conscious effort to adopt better technologies. There is no concept of mechanised farming in Chandel and Ukhrul districts as well.

No irrigation facilities are available to the cultivators in most of the villages in Manipur. This is the case, for instance, with the cultivators of Vanchengphai in Tamenglong district. They depend entirely on rainfall for cultivation. In Nungsai-Chiru village of the Senapati district, no irrigation facilities exist. However, in Hundung (Ukhrul), canals, streams, tanks and ponds are available for this purpose. In Tolloi (Ukhrul), irrigation is done only through channels by the gravitational methods.

Cultivation in Chandel-Christian (Chandel) get irrigation from river Chakpi. A kutcha dam exists. But the absence of canals limits the influence of this source to a few plots, those lying near the river. Water is also stored in a tank, but there are no pumping sets. In Dongjang (Churachandpur) the water source is a stream running down the hills. This is intercepted by a dam of 1.5 m height. The stored water flows down in unlined channels. The terrace field in Sitam (Churachandpur) are about 20-30 ha. in area and are located along the bank of the Tuibum river. There is no pumping set to lift water.

Terracing has been done to some extent on the lower slopes of the village Lower Kom Keirap (Churachandpur). In Hundung (Ukhrul) terrace fields are inherited. All households do not own it. Poor people either have no such fields or have the same in small areas. Due to non-availability of large plain tracts, terrace as well as *jhum* cultivation is practiced. In Tolloi

(Ukhrul), the hill slopes along the banks of three rivers which flow near the village have been extensively developed into terraces for wet paddy cultivation. In Tungjoy (Senapati), paddy is planted in terrace fields. Most of the terrace fields are used for monocropping while some do use it for double cropping. In Nungsai-Chiru (Senapati), on the lower slopes of the hills, especially in foothill areas, terracing has been done. The plots are long and narrow with a flat surface and can hold water. The terraced plots are to be irrigated as the porosity of the soil requires constant flow of water through the fields. Normally, this is done by diverting the water from a nearby stream.

The economic stability of the region depends greatly on the wet paddy cultivation on the flat plains. Five varieties of local rice are grown, for example, in Nungsai-Chiru (Senapati). Manure and fertilisers are also used. The average yield of paddy here is about 25 quintals per ha. as compared to 18 ha. in the hills. The Moyons of Komlathabi and Heigru-Tampak villages (Chandel) have cultivable lands on the hill slopes as well as the plains. About half of the families in Mata and Mata Mualtam (Churachandpur) practice sedentary cultivation on wetlands. These wetlands are actually the delta of nearby streams.

In the absence of any developed secondary sector employment, the rural population in Manipur depends on agriculture for livelihood. Under *jhumming*, productivity and production gradually declines and it is not sustainable over a period of time. Agriculture is having a mono-cropping pattern with paddy being the main crop.

In Tangpijol (Churachandpur), mixed cropping is being done and in the same field along with paddy some secondary crops are also grown. These are colocassia, cucumber, maize, sesamum and millets. These crops are *kharif* crops. Paddy continues to be the single major crop throughout the universe of study in the absence of irrigation facilities in the *rabi* season. Maize is grown in certain villages in the kitchen garden or on mountain slopes.

Coming to agronomics, people are in dire straits in the absence of satisfactory harvest.

Shirui (Ukhrul) has two crops a year. During the *khrif* the villagers grow mainly paddy, maize, beans, pumpkins etc. and during *rabi* they grow mainly potato, pea, broad beans, oilseeds (mustard and soyabean only), French beans etc. The following are the rough production figures of some of the crops:

Paddy	25-30 quintals/ha.
Maize	30-40 quintals/ha.
Pea	10-15 quintals/ha.
Potato	60-65 quintals/ha.

The areas under cultivation, the yields and the prices of the main crops cultivated in Tolloi (Ukhrul) are :

Crops	Area (acres)	Yield (MT/acre)	Price (Rs./kg)
Rice	360	0.7	8.00
Maize	70	1.2	2.00
Potato	40	7.0	3.00
Ginger	10	3.0	2.50
Squash	10	3.0	2.50

The approximate particulars of returns and the costs of production of the main crops are as under:

Crops	Returns/Acre		Cost (Rs.)/Acre		
	Qty(MT)	Price(Rs)	Seed	Labour	Total
Rice	0.7	5600	140	600	740
Maize	1.2	2400	60	400	460
Potato	7.0	21000	800	700	1500
Ginger	3.0	7500	400	600	1000
Squash	3.0	7500	300	300	600

The items of the village produce sold outside the village, the percentage sold outside and reserved for consumption in the village are:

Items	Qty./year	Total Cost (Rs)	Percentage	
			Sold Out	Consumed
Timber	450 cu.ft.	22,500	20	80
Potato	280 MT	8,40,000	70	30
Ginger	30 MT	75,000	60	40
Squash	30 MT	75,000	30	70
Cabbage	25 MT	62,500	20	80

The yield per acre in the valley land varies from 1900 to 2400 kgs. per acre in Kom Keirap (Churachandpur). The yield comes to 32 to 40 bags with each bag weighing about 60 kg. The price per bag currently is around Rs.180 per bag, making the returns per acre vary from Rs. 5800 to Rs. 7200. The cost of production per acre is dependent upon a large number of variables which may not be uniform for all villagers.

The major problems confronting agriculture in the universe area are as follows :

1. The soil is acidic in nature. This leads to low availability of phosphorus which gets fixed, thus leading to low response to fertiliser. Due to heavy rains and consequent leaching of silica, there is high concentration of iron leading to iron toxicity at places.
2. High rainfall and humidity create a favourable environment for a wide range of pests, diseases and weeds. Similarly, climate creates problems in the storage of grains and hay-making etc. Double-cropping is non-existent. Undulating topography, hill slopes and varying altitudes also create problems for the agriculture.
3. *Jhum* cultivation is associated with many social and cultural patterns, customs and habits.
4. The dearth of proper technology as well as poor utilisation has greatly limited agricultural production. Appropriate technology to tackle with area-specific problems is still not fully available.

A good potential for horticulture exists. If properly taken care of, it can provide good supplementary occupation to villagers. The land, mostly in the backyard is used to grow papaya, guava, jackfruit, banana, 'yongchak' etc. mostly used in self-consumption. Horticulture, on a commercial scale has not yet been tried.

Livestock

The present condition of the livestock may be termed as below average in the universe area. Infrastructural facilities like veterinary facilities are inadequate and far between.

Milk is not popular among the tribals. The unproductive cows are slaughtered for beef. Some grazing facilities are available in the villages, mostly on the foothills, but they are inadequate. The condition of the cattle is poor. The tribals do not graze the cows themselves. Milk yield is 1-2 kg. per cow. Traditionally, Zou tribals have not been very fond of milk. Due to *jhumming*, grazing land is not only shrinking but repeated cultivation makes the grass very hard for the cattle. In Parbung, Lungthulien and Senvon (Churachandpur), no cattle belong to any exotic variety. In Khemkan (Thoubal), the average number of cows/buffaloes per family was two. In Vanchengphai (Tamenglong), no cows or buffaloes are kept. Having worked out the total production of milk in village Shirui (Ukhrul) it was found that per capita milk consumption in the village was a meagre 50 ml./day (approximately). In Chandel district, cows are reared for beef.

The well-to-do among the tribals rear pigs. These are very popular because their parent stock is not expensive to buy and rearing does not require much care and labour. Besides, they can be fed with the kitchen refuse. The pigs are allowed to grow to any size for they are sold in weight, a kg. fetching Rs. 50. There is immense scope for the development of piggery in the universe area. However, piggery is not organised. Pork is in great demand in the towns and a ready market exists. Hence, efforts should be afoot to promote piggery.

There were quite a good number of households in the universe area rearing poultry. This also fetches a good price in nearby markets. Foul rearing comes as a tradition, rather than an economic activity. There is tremendous potential for the development of poultry in the universe area.

In Shirui (Ukhrul), broad terraces can be brought under paddy-*cum*-fish culture. In paddy lands in low lying areas, where yield is very low due to waterlogging, fish rearing with paddy simultaneously, as a supplementary crop, may render very good return and entail a most rational use of the land. The geographic features of the universe are highly favourable for paddy-*cum*-fish culture.

Rural Industries

The women of the North-East are famous for weaving clothes and our universe of study is no exception. The common ones are shawl, *phanek* (cloth worn by women at waist to cover the lower half) and some plain cloth. Every tribe adopts a unique pattern and colour. Shawl weaving is a labour intensive craft and it takes on an average 15 days to finish a shawl. In a year a Zou woman can weave 15 to 20 shawls, which on an average fetches Rs. 300-600 depending on texture.

There are a few carpenters, wool-knitting units etc. and a saw mill in Tungjoy (Senapati). The village being basically non-market oriented, these carpenters and wool-knitters restrict themselves to meeting the demands of the villagers only. In Moltuk (Chandel) handicrafts exist in a small way. Carpentry, bamboo works and blacksmithy come as subsidiary sources of income in Parbung, Lungthulien and Senvon (Churachandpur). The income is highly variable and is directly proportional to the interest taken by the Government agencies. The articles produced by the cane and bamboo workers in Thanlon (Churachandpur) are mats, baskets, winnowing fans, bamboo curtains, sieves, *murhas*, chairs etc.

Promotion of agro-based industries is a must in this area as it would make decentralised planning a reality and thereby help in formulating a plan strategy based on local resource endowments and felt needs of the people in the area. It would promote local entrepreneurship, generate employment, arrest mindless migration to urban areas and also check concentration of economic power through diffusion of the ownership of means of production.

Rice milling offers good scope. All the units in Thanlon (Churachandpur), for instance, are of huller type. Rubber roller – Sheller mills could not become popular due to high cost and higher capacity. Mini rice mill technology developed by CFTRI Mysore deserves all attention. Again, the by-products of rice mills offer ample scope for exploitation.

The spirit of cooperation is lacking. DWCRA appears to be the only bright spot. May be the consequent benefits of

DWCRA bring about a spirit and example of cooperation. The woman-groups are now very hopeful about their future, especially in Parbung, as apart from the cooperative department, industries department has also agreed to provide them help. It has also been trying to revive the Manipur handlooms and handicrafts marketing corporation, to procure the finished products from the work site itself and sell it in different States. For the time being, the cooperative department itself is able to lift the present production and send it to the sellers at Kohima, Dimapur and Shillong. The operations are, however, not at a large level due to transport bottlenecks.

Tribals in the sample area do not prepare cloth comparable to those of the Meitei villages. It is due to the limitation posed by the back-pressure loom by which only a cloth of very limited width can be woven. Then the tribal weavers have not taken to modernisation as has been done in the Meitei villages of the Manipur plains. Time is up they should switch over to the use of improved looms for weaving the cloth. The model is not far to seek. The handloom industry which at present is in the form of domestic industry is in a very low level of development. At best it is meeting part of the home needs. The weavers are not engaged whole time. Very small capital is invested. The produce is not meant for sale outside. The products are below standard relatively. Therefore, the question of competing in the market does not arise.

The favourable points about this industry are: (i) They have kept the traditional cottage industry alive, (ii) They are preparing rough durable cloth for home needs, and (iii) they keep themselves engaged in spare time. The possibilities of improvement and modernisation are, of course, there. The limitations, however, cannot be ignored in the nearby Meitei villages. This cottage industry is far ahead as they have adopted advanced technologies. They have improved upon the fly shuttle looms and are switching on to power looms. The market is floated with Manipuri handloom products. Another factor is that the younger tribal generation has almost discarded the home-made cloth in favour of mill made cloth. This change in style and taste has greatly limited the scope of the development of this industry. It is quite apparent that the cottage industry products have lost patronage both inside and outside rural belts.

The Tolloi United Women's Society (TUWS) is the only cooperative society of weavers in Tolloi. Shuttle looms are being used for imparting training. With the introduction of shuttle looms, a reasonably big growth can be expected. The TUWS is taking a leading role in this regard.

Rural Credit Structure

There is an imperative need for sufficient banking cover in order that the distance between the bank and the villages tagged is minimised.

The credit needs of the villages under study reflect an underdeveloped economy. About 80 per cent of the money is spent on personal consumption, festivals, religious functions or on meeting social obligations. In hilly pockets, the *jhumming* does not consume much costly input, so the quantum of agricultural loan is fairly low.

The study area is marked by low credit absorption capacity, lack of banking habit among the people and overall unsatisfactory law and order situation. The recovery of the loan advances is only in the vicinity of 6 per cent. Hence banks have adopted a rather cautious approach to lending and have lost zeal and initiative. The banks have perforce to finance IRDP only under obligation. Bank dealing is confined by and large to non-tribal groups.

As the credit needs are of unproductive purposes, the possibility of getting loans from either banks or cooperatives diminishes. Therefore, the money-lender plays a crucial role.

Private lending and repayment in the tribal pockets is marked by the fact that the village authorities will determine the modes/ways of repayment and can even punish the perpetual defaulters by transferring some of their movable property to the lender.

Apart from the problem of abysmally low recovery percentage and high C/D ratio, the banks face certain other problems in their day-to-day functioning. The branches are understaffed and overworked. No proper accommodation facilities are available in far-flung areas. Climatically some of the places record high rainfall and are excessively cold. On the top of it, there are law and order and safety problems. Since bank personnel handle money they keep on receiving demand letters from anti-social elements and throughout the day they face safety hazards. However, bank personnel are themselves responsible for such a plight to a great extent, as they are making money themselves out of institutional finance measures. In the absence of complaint, no positive action is taken in several areas.

Occupations, Incomes and Labour Relations

The real income of the villagers cannot be determined without an estimate of their income in kind.

A new kind of community participation has come about in certain villages. The households of one ward in Hundung (Ukhrul) work together in the fields of different occupants of the ward and the work is done in rotation. No ill-feeling or sense of cheating is found. In such kind of community participation, nothing is paid to the persons working. Everyone contributes labour and discharges his responsibility sincerely.

Agriculture is the main occupation. A large portion of production is for self consumption. Whatever is saved is used for exchange trade. Occasionally, the villagers sell fire-wood, wooden post, tree log and bamboo taken from the village forests.

Here, the situation is much different from other places in the country in respect of payment of minimum wages. People would work either for the wages they have themselves prescribed or go without any money, even if it means no income for some time. The actual minimum wages prevailing in the area are more than the wages fixed by the Government. All the labourers employed for whatever period, get wages fixed by them, which are always equal to or more than the minimum wages prescribed by the Government.

The employer-employee relationship in the area is a congenial one. As the number of persons going out of the villages on daily wage earning etc. is very few, this relationship is determined to a great extent by the cordial intra-village relationships based on a feeling of brotherhood, and the common bonds that bind the villagers. In general, therefore, a cordial employer-employee relationship exists in the area. It may be remarked that the villagers have a strong attachment with their village and this brings them close to each other. In fact, there exists in this area, the tribal feeling of helping each other without expecting returns. There are, indeed, quite a number of households on subsistence level. They are struggling even for the basic necessities to live. However, the redeeming factor is that the villagers have a common bond which makes it possible for these people to survive somehow even in the most trying of times. There is a feeling of brotherhood that makes the well-to-do give contributions to the needy and the villagers interact well in this regard.

Nonetheless, economic development does not take off from fraternal bonds alone. There has to be a diversification of occupations and pursuing the same on commercial and scientific lines. There cannot be an economic uplift of the villagers unless the subsidiary sector is properly developed and necessary backward and forward linkages are forged.

Rural Development Schemes

JRY, EAS and Social Forestry under the DRDA are the main employment generation programmes in the study area. The village share of JRY is rarely implemented by the villagers and is distributed among the members of the village or spent for the common expenses of the village.

In Thanlon, the Chief and the Council decide which works are to be taken under the NREP. They then meet the BDO/SDO and the DC and try to get their work included in the annual work programme. A number of culverts, a waiting shed, road construction, community hall construction, and repair of school building, construction of bridges and social forestry schemes are taken up. Under NREP and RLEGP in Parbung, Lungthulien and Senvon, many viable schemes have been executed, one of them being the Sitam irrigation project. The JRY schemes have been implemented in Tangpijol since 1989-90 for the construction of community durable assets and for providing employment in the villages. Village Shirui had not been much benefited by the NREP or RLEGP due to lack of awareness of the villagers and official apathy.

Under the asset creation scheme lots of development activities have been undertaken in the rural areas. Under IRDP, different schemes, viz. banana/pineapple garden, lemon/orange orchards, terrace cultivation schemes, coffee/cardamom plantation etc. have been given to many beneficiaries.

The following is an IRDP scheme chart in Thanlon for the financial years 1983-84 and 1988-89.

	IRDP Schemes	No.of Beneficiaries
1983-84		
	Minor Irrigation	2
	Soybean	10
	Ginger	3
	Tapioca	5
	Pineapple	5
	Wool knitting	2
	Carpentry	5
	Sewing Machines	5
	Piggery	10
	Poultry	7
	Duckery	3
	Goat-rearing	2
1988-89		
	Potato	6
	Papaya	8
	Cardamom	13
	Lemon	6
	Coffee	7
	Banana	7
	Parkia	5
	Carpentry	9
	Blacksmithy	6
	Provision Shops	4
	Rural tea stalls	8
	Weaving/Knitting	6

The beneficiaries in Komlathabi and Heigrutampak are generally identified in consultation with the village chief and the council. The implementation of the IRDP schemes is plagued by paucity of assets. Buffaloes, milch cows, pigs, ducklings, piglets, fish fingerlings all have to be purchased from far off places by the suppliers. The suppliers, at times, supply poor quality assets. Churachandpur is one of the districts selected for the implementation of the DWCRA schemes.

JRY has been able to generate some durable assets like inter-village roads, ponds, roads to paddy fields, community hall, village court, village playground etc. and has certainly been able to employ some people during the agricultural lean season.

TRYSEM beneficiaries, wherever not covered under IRDP, have not been able to bring their training to a logical conclusion.

In the past, DWCRA has not been implemented properly because some years back the money was used by the villagers for getting electricity connection/paying electricity bills. DWCRA requires a sincere monitoring and regular flow of credit by the banks. The women's groups should be educated not to spend the money for feasts/festivals/electricity connections, rather they should take up some income generating activities which can give employment to other villagers.

One of the basic prerequisites of poverty eradication is reorientation of agricultural relations so that ownership of land is shared by a larger section of population. In Tangpijol, the land ownership pattern is customary in nature and entire village land is vested in the chief. The Manipur Land Reforms and Land Revenue Act does not extend to hill areas and unless this Act is extended there is no question of land reforms. There is no incentive to the individual farmer for making any improvement on land or for taking up modern technology. It is difficult to obtain long-term or short-term loan as the farmer cannot offer his land for security. The shifting nature of cultivation and absence of individual land ownership has a direct bearing on poverty alleviation programmes.

There is a need to simplify the criteria for identifying households below poverty line and define and measure them in relative terms after they are identified in absolute terms. Just income criterion is not sufficient and there is a need to look into various disadvantages or constraints in terms of land, irrigation, electricity etc. The beneficiaries for the poverty alleviation programmes are generally identified in consultation with the village chief and the council. The villagers in Thanlon claimed that anti-poverty programmes were plagued by wrong identification of beneficiaries.

IRDP has also suffered a severe jolt on account of loss of backward and forward linkages. High casualty of animals and inadequate veterinary aid marked the near failure of animal husbandry schemes. The main reasons for the failure of horticultural schemes have been bad seeds, lack of irrigation facilities, lack of field fencing and even untimely delivery of seeds. Moreover, absence of market facilities is a major handicap and most of the products are used in home consumption.

Many location specific schemes could be started in the concerned villages but the officials lack imaginative and innovative ideas. For example, mules can be given to carry merchandise to interior areas and bring down products from remote regions to the Block Headquarters and further down.

The minor irrigation scheme (which has been a big failure) beneficiaries in Thanlon pleaded that they needed further assistance like crop loans. Moreover, they received no technical or financial assistance from other departments like horticulture, sericulture, oilseeds etc. No officials had met them after the initial subsidy whether it be the VLW or extension officers of the banks.

General Economic Conditions

There is a growing tendency among the tribals to send their children to the mainland for higher education. Further many tribals have realised the importance of movable assets like livestock and poultry which can be their own.

The villages have excellent potential in the areas of horticulture and animal husbandry. These need to be tapped to improve the economy of the village.

Development of forests is another means by which the villages having forest cover can have greater economic growth. Tree plantation for timber and fire-wood in the vast private and common village lands will bring prosperity in the future.

If the villages are electrified, power supply can be used for powerlooms, fruit processing, bamboo chipping and paper rolling industries.

Local resources may have to be tapped in a meaningful manner to increase employment avenues. Small units of bamboo chipping, or of preparing pineapple juice etc. are feasible as a plenty of both bamboos and pineapples are available locally.

Families, having someone in the government service, have a somewhat stable economy.

Development : The Social and Ethnic Connection

All the tribes in Manipur can be divided into Naga group of tribes and Chin-Kuki-Mizo group of tribes with some smaller tribes intermediate between these two groups, as ethnic transformation is in the offing. Traditional chieftainship is not common to all the tribes. Chieftains lost much of their traditional power due to the introduction of Christianity and modern education leading to multifarious changes. At present, there are six well-known Naga tribes, viz. (i) Kabui (Rongmei and Puimei), (ii) Kacha Naga (Liangmei and Zemei), (iii) Mao, (iv) Maram, (v) Tangkhul and (vi) Maring. The Chin-Kuki-Mizo tribes are : (i) Gangte, (ii) Hmar, (iii) Lushai (Mizo), (iv) Paite, (v) Simte, (vi) Thadou (Kuki), (vii) Vaiphei and (viii) Zou. Intermediate between the two groups of the Naga and the Chin-Kuki-Mizo tribes, but linguistically close to the latter than the former are numerically smaller tribes like (i) Aimol, (ii) Chiru, (iii) Koireng, (iv) Kom, (v) Anal, (vi) Chothe, (vii) Lamkang, (viii) Koirao/Thangal, (ix) Purum, (x) Monsang, and (xi) Moyon. As such, they were also known as old Kukis in anthropological literature. The majority of the people of the North Eastern States are of Tibeto-Mongoloid stock and the people of Manipur are no exception.

The Naga tribes have ethnic and cultural affinities with the people of Nagaland and the non-Naga tribes belonging to the Kuki-Chin family have affinity with the Chins of Burma and the Mizos of Mizoram. The regular evangelical activities brought the Naga societies closer to one another and at the same time instilled a sense of oneness. The Nagas thus constitute a group of people with a shared sense of peoplehood.

The Kukis are the groups of people possessing common language and common culture but which show little organisational compatibility into a compact ethnic group. The Kukis as a whole are a diverse group covering a number of tribes, sub-tribes and clans with varying manners and customs.

Many tribal villages have sprung up in the Imphal valley also. The recent trend among the educated and well-to-do people belonging to various Naga tribes is to own houses in Imphal to enjoy the amenities of modern life. The Kuki-Chin tribes have their maximum concentration in Churachandpur which is fast developing into a modern township and in order of importance second only to Imphal.

The life of the hillman is very much influenced by his surrounding environment. The hill people set up their villages on the top or slopes of high hills, covered with forests. In selecting sites for their villages they must have been guided by the consideration of security. Frequent inter-tribal conflicts made them security conscious. However, the Kuki-Chin groups preferred the foot of the hills and the rich, fertile valley areas.

Justice is available cheaply and easily in the tribal villages. The Village Council is easily accessible to everyone – rich or poor.

The role of women in the tribal society is immense. However, there are some social restrictions on them, viz., (i) Women cannot become priests, (ii) They cannot sit cross-legged, (iii) They cannot touch spears and shields, (iv) They cannot wear *Haora/Luirim, i.e.* male shawls, (v) They cannot join hunting parties, (vi) They cannot loosen their hair before the village elders, (vii) They cannot inherit the father's landed property.

Christianity has undoubtedly brought the message of modern life, a wider companionship and a new sense of dignity in these areas. Education, improved habits of living and reliance on modern medicines have got some foothold.

Those who want to get better education and are looking for job opportunities prefer to move out.

Families whose members have moved out are now realising the importance of horticultural schemes. More and more orange/lemon orchards and pineapple farms are coming up.

There has been a perceptible change in the standard of living of some people. Thatched roof is gradually being replaced by GCI sheets. Bamboo mat walling is giving place to wooden planks. The people can now afford a square meal a day. Even the poorest earn some money by working on a casual basis.

TRIPURA

Tripura is a picturesque hilly State in the North-Eastern region of the country. The area of the State is about 10,491.69 sq. km. and its population is 27,57,205 as per the 1991 census. It is bounded on the North, West, South and South-East by the international boundary with Bangladesh, while in the East, it has a common boundary with Mizoram and Assam. Although, Tripura has no claims to very high hills, yet, in a sense it is a gate-way to the Eastern Hills offshoots of the Eastern Himalayas. From Tripura starts the hilly terrain of the North-East after the vast plains of Bangladesh. A princely State of the past, this State is inhabited by various ethnic groups and has a rich cultural tradition. As tribal and Bengali cultural ethos blends here magnificently, a unique cultural genre has been born out of a co-existence of diverse ethnic groups, which at the same time, maintain their distinct cultural identities.

Tripura comprises 3 districts, namely, West Tripura (with Headquarters at Agartala), North Tripura (with Headquarters at Kailasahar) and South Tripura (with Headquarters at Udaipur).

Tribals in Tripura do not stay in a village kind of human habitation in the traditional sense of the term as applicable in the plains areas. Instead, they live in closely knit, mostly single community human congregation called *'paras'* which are remarkably different from the villages. These *paras* have several distinguishing features such as high mobility on account of *jhumming*, inherent desire of seclusion from urban cultures, self-administration etc. Majority of the *paras* were set up by different *Roajas* (heads/choudharies) and they derive their names from these *Roajas*. The age of their setting up varies from 15 years to 100 years back. Majority of the *paras* are either in reserve or protected forests or on Khas land. Most of them are having single community either Reang or Jamatia or Noatia etc.

Agriculture and Allied Activities

Agriculture is the mainstay of Tripura's economy, paddy being the principal crop. It is cultivated twice a year in a flat land. The paddy of April/August is *Aush*, that of August-November is called *Aman* and that of December-March is called *Bora*. *Jhumming* or shifting cultivation is practiced in the tribal pockets of the State.

Nevertheless, the agricultural output has not been, over a period of time, in consonance with an increase in demand. An increase in agricultural output has been offset by a sharp rise in demand resulting from the growth of population and the desire of the urban people for a better life.

About 76 per cent of the people directly depend on agriculture for their livelihood and 67.48 per cent of the total workers are engaged in farming, shifting as well as settled. About 70 per cent of the State revenue is also earned from agriculture. The total area of the State is 10,43,696 hectares. Only little more than 20 per cent of it is sown with crops while about 60 per cent is classified as forest land. Uncultivated and fallow land cover about 20,000 hectares and most of it is in fact under permanent pastures and grazing lands, much of which have been overgrazed, resulting in denuded or deteriorated forest lands. Over 83 per cent of the cropped land is given to food crops and paddy alone accounts for 81.5 per cent of the acreage devoted to agriculture. Thus only about one-sixth of the total cropped land is given to cash crops. Jute (5.66%), cotton (3.61%), oilseeds (3.10%) and tea (2.10%)

are the important cash crops. Of the total cropped land only about 8.71 per cent is currently receiving assured means of irrigation. Elsewhere, the farming is rainfed. In the valley flats and plain tracts wherever water is available during winter two crops a year are raised. In a nutshell, the agricultural economy of Tripura presents a picture of an overridingly subsistence agriculture, cultivating all the readily available land and taking two crops wherever water is available.

The cultivable land in the State can broadly be divided into two categories, viz. *lunga* land and *tilla* land. The former is a plain tract normally located between two hillocks and the latter is undulating and sloping land situated on highlands. The *lunga* land is already under the plough while the *tilla* land is partly under the area of the *jhumiyas* and is partly being reclaimed for plough cultivation. About 40 per cent of the total land of Tripura is made up of valley basins, plain tracts, mid uplands. Most of it is found in the West Tripura district.

The West Tripura district is not only the most intensively cultivated district of the State but also the most thickly populated district. From Table 3.16, it is evident that nearly half of the paddy acreage (45%) and about 43.1 per cent of the cultivated acreage is found in the West Tripura district. The district also contains relatively high acreage devoted to mesta and potatoes (including sweet potatoes).

In the Pakhirabada village of the North Tripura district, people have started the use of High Yielding Variety of paddy. The VLW of the agriculture department assists the villagers in switching over to the modern methods of cultivation. In village Kachucharra (North Tripura), wooden ploughs with a bamboo leveller are the implements for lowlands while the manual, iron plough is used on the dry, hard, upland soil. Bullocks can be hired at the rate of Rs. 5-10 day/bullock. Two farmers also own power-tillers which are rent out at the rate of Rs. 40-45 per hour inclusive of diesel charges. Pumpsets operated on diesel can be hired at the rate of Rs. 25-35 per hour inclusive of diesel charges. There are no threshers in the village. Chemical fertilisers and quality seeds are made available at the store of the agriculture department.

Table 3.16 : District-wise Distribution of Agricultural Acreage and Production of Major Crops – 1976

Description	West Tripura		North Tripura		South Tripura		Tripura	
	Area	Prdn.	Area	Prdn.	Area	Prdn.	Area	Prdn.
Rice	132.59	146.65	80.05	83.40	86.29	90.00	298.93	324.05
Wheat	0.12	0.26	0.25	0.47	0.21	0.55	0.58	1.28
Pulses	1.03	0.37	1.07	0.40	1.09	0.45	3.19	1.22
Potato and Sweet Potatoes	1.55	13.64	1.48	10.83	1.21	15.20	4.26	41.67
Oilseeds	1.37	0.49	2.45	1.04	1.84	1.04	5.66	2.57
Jute	2.31	3.44	1.37	2.18	2.76	3.38	6.44	9.00
Mesta	3.77	4.38	2.06	2.07	3.46	3.45	9.29	9.90
Cotton (ginned)	0.40	0.06	1.20	0.25	0.40	0.08	2.00	0.39
Sugarcane	0.39	15.00	1.09	37.50	0.69	33.50	2.17	86.00
Irrigated Area	12.766		4.969		11.925		29.660	
Irrigated area as per cent of total irrigated area.	43.05		16.75		40.20		100.00	

Note : Area is given in thousand hectares and production is given in thousand tonnes.
Source : Directorate of Economics and Statistics, Agartala.

Agriculture in Lebachhara (South Tripura) can be broadly divided in four parts : Cultivation on *Naal* or *Lunga* (low) land, on high (*tilla*) land, *jhum* cultivation and cultivation in house garden. Paddy is the main crop on *Naal* or *Lunga* lands. *Tilla* land considered useless till recently is being used for plantation at places. *Jhum* cultivation is practiced by tribals on *Khas*/forest land. Almost all inputs like seeds, fertilisers, plant protection chemicals etc. are supplied by the department of agriculture at a highly subsidised rates.

In Trishabari (West Tripura), chemical fertiliser is sold by the agriculture department through their VLW stores. Seeds and pesticides are also distributed through the same. The supply is insufficient. Tilling is mainly done by bullocks but some farmers also hire power tillers from the agriculture department.

Modern agricultural implements are slowly becoming popular in Borkathal (West Tripura).

The area irrigated in Durgapur (North Tripura) is 31.4 hectares which is only 5.3 per cent of the total area and 6 per cent of the net sown area. In Lebachhara (South Tripura), most of the land is under rainfed cultivation with single cropping. Irrigation facilities in Chenchuria (West Tripura) are quite poor. The facilities included a deep tubewell constructed by the Government and a Cherra (small stream) passing through the village.

The principal crop in Durgapur (North Tripura) is paddy. It is cultivated over 80 per cent of the net cropped area. Area-wise distribution of crops is as follows:

Sl. No.	Crop		Area (hect)
1.	Paddy	Aus (early Kharif)	413.6
		Aman (Late Kharif)	491.4
		Bofo (Rabi)	17.2
2.	Wheat		4.1
3.	Pulses		14.2
4.	Vegetables		31.3
5.	Oil Seeds		11.7
6.	Orchard		23.8
7.	Others		16.7
	Total		1024.00

The average yield of low variety paddy per acre in Kanchan Bari (North Tripura) is 25 maunds. The price per maund is Rs. 80. Hence returns per acre is Rs. 2000 out of which Rs. 805 goes to inputs. In case of HYV paddy, the production per acre is 1800 kg. so the returns per acre are Rs. 3600. The cost involved is Rs. 1100. Hence net profit per acre is Rs. 2500.

In Holakhet (South Tripura), apart from paddy, the production levels of potato are also in excess of the village demand.

The area under paddy in Chenchuria accounts for 77 per cent of the gross area of 790.576 hectares followed by area under 'Mesta' (21%). The area under vegetables, oilseeds, fruit orchards and rubber account for 2 per cent of the gross cultivated area only.

The following is the economics of principal crops in Trishabari (West Tripura) :

Crop	Cost of Cultivation (Rs./acre)	Return (Rs./acre)
Paddy	1,800	4,000
Wheat	1,000	2,800
Mustard	1,500	3,500
Potato	5,000	10,000
Tomato	1,500	5,000
Brinjal	2,000	5,500
Cabbage	1,000	4,000
Cauliflower	1,000	4,000

Regarding horticulture, it has been found in the probationers' study that the following plantations are carried out : pineapple, jackfruits, arecanut, coconut, lemon, papaya, shepha, guava, banana etc. Horticulture is a part of the life of the villagers but commercial exploitation is missing.

By way of suggestions, one can say that irrigation facilities should be created to ensure optimum use of land. Paddy-cum-fish culture should be encouraged. Proper crop cycle should be maintained to sustain the fertility of the soil. Villagers are not aware of crop rotation techniques.

Though the quantum of seeds and fertilisers has increased manifold during the past decade, the supply is far from being sufficient.

Middlemen bring vegetables to market points and earn heavy profits. Rice and wheat are also sold at these points. Primary marketing societies should be strengthened to eliminate the middlemen.

It can be seen that the cultivation of vegetables is fairly profitable. After the introduction of the True Potato Seed, the profitability in growing potato will further increase. This explains the shift in the cropping pattern. Areas adjacent to an irrigation source have been found more amenable in this regard.

Due to lack of irrigation and good quality of seeds, the production of wheat, pulses and mustard is quite low and unprofitable. There is a scope to increase the productivity of these crops by adopting modern technology. Cooperative farming may prove to be successful as individual farmers do not have the means to go for mechanised farming.

There is enormous scope for improving irrigation facilities in the villages through the provision of seasonal bandhs and irrigation channels.

It is gratifying to note that the Agriculture Department of the Government of Tripura is running at a number of places, where power tillers are given on hire to farmers. The objective of opening these centres is to enable small farmers to make use of mechanical means of cultivation, since they cannot afford to purchase costly agricultural implements.

Considerable improvement in incomes can result from adoption of advanced techniques in sugarcane, jute, rubber cultivation and horticulture. Tribal farmers want to take up rubber plantation on a large scale provided land is allotted to them. This indicates that they are now realising the benefits of cash/non-conventional crops and would like to shift towards these crops if some help is provided by the government. The waste *tilla* lands can be used for intensive horticulture on commercial lines.

There is hardly any notion of agricultural credit. The flow of such credit would have gone a long way in determining the quality of inputs and productivity.

Livestock

It is evident from the study area that the animal husbandry department has failed to make much impact. The department has given exotic varieties to some farmers, but in the absence of forward and backward linkages, not much improvement can be expected.

Non-availability of good quality seed is a big problem in the State. Procuring from other States is very costly due to high transportation costs. That is why area under feed crops should be increased.

Exotic varieties of cows in sufficient numbers and adequate veterinary services should be provided to the farmers. Once milk production is increased, substantial suitable forward linkages can be thought of. At present, milk production is woefully low in the State. *Desi* cows yield less milk and are less prone to diseases. Jersey cows yield more milk but are high prone to disease. So a 66 per cent Jersey and 34 per cent *Desi* serum level hybrid is the optimum level which would be less disease prone, more milk yielding and better adjusting to the Tripura condition. Use of artificial insemination is, nonetheless, poor due to lack of refrigeration and transport lags.

There are several tanks in the region. The idea of dovetailing duckery with fishery is yet to strike firm roots here.

Due to the popularity and success of piggery schemes among the tribals of Tripura, the Centrally Sponsored Special Piggery Development Programme (SPDP) is implemented here. Under this scheme, three *Desi* females and one exotic male will be supplied to the beneficiary. Including all incidental charges, the total outlay of the scheme is only Rs. 6,450 per beneficiary while the subsidy component for small and marginal farmers and agricultural labourers is 25 per cent and 33-1/3 per cent respectively. Subsidy for ST beneficiaries is 50 per cent subject to a maximum of Rs. 5,000 per beneficiary. The scheme needs to be expanded and popularised.

According to the norms of the fishery department, a water area of one hectare should yield a minimum of 2000 kg. of fish per year. However, as in Sonaimuri (North Tripura), the actual yield is only 500 kg. of fish per hectare per annum.

Floods cause the ponds overflow, damaging pisciculture. There is also witnessed lack of entrepreneurship in the villagers. If the villagers develop entrepreneurship, they can develop ponds suitable for pisciculture along commercial lines.

In some of the *paras* of Gandachera (South Tripura), there are the possibilities of creating reservoirs near the *paras* by constructing bunds.

Livestock, if developed properly, will go a long way in reducing the pressure on agriculture. In fact, it is the only way to reduce poverty in the area as otherwise the area does not hold much promise. With large scale demand, marketing is no problem. Livestock development combined with horticulture will definitely lead to the emergence of a truly mixed farming in the State.

Rural Industries

Being far away from the mainland markets and due to appalling absence of infrastructural facilities, there are no major industries in Tripura. Rural artisans, by and large, do not take up their industry as a full-time vocation, rather they work in conjunction with other activities such as agriculture, petty business etc.

Rural industries in the surveyed villages of all the three districts of Tripura include weaving, cane and bamboo work and certain miscellaneous industries.

The Manipuris in Durgapur (North Tripura) are engaged in weaving which is a traditional pursuit. Weaving is done by the Manipuris for meeting their own needs but there are some families which are selling the cloths in the market also. The common products are bed-sheet, towel, *pachra* etc. With necessary official support, weaving may become a good economic activity. There are about 100 weavers in Kanchanbari (North Tripura). In June 1990, the Tripura Handloom and Handicraft Development Corporation a Public Sector Undertaking of the Government of Tripura, set up a weaving centre, to impart training to women interested in learning afresh or developing the skills they already possessed. There are two schemes of the Rural Development Department to assist tribal weavers – supply of yarn at 75 per cent subsidy and supply of free yarn. The non-tribals are assisted by the Industries Department in upgrading their pit loom. Daily earnings of a weaver range from Rs. 9-15 depending on the skill.

This is a vanishing skill in Lachuchhara because of low returns despite hard labour.

Handicrafts are a part and parcel of the tribal life. All tribal families in Gandachera (South Tripura) produce some kind of handicraft. By and large, the handicrafts produced are textile, basket, wood-work, cane and bamboo articles, *dari* and so on. Most of their own garments are produced by them. Many of the articles produced are sold in the nearby market. Birchandra Manu (South Tripura) has no industry except weaving.

Coming to West Tripura, there is a Handloom Cooperative Society in Purba Barjala, which has also received loom from the Industries Department for the construction of shed and for working and share capital. The main village industry in Chenchuria is weaving. It is common here due to Manipuri population.

Some women in Pakhirbada (North Tripura) can make small baskets, mats etc. using sliced bamboo. They sell it in the nearby markets to supplement their income. Bamboo work comes as a vocation in Birchandra Manu (South Tripura). Some families in Lebachhara (South Tripura) are also involved in making handicraft products from bamboo. They sell it in the weekly market in Nutan Bazaar.

The Rudrapals in Durgapur (North Tripura) are engaged in pottery. In fact, the Rudrapal community is traditionally engaged in pottery all over Tripura. There are a few carpenters in Pakhirbada (North Tripura), belonging to the Namasudra community. *Beedi* is manufactured in Holakhet (South Tripura).

The main problem in the weaving industry is that it has a seasonal demand. The items produced by the members of the Society in Chenchuria are sold only in the winter season. Thus, the weavers get job only for 3-4 months in a year (that too on rationing basis) and their earnings range between Rs. 100 to 300 per month. Thus weaving remains mainly a supportive economic activity, in which mostly women are engaged. Even the Cooperative Society achieved more than 50 per cent of its annual turnover during 3 winter months only. The industry can be developed, only if the State Government takes up responsibility of more aggressive marketing of the finished products of the weavers within and outside the State. The weavers may also have to modify the needs of the market, especially the markets outside the State.

Hand spinning is generally not practiced. The main reason is that the cotton produced in the State is short staple cotton, which is not suitable for making yarn. Hence, the yarn used in weaving is mostly procured from outside the State.

Weaving, if developed systematically, can turn out to be a profitable venture. Even now, in a day, a person in Birchandra Manu can weave *pachras* or sheets that fetch upto Rs. 60. Deducting the cost of yarn, the profit will be around Rs. 15 to 20.

The quality of thread is not good. The colours are not fast. The cost of the weaved product is high. As compared to this the cloth of the mills is much cheaper. So, marketing has to be done in an effective way. The productivity of the units to be set up in future should be high. This would lower the cost of the products.

Bamboo artefacts used to fetch decent prices earlier but the industry is now facing threat of extinction because of its non-viability. Dwindling jungles have resulted in the high cost of bamboos, making this vocation unattractive. Competition from refugees too occurs who are also engaged in making these handicrafts and selling it at cheaper prices. Chakma refugees in Lebachhera appear to be better artisans than natives.

KVIC can intervene and provide technology for better extraction of sugar and packing of gur.

Mechanised and improved *ghani* would go a long way in improving the economic viability of oil extraction.

Rural Credit Structure

The area under study is badly in need of financial assistance. Nonetheless, repayment position *vis-a-vis* Bank credit being tardy, it is neither forthcoming nor being channelised into meaningful pursuits.

In recent years, a large number of bank branches have been opened in the rural areas of Tripura to help the rural folk. Various departments of the State Government provide loans to beneficiaries under different schemes. In most of the cases the amount has been consumed by the beneficiaries. People have developed a psychology that Government loans are not to be repaid. Now it has become difficult to find beneficiaries because banks do not give loans to the defaulters.

The functioning of LAMPS and PACs, once prominent credit institutions, have come to a standstill over the last few years, due to financial crunch. Plagued by a chronic paucity of funds and persistent mismanagement, the LAMPS and PACs all over Tripura are facing a major financial crisis. These bodies are now devoid of many credit functions. For example, the Borkathal LAMPS maintains one consumer cooperative store and one power tiller.

Occupation, Incomes and Labour Relations

Agriculture is the main occupation in the study area. However, in certain villages, people also engage in agricultural labour, pisciculture, horticulture and livestock breeding.

Income-wise break-up of the families in Kanchan Bari (North Tripura) is as follows :

	Annual Income	No. of Families
1.	Upto Rs. 2,400	152
2.	Rs. 2401 - 4800	530
3.	Rs. 4801 - 6400	134
4.	Above Rs. 6400	269
	Total	1085

Evidently, 152 families belong to the destitute group. 816 families are below the poverty line.

Land ownership and family incomes in Holakhet (South Tripura) are as follows:

Cultivable Average Land (in Kanis)	Income Rs. 0-300	Income Rs. 301-600	Income Rs. 601-1000	Income Rs. 1001-1500	Income Rs. >1500	Income
0.00-2.49	15	6	2	2	—	396
2.50-4.99	3	4	1	—	—	438
5.00-7.49	1	1	—	2	—	825
7.50-9.99	1	1	—	2	—	1580
10.00 & more	1	—	—	—	—	550
Total	21	12	4	6	2	570

Out of the 40 families surveyed in Lebachhara (South Tripura), the monthly income distribution comes as follows:

Rs. 300 - 500	10
Rs. 501 - 1000	21
Rs. 1001 - 1500	6
Above Rs. 1500	3

This figure is only a rough average estimation.

No labour conflict or tension was reported in Srirampur (North Tripura). Minimum wage for the unskilled workers in the State is Rs. 23.65. However, the market rate varies from Rs. 30 to Rs. 40 depending on the season. Not a single incidence of bonded labour was found. In Pakhirbada (North Tripura), the actual wage earned by the agricultural labourer is Rs. 20 per day (as against the prescribed minimum wage of Rs. 16 per day). Wage rate prevailing in Lebachhara (South Tripura) was Rs. 30 to Rs. 40 per day. But due to the influx of refugees it has gone down to Rs. 20-25 per day. Disparity between male and female wages is evident in Trishabari (West Tripura).

Although it cannot be said that the people get work round the year in Tripura, but whenever they get work, they get more than the minimum wages. During survey in Chenchuria (West Tripura), it was observed that some very poor families (which possibly would have been exploited in many other places) were also getting the minimum wages for the work done by them. The issue of enforcing the Minimum Wages Act is really non-existent either for the people or for the government. In fact, due to relatively higher wages, labourers from other parts of the country, e.g. Bihar, Orissa etc. are also attracted to this State.

Landless labourers, tenants and artisans are, by and large, below the poverty line, with meagre incomes. In other categories, especially in the case of government employees, the average income is relatively good. This is true for the entire State. The statistics of West Tripura district will be revealing in this regard. 37,726 families are above poverty line in the district and there are 36,806 government employees in these families.

From the sample data collected in Trishabari (West Tripura) it can be seen that a respondent earns Rs. 12,000 per year from his fish tank. Similarly a trader also earns the same amount. It indicates that those who are willing to take some initiative are being rewarded.

Despite the payment of minimum wages in the open market, people still come flocking to the government's employment generation programmes. This paradox cannot be explained by the classical theory of economics. If people are willing to sell their labour at minimum wage rate, it means lack of adequate demand of labour in the open market and, therefore, the market rate of labour should be less than or equal to the minimum wage rate. According to one explanation, people engage themselves in government's employment generation programme because they do not have to work as hard. It is also said that prevailing market wage is paid to the workers in Government's programmes also. They work for less number of days and get payment for more number of days.

Now-a-days, with the fragmentation of holdings and the withering of the joint family system, more families are looking to service and business as the source of livelihood and of family income.

The instances of bonded labour are absent. But the repayment of short term loans taken from the landowners, through the labour for him, is also a common practice. It can be said with reference to the Holakhet (South Tripura) survey that the wages paid for this period are partial, and are to be adjusted against the debt. The rates of interest are stiff, ranging from 5 to 7 per cent monthly. Most of these loans are taken for subsistence needs and are on the basis of verbal understanding. These loans are usually taken from a local lender.

Bengali women rarely go for earning wages in the market or for participating in the agricultural activities with their menfolk. Instead, they remain at home, taking care of cattle and working on house garden, if necessary. Taking a cue, tribal women also, in Lebachhara (South Tripura) do not like to work in the fields of others for money. All these women, however, go for Government employment schemes and obtain wages for little or no work done.

In a situation where the Government provides for work, chances of victimisation are less. There is a labour card system and a labour register maintained by the Panchayat Secretary of the Gaon Sabha in Kanchan Bari (North Tripura).

Wage discrimination on the basis of sex exists in certain pockets, not all.

A policy decision has been taken by the Government in 1978, according to which, destitute persons whose livelihood depends on selling of fire-wood would be identified by the panchayats and given a loan identification card on the basis of which they will be allowed to collect dry firewood without payment of royalty for sale in local markets. Otherwise, the forest department would charge Re. 1 for a bamboo bundle of 4′ 6″ diameter. Firewood royalty is Rs. 5 per bundle. But people from Pakhirbada (North Tripura) do not pay any royalty because no forest checkpost is on the way from Pakhirbada to Kailasahar.

Rural Development Schemes

Three employment generation programmes are being implemented in Tripura: Jawahar Rozgar Yojana, Employment Assurance Scheme, State Rural Employment Programme.

In the study area, though agriculture is the main occupation, those having meagre land are dependent on these employment generation programmes, especially during lean seasons. The assets created under various schemes in Pakhirbada (North Tripura) include four RCC wells, Balwadi, one Anganwadi

Centre, two schools, 10 km. of roads, irrigation drains, bamboo bridges, Panchayat Ghar, a community hall etc.

The usual schemes taken up under the SREP in Matai (South Tripura) are the construction of village roads, excavation and maintenance of village tanks, construction of Panchayat Ghars etc. Funds for the SREP come from different departments, viz. Rural Development, Panchayat and MIFC (Minor Irrigation and Flood Control).

Group housing is an important scheme taken up under the NREP and RLEGP in Chenchuria (West Tripura). The prevailing wage rate was Rs.14 per day, a part of which was given in kind (i.e. in the form of rice). As regards SREP, a part of the funds is distributed as Grant-in-aid, popularly known as Dhoti-Sari scheme. In Trishabari (West Tripura), the schemes taken up under the JRY are mainly the construction of Panchayat Ghar, digging of ponds, construction of community centres, construction of passenger sheds, construction of brick soled roads etc. The other employment generation programme SREP has also been an effective tool in meeting the employment needs of the poorest sections of the village in lean season. In Borkathal, the Rural Water Supply Programme (RWSP) is utilised to resink the old tubewells and to repair/maintain the existing tubewells.

The Fisheries Department, as a part of its vertical and horizontal schemes to increase the production and water area under fishery, assists the farmers in maintaining the *pukurs* (fish ponds) and supplies the inputs at subsidised rates.

IRDP is the main asset creation programme in the study area. However, it was found that the IRDP looms are usually diverted to other purposes. Besides, the assets once created through the loan amount are not maintained by the beneficiaries.

The following Table 3.17 gives an idea of the coverage of Holakhet (South Tripura) by various rural development programmes.

Among asset creation schemes, IRDP and MMLP (Margin Money Loan Programme: by the SC/ST Corporation) are quite important. Besides, the Department of Agriculture gives subsidy upto 50 per cent in the purchase of durable agricultural implements, like power tillers, pump sets etc.

Table 3.17 : The Coverage of the Rural Development Programmes

	SC	ST	Muslim	Others	Total
JRY/SREP	7	2	4	10	23
IRDP					22
Rice Mill	–	–	1 (1)	4 (3)	5 (4)
Petty Shop	1	–	– (1)	4	5 (1)
Goatery/Cattle	1	1	3 (1)	– (1)	5 (2)
Land/Agri.	1 (1)	–	1 (1)	1	3 (2)
Rural Artisan	2	1	–	1	4
RMNP	–	–	–	1	1
Loan Mela	–	–	–	4 (2)	4 (2)
Agri Deptt. Sche.	–	–	–	8	8
Fishery Deptt. Sch.	1	–	1	1	3
Others	–	–	–	3	3

Note : Brackets indicate diversion or consumption of assistance.

Employment generation programmes have helped in mitigating rural poverty in Tripura to some extent. In lean seasons, people find it difficult to get employment. EGPs provide employment to the needy and also create some durable community assets in the process. The Government has been able to make positive impact by providing gainful employment to the people, creating rural infrastructure and providing basic amenities to the people.

The assets created under the JRY are relatively durable in nature as compared to the other employment generation programme SREP as there is sufficient provision for the material component in the JRY. SREP also has been effective in meeting the employment needs of the poorer sections of the village in lean seasons.

Besides the Block, the other agencies involved in the implementation of employment generation programmes are : fisheries, agriculture, forest and ADC. Since there is practically no coordination among these departments, real expenditure could not be known during the survey, for instance, in Lebachhara. Lack of coordination also results in duplication of work. Panchayat Secretaries are supposed to maintain asset registers but no such registers are maintained in Lebachhara. Despite all lacunae and leakages, EGS are extremely vital in supporting the population in lean agricultural seasons.

Even though the people are expected to produce an output commensurate with the wage given, usually people do not work hard, and the money is distributed virtually as an unemployment dole.

In the North Eastern region, modern developments in the trade and industries sector have not taken place. As such the Government is the only major machinery which can provide employment to the people. The economy of this region is very much dependent on the development schemes of the Government.

IRDP is almost a total failure. The repayment position of the IRDP loan component has been very poor and there had been many cases of diversion of the IRDP money to meet other pressing needs. The assets created are also not sustainable in nature, except the commercial ventures, mainly due to lack of forward and backward linkages.

Most of the Mark-II tubewells work only for the first few months. However, sanitary latrines are successful.

A dependency syndrome has been created. People are just unwilling to take initiative. Some people have the audacity to ask for SREP work for repair of their houses. Mark-II tubewells lay idle for want of some minor mechanical parts worth Rs. 30, but they were not repaired by the concerned community. It has come to notice that some IRDP beneficiaries have refused to receive IRDP amount unless it is disbursed at their doorsteps.

The dependency on the Government, in Tripura, is more so for the tribals. In fact, it is turning harmful for them because every scheme that is taken up for welfare is taken as another chance of getting money from the Government. This easy money is squandered in boozing and other activities within a short period of time and they return back to their old way of life. This habit is encouraged by the politicians who want to be populist. Government money is being doled out to the people on every occasion, be it, death, birth, festival, calamity, disease, thunder, fire or marriage. All that is required is an application with a recommendation from the Chairman or any other politician stating that the petitioner is a *bona fide* ST member and is in need of assistance. Public demand is only for gratuitous relief and SREP started by the Left Government in 1980-81. The SREP has gained notoriety as it is taken as a scheme of distributing funds without commensurate work. People come in the morning, show their face to the Chairman, work for some time and take their money.

In schemes where the beneficiaries are to be selected by the Panchayat, without any restraining guidelines, the lion's share is taken by the general category families. Their dominance in the village apart, another factor is the linkage of these schemes to some asset ownership, e.g. land or *pukurs* etc.

General Economic Conditions

Due to the absence of assured irrigation water and also due to the total dependence of the agriculture on rains, improved varieties and agricultural practices are not being taken up in the study area. Wherever the watertable is high, the overflows can be installed in large numbers to exploit the ground water.

In the uncultivable, amenable areas, rubber plantations can be taken up under the technical guidance of the Tripura Rehabilitation Plantation Corporation (TRPC). Due to the lesser gestation period required and the long productive life, it is most suited to the tribal people.

Sericulture activities can be taken up in suitable pockets on an experimental basis, to begin with.

Due to indiscriminate felling, the forest cover has gone down drastically in the recent years. Afforestation under the employment generation programmes, viz. NREP, SREP etc. can be taken up with fuel, firewood and timber plants.

Short-sighted rural development policies and programmes have resulted in immediate gratification of the people but with harmful long term effects. The Government should come up with long term perspective plan and direction for rural development. The present strategy of doling out money should be strictly stopped. The Government should prepare sectoral plans to suit the different sections of the society. Instead of attempting to help every person in the village it should select those who are willing and striving to come out of their poverty but are unable to do so due to lack of resources and skill. They should be assisted and guided in a comprehensive manner till they are able to manage themselves. The demonstration effect will ensure that some others also become desirous and the chain will continue. Meanwhile development of infrastructure should continue at full pace. Development of canal and irrigation channels should be accorded top priority in infrastructure development. Tourism and electricity infrastructure also should be taken due care of. Resources from all concerned departments will have to be pooled together. It would also require an exceptional degree of coordination among various departments, which, as the realities exist, is not likely to materialise in the near future. An integrated approach to rural development remains, in any case, the need of the hour. This should be within the frame of a long-term approach. Going piecemeal and abandoning it mid-way will be more harmful than going without it.

Apart from plantations (including rubber), horticulture-based activities like growing of pineapples for which the land is suitable – coupled with improvement in the quality of livestock, can go a long way towards the strengthening of the village economy.

Villagers are gripped in a dependency syndrome. NGOs can play a very useful role at this juncture. They can create a spirit of cooperation and self-dependence. Tripura should be linked with Guwahati in order to integrate the economy of the State with the rest of India. Transport is one of the most crucial factors affecting the economy, because it will facilitate effective utilisation of the rich natural resources of Tripura and proper industrial growth. Unless this is done, the economy of rural Tripura will continue to remain backward.

Development : The Social and Ethnic Connection

The following table presents a list of Scheduled Tribes in Tripura with reference to the Scheduled Castes and Scheduled Tribes Orders (Amendment) Act, 1976.

Sl. No.	Name of the Scheduled Tribe
1.	Bhil
2.	Bhutia
3.	Chaimal
4.	Chakma
5.	Garo
6.	Halam
7.	Jamatia
8.	Khasia
9.	Kuki
	[including the following sub-tribes: Baite, Belajhut, Chhalya, Fun, Hajange, Jangtei, Khepong, Kuntai, Laifong, Lentoi, Mezel, Vamte, Paitu (Paite), Rangchan, Ranghkole, Tahungluya].
10.	Lepcha
11.	Lusai
12.	Mog
13.	Munga/Kaor
14.	Noatia
15.	Orang
16.	Riang
17.	Santal
18.	Tripuri/Tripura/Tippera
19.	Uchai

Out of the 19 tribes, 5 are the aboriginal tribes. They are Tripuri, Noatia, Halam, Jamatia and Riang. The Moghs, Chakmas and Kukis came later; Mogs and Chakmas from Chittagong Hills and Kukis from Lushai and Jaintia Hills. The rest of the non-indigenous tribes came mainly as tea garden labourers from Bihar, Orissa and Madhya Pradesh and ultimately settled there. The Tripuris or Tripurias were the most dominant tribe in the State.

A glance at the population statistics of the State as a whole, on the following table shows the massive influx of immigrants from erstwhile Pakistan and present Bangladesh since 1947 and the union of the Princely State of Tripura in 1949. There is a complete reversal of the demographic patterns with the then majority tribals becoming a minority community in their own State. This, coupled with the increasing pressure on the meagre cultivable land available, led to a conflict situation between the two communities. The emergence of the TNU (Tribal National Volunteers) and the insurgency activities are a direct result of this conflict of interest.

Table 3.18 : Population Statistics of Tripura During Seventy Five Years

Year	ST	Others	Total	Variation
1911	111303	118310	229613	N/A
1921	171610	132827	304437	74824
1931	192249	190201	382450	130560
1941	256991	256019	513010	130560
1951	237953	407754	645707	132697
1961	360070	781935	1142005	496298
1971	450544	1105798	1556342	414337
1981	583920	1453058	2053058	496716
1991	697376	1753624	2428818	375760

Refugee influx has had far reaching consequences on the economy, society and culture of the State. This has been viewed both as an important growth booster and also as a heavy burden on the State's economy in different quarters.

The large scale immigration of displaced persons has so changed the demographic profile of the State that the Bengalis now outnumber the tribals. This demographic change has led to the intensification of the pressure on lands. The lands of the tribal people are also being alienated to the Bengali settlers. It cannot be disputed that the interests of the tribals have been affected by the settlement of the refugees in the State on a large scale. At this moment when the tribals have been showing much interest in settled wet rice cultivation in place of shifting cultivation, the non-availability of adequate amount of valley lands (*Lunga*) has emerged as the biggest constraint. It is also alleged in certain quarters that the development expenditure meant for the tribal people exclusively have been diverted to the area where benefits accrue mainly to the non-tribals. Thirdly, as the Bengali settlers are generally more advanced culturally, they naturally dominate over the tribal people in political, social and economic fields.

It would be over-simplistic to conclude that all the ills afflicting the tribal people are the consequences of refugee rehabilitation in the State. In fact, the tribal people have benefited in a number of ways as a result of the settlement of the

Bengali refugees in the State. The most important of all is that the tribals have been acquainted with settled cultivation by contacts with the immigrants. The refugees brought about dynamism in the tribals' self-sufficient economic system. The tribals became familiar with higher techniques of production through contacts with the refugees.

It is gratifying to note that in matters of residence, fetching water from community well, access to places of worship and to village commons, the Scheduled Castes face no discrimination. A number of factors are responsible for this:

(i) Partition of the country saw the rooting out of the population from the erstwhile East Pakistan and their subsequent settling down in Tripura in the following years. The refugees have been common sufferers, irrespective of caste and creed.

(ii) There has been no landlordism in Tripura and the distribution of land has been homogeneous.

(iii) Bengal has witnessed several socio-political movements during the nineteenth and twentieth centuries. These movements, including the left front government which has been ruling Tripura, have disseminated the spirit of equality.

(iv) The villagers share the same culture and language. Hindus and Muslims celebrate festivals like Durga Puja and Id together.

The villagers live in homogeneous clusters. People of a given community live together. There is no particular reason for this lifestyle, except that the kins tend to stay together on a *tilla*. The clusters are interspersed.

The sanskritisation of the people has not taken place. They still follow old simple rituals which do not require much assistance from the priests. By and large, the people were the followers of Chaitanya, who preached equality of men. This spirit has not yet been corrupted by the forces from the mainland due to the isolation of this place.

In the whole of Tripura, there have been very few instances of Hindu-Muslim clashes. Communal clashes have occurred between tribals – the original inhabitants of this State and the Bengalis – the migrants. These migrants have considerably outnumbered the tribals and have captured all seats of power. This led to a massive communal riot between the Bengalis and the tribals in 1980. The root cause of the insurgency in this area also lies in the tribal-Bengali dichotomy. But there are no instances of clashes on the basis of religion. In fact, the division of the people along political party lines is much more marked than one along religious lines. The people of this area were totally unconcerned about the Ram Janma Bhoomi-Babri Masjid issue.

Women enjoy a very respectable position in the Tripura society. They do contribute to the family income by day labour and by weaving of bamboo baskets etc. They also get equal wages as men for doing day labour. The women cover their head with *sari* while talking to the elders, but do not practice *purda* system at all. There is co-education in the school. The girls are given the same food as their brothers.

People do not follow their religious customs very diligently. The Hindus do not follow many of the rituals their counterparts follow in the mainland. In fact there are very few temples in the sample universe. The Manipuri community has a hall, for instance, in Ichabpur village (Pakhirbada sample area), which they use as a temple. The Muslims do not have many rituals after birth or death of a person. Except for very aged men, nobody has the typical Muslim appearance. Nobody has beard or the tuft of hair under the chin or wears the typical Muslim cap. The women do not observe *purda*. They are dressed in colourful clothes. Religion is not a very important factor in the villages under study.

NOTES

1. Menezes, L.M., Press Note (NEC), April 24, 1992, Guwahati, pp. 2-3.
2. Baishya, Prabin, "Industrial Development of the NE Region: A Study in Regional Imbalance", in *Journal of the North-Eastern Council* (Shillong : January-March 1994), pp. 5-6.

3. Venkata Rao, N. and Reddy, B.S.N., "Structural Changes in Land Relations and Technological Implications in North-Eastern India", in *Journal of the North-Eastern Council* (Shillong : July-September, 1988), pp. 10-11.
4. Hazarika, M.P., "Shifting Cultivation — A Perennial Problem in the North-East" in *Journal of the North-Eastern Council* (Shillong : July-September, 1988), pp 17-19.
5. Sarkar, A.N., "Agriculture : A Profile of Planned Development in North-East", in *Journal of North-Eastern Council* (Shillong : October — December, 1993), p. 31.
6. Sarkar, A.N., "Multiple Cropping Strategies for Achieving Higher Agricultural Productivity in the North Eastern Region", in *Journal of North Eastern Council* (Shillong : July-December, 1992), p. 24.
7. *Ibid.*
8. Paul, B.K., "Technology Need for Rural Development in the North-Eastern Region — Part-II" in *Journal of the North Eastern Council* (Shillong : January-April, 1986), p.19.
9. Sarkar, A.N., "Development of Commercial Plantations in North Eastern India" in *Journal of the North Eastern Council* (Shillong : January-March 1992), p.17.
10. *Ibid.*, p. 21.
11. *Ibid.*, p. 27.
12. Sarkar, A.N., "Low Cost Mushroom Cultivation : A Viable Means for Poverty Alleviation in North-East India" in *Journal of the North Eastern Council* (Shillong: April - June, 1992), p. 5.
13. Goswami, S.N., "Water Resources of North Eastern Region : Potential and Utilisation" in *Journal of the North Eastern Council* (Shillong : April-June, 1993), p. 5.
14. Bora, P.C., "Agricultural Development in North-East Region of India" in *Journal of the North Eastern Council* (Shillong: January-April, 1985), p.16.
15. Sarkar, A.N., "Agriculture : A Profile of Planned Development in North East" in *Journal of the North Eastern Council* (Shillong : October-December, 1993), p. 32.
16. Nigam, M.P., "Mulberry Sericulture in the NE Region — Some Suggestions for Development" in *Journal of the North Eastern Council* (Shillong : April-September 1989), pp. 51-53.
17. Lipton, A.P., "Scope and Problems of Fish Culture in Tripura" in *Journal of the North Eastern Council* (Shillong : Jan-Feb. 1984), p. 19.
18. Sinha, M., "Systematic Plan for Fisheries Development of North-Eastern States in Journal of the North-States" in *Journal of the North Eastern Council* (Shillong : April-June, 1991), pp. 14-14.
19. *Ibid.*, p. 11.
20. Saikia, Sunil K., "Problems of Small Units in North-Eastern Region", *Yojana*, November 30, 1992, pp. 27-29.
21. Mookerji, K.K. and Potty, V.H., "Agro-based Industries Potential of North Eastern Region" in *Journal of the North Eastern Council* (Shillong: January-February, 1994), pp. 22-25.

22. Chhibbir, V., "Industrial Development of Manipur" in *Journal of the North Eastern Council* (Shillong : March-April 1984), p. 22.
23. Paul, B.K. and Basu, T., "Appropriate Technology for Development of Small Scale Industries in North Eastern Region" in *Journal of the North Eastern Council* (Shillong : July-August 1986), p.7.
24. Phukan, S.D., "The Role of NEC in Entrepreneurship Development and Present Industrial Policy" in *Journal of the North Eastern Council* (Shillong : July-September, 1993), p. 2.
25. Singha, Rajamani, "Handloom Industry in North Eastern India : A Comparative Analysis" in *Journal of the North Eastern Council* (Shillong: January-March, 1994), p.17.
26. Sarkar, A.N., "Role of Cooperatives in Agriculture & Allied Activities in North Eastern Region" in *Journal of the North Eastern Council* (Shillong: April-June 1994), p. 28.

REFERENCES

NORTH-EAST

Adiseshiah, Malcolm S. (ed). *Planning Perspectives for the North-Eastern and Eastern Zone* (Lancer Publishers Pvt. Ltd., New Delhi), 1992.

A Study of the Land System of Meghalaya (Law Research Institute, Eastern Region, Guwahati High Court, Guwahati), 1990.

A Study of the Land Systems of Mizoram (Law Research Institute, Eastern Region, Guwahati High Court, Guwahati), 1990.

Bhattacharjee, J.B., *Sequences of Development in North-East India* (Omsons Publications : Guwahati, New Delhi), 1989.

Chib, S.S., *North Eastern India* (ESS ESS Publications : New Delhi), 1984.

Constantine, R., "Manipur Marches Ahead" in *Yojana* (New Delhi : 16-31 August, 1982). Pp. 75-83.

Das Gupta, Malabika, Arun Kumar Gangopadhyaya, Tanmay Bhattacharya, Mahadeb Chakraborti, (eds). *Forestry Development in North-East India* (Omsons Publications: Guwahati, New Delhi), 1986.

Datta Ray, B., *The Emergence and Role of Middle Class in North-East India* (Uppal Publishing House: New Delhi), 1983.

Deka, Dinesh, "Tripura — The Land of Romance" in *Yojana* (*op.cit.*), pp. 104-106.

Development of Horticulture, Plantations and Forests in North-Eastern Region (Agriculture Refinance and Development Corporation : Bombay), 1975.

Dutta B.B., *Land Use Pattern in North-East India* (Gagan Publishers : Ludhiana), 1986.

Goswami, Atul (ed) *Land Reforms and Peasant Movement : A Study of North-East India* (Omsons Publications: New Delhi, Guwahati), 1986.

Horam, M., *North-East India : A Profile* (Cosmo Publications : New Delhi), 1990.

Mahajan, V.S. (ed), *Emerging Patterns of North-Eastern Economy* (Deep and Deep Publications : New Delhi), 1987.

Mali, D.D., P. Deka, *Industrial Development in North-East India* (Omsons Publications : Guwahati, New Delhi), 1987.

Saikia, P.D., U. Phukan, *Rural Development in North-East India* (B.R. Publishing Corporation : Delhi), 1989.

Samanta, R.K., *Rural Development in North-East India : Perspectives, Issues and Experiences* (Uppal Publishing House : New Delhi), 1991.

Shukla, S.P. and A.K. Agarwal, *Agriculture in North-Eastern Region* (National Publishing House : New Delhi), 1986.

Singh, J.P., *Human Resources of North-Eastern India* (Inter-India Publications: New Delhi), 1982.

Thakur, Pankaj, *Profile of a Development Strategy for India's North-East* (Span Publications Pvt. Ltd.), 1988.

Yogi, Anand Kumar, *Development of North-East Region : Problems and Prospects* (Spectrum Publications: Guwahati, Delhi), 1991.

MANIPUR

A Study of the Land System of Manipur (Law Research Institute, Eastern Region, Gauhati High Court, Guwahati), 1985.

Brown, R., *Statistical Account of the Native State of Manipur* (Sanskaran Prakashak : Delhi), 1975.

Chaki-Sircar, Manjusri, *Feminism in a Traditional Society : Women of the Manipur Valley* (Shakti Books/Vikas Publishing House : New Delhi), 1984.

Chakravartti, Rama, *People of Manipur : Anthropogenetic Study of Four Manipur Groups* (B.R. Publishing Corporation : Delhi), 1986.

Constantine, R., *Manipur : Maid of the Mountains* (Lancers Publishers : New Delhi), 1981.

Das, Rajat Kanti, *Tribal Social Structure* (Inter-India Publications : New Delhi), 1988.

Dena, Lal, *British Policy Towards Manipur : 1891-1919,* (Publishers not mentioned), 1984.

Dev, Bimal J. and Lahiri, Dilip K., *Manipur : Culture and Politics* (Mittal Publications : Delhi) 1987.

Dun, Captain E.W., *Gazetteer of Manipur* (Vivek Publishing Company : Delhi), 1981.

Economic Review 1981-82, Directorate of Economics and Statistics (Government of Manipur, Imphal).

Gangte, T.S., *The Kukis of Manipur : A Historical Analysis* (Gyan Publishing House : New Delhi), 1993.

Ghosh, G.K., *Tribals and their Culture in Manipur and Nagaland, Vol. 3* (Ashish Publishing House : New Delhi), 1992.

Goswami, Atul, *Land Reforms and Peasant Movement* (Omsons Publications: New Delhi), 1986.

Gougin, T., *History of Zomi* (Published by the Author), 1986.

Gougin, T., *Discovery of Zoland* (Published by the author), 1980.

Government of Manipur Revised Tribal Sub Plan : 1986-87 (Department for Development of Tribals and Backward Classes, Manipur).

Government of Manipur Draft Special Component Plan for Scheduled Castes 1990-91 (Department for Development of Tribals and Backward Classes, Manipur).

Grimwood, Ethel St. Clair, *My Three Years in Manipur* (Vivek Publishing House: Delhi), 1975.

Hodson, T.C., *The Meiteis* (B.R. Publishing Corporation : Delhi), 1975.

Hodson, T.C., *The Naga Tribes of Manipur* (Low Price Publications : Delhi-52), 1989.

Johnstone, Sir James, *Manipur and the Naga Hills* (Vivek Publishing House: Delhi), 1971.

Kabui, Gangmumei, *Anal : A Transborder Tribe of Manipur* (Mittal Publications : Delhi), 1985.

Kirti Singh, M., *Religion and Culture of Manipur* (Manas Publications : Delhi), 1988.

Mahajan, V.S., *Emerging Pattern of North-Eastern Economy* (Deep and Deep Publications, New Delhi), 1987.

Meitei Villages: Imphal (East Block, Manipur Rural Development Plan (Research and Development Unit : Association of Voluntary Agencies for Rural Development, New Delhi), 1976.

Panchani, Chander Sheikher, *Manipur: Religion, Culture and Society* (Konark Publishers Pvt. Ltd.), 1987.

Pandey, S.N. (ed), *Sources of the History of Manipur and the Adjoining Areas* (National Publishing House: New Delhi), 1985.

Roy Burman, B.K., *Towards Poverty Alleviation Programmes in Nagaland and Manipur* (Mittal Publications: Delhi), 1984.

Roy, Nilima, *Art of Manipur* (Agam Kala Prakashan : Delhi), 1979.

Sanajaoba, Naorem (ed.), *Manipur : Past and Present : The Heritage and Ordeals of a Civilization, Vol. 1* (Mittal Publications : Delhi), 1988.

Singh, K.M., *History of Christian Missions in Manipur and other Neighbouring States* (Mittal Publications : New Delhi), 1991.

Singh, K.M., *Hijab Irabot Singh and Political Movement in Manipur* (B.R. Publishing Corporation : Delhi), 1989.

Singh, Ravindra Pratap, *Electoral Politics in Manipur : A Spatio-Temporal Study* (Concept Publishing Company : New Delhi), 1981.

Singh, Lairenmayum, Iboongohal, *Introduction to Manipur* (Published by S. Ibochaoba Singh, Imphal), 1987.

Singh, N. Tombi, *Manipur – A Study* (Publishers not mentioned), 1972.

Soppitt, C.A., *A Short Account of the Kuki-Lushai Tribes on the North-East Frontier* (Firma K.L.M. Ltd. on behalf of Tribal Research Institute, Aizawl), 1976.

Thakur, Pankaj (ed.), *Profile of a Development Strategy for India's North-East* (Span Publications Pvt. Ltd. : Guwahati), 1988.

Seventh Five Year Plan 1985-90 and Annual Plan 1985-86 (Manipur).

Techno-Economic Survey of Manipur : Economic Report (Report of the National Council of Applied Economic Research), Manipur Administration, Imphal, 1961.

TRIPURA

Adhikari, O.S., *The Problem of Indebtedness among the Tribals in Sadar Sub-division of Tripura* (Directorate of Research, Department of Welfare for Scheduled Tribes and Scheduled Castes : Government of Tripura, Agartala), 1982.

A Guide for the Entrepreneurs (Directorate of Industries, Government of Tripura, Agartala), May, 1989.

A Study of the Land System of Tripura (Law Research Institute: Eastern Region, Guwahati High Court, Guwahati), 1990.

Barman, Debapriya Deb, *Treatise on Traditional Social Institutions of the Tripuri Community,* (Directorate of Research, Department of Welfare for Scheduled Tribes and Scheduled Castes, Government of Tripura), 1983.

Bhattacharya, A.C., *Progressive Tripura* (Inter-India Publications : New Delhi), 1985.

Bhattacharya, Gayatri, *Refugee Rehabilitation and its Impact on Tripura's Economy* (Omsons Publications : New Delhi, Guwahati), 1988.

Bhattacharjee, Pradip Nath, *The Jamatiyas of Tripura* (Department of Welfare for Scheduled Tribes and Scheduled Castes, Government of Tripura), 1983.

Bhattacharjee, Pradeep Nath, *Lokabritter Aloke Koloi Sampraday* (Directorate of Research, Department of Welfare for Scheduled Tribes and Scheduled Castes, Government of Tripura), 1983.

Bhattacharya, Banikantha, *Tripura Administration : The Era of Modernisation (1870 - 1972)*, Mittal Publications : Delhi), 1986.

Biswas, A.B., A.K. Saha, S.P. Das Gupta, and C. Chakravarti, *State of Environment in Tripura* (Prepared by the Centre for Study of Man and Environment, Presidency College, Calcutta for the Department of Science, Technology and Environment, Government of Tripura, Agartala), 1989.

Chakravarti, Mahadev (ed), *Administrative Report of Tripura State Since 1902, Vol.1-4* (Gyan Publishing House : New Delhi), 1994.

Chatterjee, S.N., *Tripura : A Profile* (Inter-India Publications : New Delhi), 1984.

Chaudhuri, Saroj and Bikach Chaudhuri, *Glimpses of Tripura* (Tripura Darpan Prakashani : Agartala), 1983.

Chib, Sukhdev Singh, *This Beautiful India : Tripura* (ESS ESS Publications : New Delhi), 1988.

Deb, D.B., *The Flora of Tripura State, Vol. II* (Today and Tomorrow's Printers and Publishers : New Delhi), 1983.

Devvarman, S.B.K., *The Tribes of Tripur,,* A Dissertation (Directorate of Research, Government of Tripura, Agartala), 1986.

Dutta, Dr. Jyotish Chandra, *An Introduction to the History of Tripura* (Book Home : Calcutta), 1984.

Gan-Chaudhuri, Jagadis, *A Political History of Tripura* (Inter-India Publications : New Delhi), 1985.

Gan-Chaudhuri, Jagadis, *An Anthology of Tripura* (Inter-India Publications: New Delhi), 1985.

Gan-Chaudhuri, Jagadis, *Tripura : The Land and Its People* (Leeladevi Publications : Delhi), 1980.

Gan-Chaudhuri, Jagadis, *The Corpus of Tripura* (Inter-India Publications : New Delhi), 1990.

Gan-Chaudhuri, Jagadis, *The Riangs of Tripura* (Directorate of Research, Department of Welfare for Scheduled Tribes and Scheduled Castes, Government of Tripura), 1983.

Ganguli, J.B., *The Benign Hills : A Study in Tripura's Population Growth and Problems* (Tripura Darpan Prakashani : Agartala), 1983.

Ghosh, Kamalini, *Tribal Insurrection in Tripura : A Study in Relative Deprivation* (Booklinks Corporation : Hyderabad), 1984.

Menon, K.D., *Tripura District Gazetteers : Tripura* (Department of Education, Government of Tripura, Agartala), 1975.

Roychoudhury, Nalini Ranjan, *Tripura through the Ages* (Sterling Publishers Private Ltd. : New Delhi), 1983.

Saigal, Omesh, *Tripura:Its History and Culture* (Concept Publishing Company : Delhi), 1978.

Singh, Ram Gopal, *The Kukis of Tripura: A Socio-Economic Survey* (Directorate of Research, Department of Welfare for Scheduled Tribes and Scheduled Castes, Government of Tripura), Year of publication not given.

Socio-Economic Survey of the Cobbler Communities of Agartala Municipality and its Adjacent Areas, (Directorate of Research, Department of Welfare for Scheduled Tribes and Scheduled Castes, Government of Tripura, Agartala), 1980.

Strength of Achievement Motivation and Personality of Two Cultural Groups in Tripura (Directorate of Research, Department of Welfare for Scheduled Tribes and Scheduled Castes, Government of Tripura, Agartala), 1982.

Thakurta, S.N. Guha, *Contract Labour in Construction Industry* (Firma KLM Pvt. Ltd. : Calcutta), 1980.

The Kaipengs (Directorate of Research, Department of Welfare for Scheduled Tribes and Scheduled Castes, Government of Tripura, Agartala), 1980.

Varman, S.B.K. Dev, *A Study over the Jhum and Jhumia Rehabilitation in the Union Territory of Tripura* (Directorate of Research, Department of Welfare for Scheduled Tribes and Scheduled Castes, Government of Tripura, Agartala), 1971.

4

NAGALAND

KAMAL KUMAR SHARMA

INTRODUCTION

This Report is based on the Socio-Economic Survey Reports prepared by the IAS probationers, allotted to Nagaland Cadre from the period 1986-1992. These officers were:

1. Sh. D.K. Bhalla (1986)
2. Ms. Vasudha Sharma (1987)
3. Sh. Pankaj Kumar (1987)
4. Sh. G.V.V. Sharma (1987)
5. Ms. S. Aparna (1988)
6. Sh. Rajiv Bansal (1988)
7. Sh. T.T. Toy (1989)
8. Sh. Jyoti Kalash (1990)
9. Sh. S. Imchen (1991)
10. Jan-e-Alam (1991)
11. Sanjay Kumar (1992)

Nagaland, the sixteenth State of Indian Union was inaugurated on December 1, 1963. By an Act, called the Naga Hills Tuensang Area Act, 1957, the former Naga Hills district and the Tuensang Frontier Divisions were transferred from Assam State and N.E.F.A. (now Arunachal Pradesh) and formed into a new State, Nagaland.

The State of Nagaland covers an area of 16,527 square kilometres and lies between 25°6′N to 27°2′N latitudes and between 93°2′E and 95°15′E longitudes. It is bounded by Assam in the north, north-west and west; Burma and Arunachal Pradesh in the east; and Manipur in the south. Excepting some plain areas in the south-western side like Dimapur, the rest of Nagaland is completely hilly region. The altitude varies between 194 and 3,048 metres.

The State comprises 7 districts, namely Kohima, Phek, Wokha, Zunheboto, Mokokchung, Tuensang and Mon. There are 1,119 villages out of which 7 villages are uninhabited. There are only seven towns in the State as a whole.

The State is full of hills and gorges covered with dense evergreen forests. There are plenty of streams flowing in the different parts of the State. The important rivers of Nagaland are the Dhanirun, Doyang, Dikhu, Jhaiyl etc. Most of these rivers flow through the Assam plains to join the mighty Brahmaputra.

There are basically two seasons. The summer starts generally from April and ends in March. The maximum temperature is about 28°C and the winters are very cold. The State economy is predominantly agriculture. The hilly terrain does not allow large scale agricultural activities. Jhum cultivation is still practiced in many areas.

According to D.K. Bhalla, 1986, "There was not much development between 1947 and 1962 till the grant of statehood. After 1962 the funds started pouring in fast and there was an effort to develop the State quickly. But unlike other parts of the country where pre-independence era signifies something of a feudal, decadent order and post-independence era an end of it all, it was not so here. There was no sharp change in land ownership pattern or values of the people in villages or life-styles. Only they become accustomed to more easier ways of life and more basic facilities like roads, water supply, electricity, education, buildings etc. There was no *zemindari,* no *begar*, no *sati*, no child marriages and so no question of their abolition ever arose. There were no outside settlers, no problems of migration or urban congestion came up."

According to Rajiv Bansal (1988), "A socio-economic survey in this region of India has to be conducted keeping in view the special circumstances in which these States have developed". The Naga tribes have for ever been famous for their practice of head hunting. It was only in 1930s that the British first made their in-roads into this hostile area. It took a few decades for the British Army to establish British control over these warrior tribes. The sole objective of the British Government was to maintain peace in the region. The year 1872 saw the first British Missionaries enter the area. The religious zeal bore fruit and within a few decades most of Nagaland had adopted Christianity. The Indian Independence witnessed upsurge of insurgency with one faction wishing to secede from the nation. Generous Central Aid followed to subdue the insurgent activities. Statehood followed on 1st December, 1963. Insurgency again got an upper hand and it was only after 1975 that relative peace was established. However, the peace till this date is an uneasy one.

In the light of the turbulent history of the State a socio-economic study reveals unique characteristics in this area. The village economy is an agricultural one. The traditional system of leadership and ownership and control of land continues to hold force to this day. Generally, there is a little economic inequality. Absolute poverty is not to be seen anywhere. The poorest of the poor has enough to eat and live. The standard of living of the villagers is on the whole quite high. Within the last two decades or so, much development has been achieved in road network, water supply, electricity supply, health care and education. However, much more yet remains to be done. Corruption and nepotism are the bane of the society and have come to stay.

The survey definitely has its limitations. These limitations have arisen mainly because of non-availability of data. The survey has been made more meaningful with the in-depth study of the land tenure system.

SUMMARY

Area – 16,579 sq. km.

Demography (1991) – Population: 1,209,546. Population Growth: 56.86 per cent. Density: 73 per sq.km. Sex Ratio: 890 females for every 1,000 males.

Economy – Labour Force (1991) : 44.20 per cent of which 75.26 per cent in the primary sector, 3.48 per cent in the secondary sector and 21.26 per cent in the tertiary sector. Per Capita Income (1989-90) : Rs. 3,529 at current prices. Per Capita Annual Consumption: N.A. State Domestic Product (1990-91): 404 crores (quick estimates).

Education – Literacy (1991) : 61.7 per cent. Rural, 57.2 per cent; Urban, 83.1 per cent. Female Rural Literacy: 50.36 per cent (seven years and above). Primary Schools (1989-90) : 1,286. Upper Primary, 341. School Enrolment (1989) : 269,935 (including nursery schools). Primary schools, 140,232; Secondary schools, 56,345. Primary School Teachers (1992-93) : One for every 19 students.

Health – Life Expectancy: N.A. Infant Mortality Rate (1990-92): 10 per 1,000 born. There is one physician for every 5,401 inhabitants (1989) and one hospital for every 36,652.91 inhabitants (1989). Primary Health Centres (1992): 33.

Others – Access to Potable Water (1991): Rural, 55.60 per cent; Urban, 45.47 per cent. Number of Fair Price/Ration Shops (1992) : Rural, 202; Urban, 271. Road Mileage (1987-88): 355 per 1,000 sq. km. Poverty Ratio: N.A. Villages Electrified (1993): 99.8 per cent.

Table 4.1 : Area, Total Population, Density, Rural and Urban Population of Districts in Nagaland

Sl. No.	Districts	Area (sq.kms)	Total Population (1991)	Density (per sq.km)	Rural (1991)	Urban (1991)
1.	Kohmia	4,041	387,581	95.91	270,185	117,396
2.	Mokokchung	1,615	158,374	98.06	133,571	24,803
3.	Mon	1,786	149,699	83.82	138,909	10,790
4.	Phek	2,026	102,156	50.42	93,790	8,366
5.	Tuensang	4,228	232,906	55.09	211,888	21,018
6.	Wokha	1,628	82,612	50.74	68,235	14,377
7.	Zunheboto	1,255	96,218	76.67	84,745	11,473

THE VILLAGE

According to S. Aparna (1988), traditionally, Naga villages have been autonomous, almost insular socio-political units. With the establishment of the modern political system consisting of a elected legislature and assembly constituencies, as also the present facilities for transport and communication, this insularity is being eroded. However, the village still retains, to a large extent, the decisive say in internal matters. Every villager of Chiechama owns his house. Even the lone landless family was allotted a plot by the Government and he managed to build his house on it. There are 564 households. The main building materials in use are timber, bamboo, mud and plaster for the walls, thatch or more often CGI sheets for the roof and mud plaster or wooden planks for the floor. A few of the villagers have built RCC houses. Only about 50-60 houses still have thatched roofs. Barring the RCC and Assam type houses, others are self-constructed.

According to Rajiv Bansal, (1988), the sacred land devoted to the deity was called *Aphu* and the location of Aphu symbolises the inauguration of the village to be set up and this sacred land owned as common village land. Sites in the neighbourhood of the *Aphu* were chosen by the founder clans who participated in the formation of the new village. Other clans were allotted lands at a distance from the *Aphu* in order of the role played by the clan in the formation of the village. These land sites which were for residential purposes were called *Yimkum*. In addition, sites for the construction of the Church, Panchayat hall, granary, schools, Health Centre, and playgrounds are also held as common village land.

According to Vasudha Sharma (1987), a traditional Angamic village was located on a hill top to guard against enemies, but the villagers did not clear away forests of the hill tops for cultivation, because they understood fully, the importance of tree-cover on the mountains for timely rains and fertile soils. They preferred to walk several kilometres down the hill to cultivate lands, even though it meant a lot many short term problems by way of putting in extra energy and time.

Houses are situated in the villages in rows or clusters according to convenience. If the terrain is narrow than the houses are located on the slope of the ridge. If it is a patch of uneven land then the houses are situated in clusters.

The sense of equality and fraternity is so well-established that in spite of the increasing gap in economic status, that is being brought about by development, the question of social segregation or disparities does not arise.

Very few houses have facilities of bathrooms and lavatories, but this seemed more because of age-old habits rather than due to any economic reasons.

The people have a very well developed aesthetic taste and are very fond of flowers. Several houses boast of well kept kitchen gardens with at least one banana tree present in almost every such garden.

In most Angami villages, there are several *khels* or clans, who have their own separate clan-chiefs, separate *gaon burra* (GB) to settle intra-clan disputes and their own lands.

According to Temjen Toy (1989), a *khel* is a geographical division of the village. Normally, a *khel* is inhabited by members of the same clan or a few clans. Each *khel* has a selected leader who is known as the *Gaon burra* or GB.

One very interesting feature of the houses in Jakhama is that they face the east. This was so since time immemorial, and the real reason behind this was unknown. The village gate is a large structure made of wood. It has no wooden door.

According to S. Imchen (1991), because of isolation every village had to develop its own things. From this point of view every Naga village is situated on the top of a hill or at least on its spur or neck, but never on the base. In general the defence arrangement has a triple line of defence. There are two stone walls and a ditch in between. The ditch is crossed by a single plank to enable the villagers to go out and come back. Every village has *khels* and every *khel* had such a plank to cross. Every *khel* of a village has got one or more water wells. These are the only source of water.

The villagers had a great reluctance to divulge any information of a personal nature as also regarding their earning. It was largely felt that if they divulge their true income, they would be taxed or pay higher house-tax, the only tax they pay at present. Moreover whatever infrastructure exist in the village does not provide any service worth the name. Power supply is at best erratic and the dispensary has no stock of medicines and life saving drugs to mention a few. The Sema political system is particularly suited to colonization as it is customary for the eldest son of a Sema Chief to take, when he is old enough, a colony from his father's village and found a new village at a convenient distance.

In this regard it would be worth to quote from J.H. Hutton's views on the society of Sema Nagas. The basis of Sema society is the village *(ippefu)* or part of a village *(Asah)* is under the control of a Chief. This system had its origin in the system of colonisation by a Chief's son accompanied by a number of his father's defendants *(mughemi)*. The former when marks the boundary of a new village the land for the new village is either acquired as a result of successful hostilities or by bringing under the use of uncultivated reserved land. The land in the latter case is demarcated by fencing and whole land is reserved for himself. Ordinarily besides a certain amount of land, which is owned/taken up by him most of his land is yearly passed on to his dependants to cultivate. Certain amount of land would be kept as reserve for the villagers to gather fuel, building materials etc. But this land is also under the control of the chief.

This is the cause, majority of land is under the Chief's control. However, these days, due to a number of factors some amount of fragmentation has taken place. Firstly, when this area was brought under British administrative law and order, the avenues of founding new villages were increased by effecting other tribes. Thus, all the sons of a chief were forced to remain as hereditary owner of the village and became heirs, though as per customs and partition of property never took place in the first generation but division of property took place from the second generation onwards. Consequently, today the original lineage chief still controls the bulk of the land but it is not concentrated in one single individual. The situation prevailing today is that the member of a family controls the land is also in most of cases a *gaon-burra* (Chief) of a *khel* in a village. Added to this is the fact that with economic development new avenues have been opened apart from agriculture, government job, for instance. The government employees are able to generate their surplus incomes and hence involved in the purchase of land. In the village as per the data available, government employees own the largest land next to the EBS. Conversely, the number of large landhoding families has declined over the years and are left with small holdings varying from one to two acres.

According to Jan-e-Alam (1991), it can be inferred that the locational advantage of a Naga village on a hill top is that the villagers are protected from outsider's raids even though it is disadvantageous from an economic point of view. The preference for a high altitude location of the village is hard to explain as cultivators sometimes have to walk down 5 to 10 km to cultivate their fields, while they are returning from agricultural fields they have to also climb up to their village with a heavy load of firewood or foodgrain produce.

Hordes of people (old and young) used to raid other villages usually during the day time when menfolk of the targetted village were busy in their fields.

Table 4.2 : Classification of Villages by Revenue, Non-Revenue and Villages fall under Township : Meziphema Block

Sl. No.	Name of Tribe Community	Number of Revenue Village	Number of Non-Revenue Township	Villages fall under township	Total
1.	Angamis	22	3	3	28
2.	Aos	1	2	-	3
3.	Garos	4	-	-	4
4.	Kacharis	12	-	1	13
5.	Kukis	6	2	-	8
6.	Nepali	1	-	-	1
7.	Sangtam	1	-	-	1
8.	Sema	30	62	1	93
9.	Yimchunger	-	2	-	2
10.	Mixed tribes villages	10	-	10	20
	Total	87	71	15	173

Source : Based on information from Block Development Office, Medziphema.

According to Sanjay Kumar (1992), the villages in Nagaland may be classified into three categories, viz. revenue paying, non-revenue paying village and the villages falling under the townships. The revenue villages are those villages, which are recognised by the Government of Nagaland and non-revenue villages are those villages, which are not yet recognised by the Government of Nagaland. Every household in the revenue villages pays a sum of Rs. 5 per house annually as the house tax to the government. The unrecognised villages in the Block are mostly Sema villages, which are located on the foothill of Dhansiripar, Medziphema, and Nihoku circles. Most of them are now placed in recently created Kuhoboto Block in Nihokhu circles.

It appears that out of the total number of 173 villages, 87 or 50.28 per cent revenue paying villages and 71 (41.04%) are non-revenue villages. The villages that fall under townships are 15 (8.67%).

Summary and Issues

Based on the reports submitted by the probationers it is clear that Nagas live in villages. These villages are mostly located on the hill tops for security reasons. From here they can keep a watch on the invading "enemies" and also can resist such forces better.

- The villages of Nagaland are self-sufficient and independent units. Each has its own cultivated land, water source, domestic animals, etc. The defence of the village is given top priority. A proper fencing of the site with bamboo spikes, pali shades is done to guard from the outside attack.
- Village gates were erected at strategic places. A narrow and deep path leads to the gate in some tribes. The gates are without the door. There are beams placed in a criss-cross style at the gate. This helps the guard to see the approaching enemy.
- At present no such strategy is being followed. Houses have appeared all over. Today lot of local politicians and bureaucrats are constructing houses in Dimapur. This is the rail head and has better transportation and communication facilities.
- The Naga villages are in a state of flux. Like any other part of the country, consumer items have become important. Migration has started to some extents to places like Dimapur, Kohima, Mokokchung etc.

LAND AND AGRICULTURE

According to Vasudha Sharma (1987), lands are distributed on two bases – individual basis as well as community basis. In the case of Botsa, half the total land of village belongs to the community and the rest half is divided among the individuals. The descendants of those who had established the village have more land than others, but the general principle followed is that at the time of establishment of the village, the general people got as much land as much they were capable of cultivating. If on subsequent divisions in every generation, any person gets less land than enough for him to survive, he can ask the community to let him cultivate a portion of its land and the community usually agrees to it on condition that he does not hold proprietary or hereditary rights on this land. In this way, even the poorest of the poor of the village has at least an acre of land for cultivation.

As mentioned above, land is abundant in the village. A medium-income family can boast of approximately 4-5 acres of land. Soil is a fertile loam and water for irrigation is plentiful. There are numerous streams through which Botsa not only gets enough water for itself all the year round, but supplies water to five villages in the neighbourhood. The result is that Botsa people do not practice *Jhum* cultivation. All their fields are well-terraced and only wet rice cultivation *(Panikheti)* is being done. So, all the lands are wet lands. Selling of the lands is most uncommon in the village.

Only local varieties of rice are grown. The village has never received any improved varieties from the agriculture department. They themselves did not seem very keen on experimenting with new varieties, because they are not producing for market and they prefer the local varieties for consumption.

Average yield of rice is reported to be about 7-8 quintals per acre. The pattern of land distribution in Nagaland in general, but in Angami areas in particular, is probably the best and the most egalitarian existing anywhere in India. There are no landless poor and no agricultural labourers. Everyone owns the house and the land he lives in and works on. In addition, if anyone is willing to cultivate any more land, he can utilise the community land for the purpose. The rich people who are large landholders also lease out land to those who do not have enough, but the rents are nominal. Tradition normally determines the value of land which is oriented to status rather than to productivity and paid rents are determined entirely by tradition. No doubt, there are inequalities of income and standards of living, but there has been till now, very little accumulation for investment and the productive system has remained almost static over a very long time.

Another area where Nagaland is different is that in the inner line area, there is no system of land revenue. There has been no cadastral survey either. There is no government land within the inner line except for what it has acquired from individuals or communities for public purposes.

Age old implements are being used. For example, there has been no change in the type of plough used since plough came to be used first in terraced fields. No fertilisers or even green manures are used. No High Yielding Varieties of rice are in use. The reason for this is partly the lack of development of varieties specifically suitable to this region through proper agricultural research.

But the people are sentimentally very much attached to their own piece of land. Therefore, exchange of lands is not a normal practice.

Building of field huts is not necessary, because no protection is needed for the produce either from human beings or from pests. There is no risk of theft or any other type of damage to the crop from any human being. The age-old honesty and self-respect of the Nagas contributes mainly to this fact. As for pests, one has to strain one's eyes and ears for hours or even days together in Kohima to watch or hear the slightest hint of a bird or any other crop-pest-even children specialise in the *shikar,* the moment they can spot it.

Irrigation is wholly by a number of small streams which are rain-fed. Since these streams suffice and the cultivators have made channels to their own fields and the rainy season is very long, there is no need of any other source of irrigation.

Houses are not bought or sold normally, so site values are difficult to determine.

According to G.V.V. Sharma (1987), they grow rice mixed with maize, chillies, potatoes, squash, sorghum and some varieties of oil seeds. All this is done by *Jhum* cultivation. The *Jhum* cycle is now 8 years long, i.e. they start working the jungle in the same place which was worked 8 years ago. Nobody has ventured to do *Panikheti* partly because of lack of sufficient water sources. No initiative for construction of water harvesting structures has been seen and perhaps that would lead to some structural difficulties within the village. There is a kind of vicious circle in the sense that water sources are required for terrace cultivation to be possible but the very fact of *jhumming* leads to lack of permanent attachment to any particular pieces of land. This precludes any effort for water harvesting structures catering to any piece of land. Further *jhumming* having been the practice since time immemorial people have a strong disinclination to any change. Added to all this is the fact that terrace cultivation would mean immense hard work at the beginning.

Land Utilization

According to Pankaj Kumar (1987), in the absence of any concrete data available in the District Agriculture Office the statistics about land utilisation is based on guess-estimates. The total cultivable area is about 35,000 acres. Almost all of it is under *Jhum* cultivation. Terrace cultivation is practiced in a very limited manner in the village (in fact, this is true of the district as a whole).

Land Tenure

All land belongs to the villagers. In the village every *khel* or clan has got its own land. There is no *patta* or *rayati* system. In the clan again, every individual family has got its own land. This family land goes on sub-dividing itself as the members of the family increase in number. When the land falls short for any particular family, the family may be allowed to cultivate the *khel* land or the village land. However, land is purchased or sold within the village itself because there is a strong aversion among the villagers to sell land outside the village. The transaction is carried out verbally in the presence of some responsible person of the village. Now-a-days such sale is generally written as many people can read or write.

Pests and Diseases

Total crop failure due to crop disease, floods, cyclone or pests has not occurred in living memory. Main pests are stem borer and grasshopper. Their incidence is not severe, however, and this coupled with the efforts of the agriculture department practically assures a safe harvesting.

Crop Yield

No firm estimates are available about the average crop yield per acre. An attempt was made to ascertain the average yields by putting questions to the villagers and to the field staff of agriculture department. The results are summarised in Table 4.3 below :

Table 4.3 : Average Crop Yield per Acre

Crop Yield	(No.of tins)	Yield (kg.)	Value (Rs.)
Joba tear (*Jhum*)	0	420	360
Maize (*Jhum*)	40	600	1000
Millet (*Jhum*)	25	325	500
Paddy	0	600	1250

The inputs are the seeds and the labour. In case of paddy cultivation, another input is the preparation of the terrace fields. The village is not self-sufficient in food crops, particularly, rice. The agricultural produce is sold in market in small quantities by individuals in the nearby Tuensang town and it mainly consists of fruits and vegetables.

According to Rajiv Bansal (1988), the system of land ownership in this tribal area is quite distinct from that of plains area. Broadly, the entire village land is divided into three categories, i.e. village land, clan land and individual land. The percentage of land under each category varies from village to village and in the absence of any land survey, it is impossible to determine this percentage. However, it can be said that the major portion of the land is clan land.

Before the cultivation season, the clan members collectively decide as to which areas are to be taken up for *Jhum* cultivation. Once these pockets or *khetis* areas are decided the process of allocating the same comes into action. For this purpose, all the households in the clan are arranged serially in descending order according to age. The senior most clan member is then given the first chance to select one *kheti* area. This ensures that the older people are able to get land near the village and also get the best land. The system is based on the fact that older people will not be able to contribute hard labour like the youngsters.

After the eldest clan member has exercised his chance, opportunity is given to the second eldest member to choose his *kheti*. In this way according to age each clan member chooses his land. In this manner, it may so happen that the younger clan members either do not get land or get land which is unsuitable for cultivation or get land which is insufficient to meet their requirements. In this situation, the younger members can request for land from the senior clan members who have excess land. It is here that respect for elders comes into play. If the elder members feel that the younger ones who require land are respectful, then they can give a portion of their land to the younger ones. However, they are within their right to refuse.

In a situation in which the younger clan members cannot secure land from the senior members for want of surplus land or due to lack of respect, the young members can borrow land from members of other clans at a price or 'tax'. This tax equals the amount of seed planted in the land, i.e. if a person leases out land sufficient for planting 5 tins of seed then he has to give 5 tins of paddy as tax to the owner. In this manner, each clan member awaits his turn to come of age and improve his chances for getting land.

Individual land can be obtained by three methods. One is by way of inheriting ancestral property. It may be noted here that inheritance is through the male line only and women do not inherit any share of landed property. However, in case a person dies without leaving behind a son then the property passes on to the eldest son of the brother of the deceased person. The second way to obtain individual land is to take a portion of the clan *jhum* land and develop it for terrace cultivation. The land right is given to him in recognition of the hard labour he has put in to develop it. The third way to acquire individual land is to purchase it at a price.

The system of clan land has its basis on age and respect for elders. Each clan has a certain area based on the size of the clan. The founder clans were entitled to the best portions of the land. The system of allocation of land for cultivation to the clan members makes interesting study. The clan land is normally not contiguous and is held in pockets called *khetis*. These *khetis* or pockets are not equal in area. Also, while some *khetis* are adjacent to the village, others are situated at one to two hours walking distance. Further some *khetis* are on slopes suitable for *Jhum* cultivation and others are cliff lands.

According to S. Aparna (1988), two styles of agriculture are practiced namely terrace rice cultivation and *Jhum* or dry rice cultivation. Unlike other Naga tribes, the Angamis and the Chakesangs have been practicing terrace cultivation since time immemorial.

The main implements being used are the spade and the pickaxe, the traditional all-purpose *dao*, manual plough and sickle. Animal power is not used. The paddy seed is stored out of the last harvest. Fertilisers are not being in any appreciable level due to low availability, and hardening effect on soil etc. Manuring of the fields is practiced.

In the State, government does not own the land but ownership is private, vested in the chiefs, clans or individuals. In the village, therefore, bulk of the land belongs to the village chiefs and some individuals with varying sizes of land.

Therefore, common property resources in the sense that all members of the community have equal rights over it include only the government buildings like the schools and dispensary, forest under village reserve, footpaths, public wells and mountain streams within the area under the village jurisdiction.

The village footpaths, public wells and streams are freely used by everyone whatever his/her social status may be. Regarding public wells, each *khel* has generally one catering to its need and is situated at an altitude below the village and about 1/2 to 1 km distant. The footpaths to the wells and the wells themselves are cleaned and kept is good repair by the community as a whole as the chief *gaon burra* declares one day in a year compulsory for all able-bodied members to do community social service.

In the mountain streams, all villagers are free to fish with nets and traps. However, use of chemicals is totally banned, and anyone caught doing so is fined Rs. 10,000. Use of water for irrigation by means of diversion channels is also open to anyone.

According to Temjen Toy (1989), the average land holding is between two to three acres. This fact is also borne out by the entries in the questionnaire. The figure given below, based on the sample drawn for the questionnaire, shows that more than 75 per cent of the people own between 2 to 5 acres.

It should be borne in mind that in Nagaland, there are no official records of land holdings. Moreover, there are no land ceilings. This makes it very difficult to use statistical tools in the calculation of land records. All figures are, therefore, based on rough estimates.

Agricultural Practices

The average annual rainfall in the area is about 80 inches, and the rainy season starts in June and continues till September end.

Cultivation is carried out in two seasons – summer and winter. However, different crops are sown and harvested in different months.

As can be seen, there are two types of cultivation carried out in Jakhama – terraced and *jhum*. Under terraced cultivation, paddy is grown during the wet season, and potato during winter when the fields are dry. Under *jhum*, the forest is cut in January, burnt in February, and the crops sown in March.

Technique

There has been no change over the years. Spades are the only implements used during cultivation. The use of bullocks, tractors, etc. is yet to be made.

Cowdung is used as manure. This is obtained from the cattle the farmers keep at home. The use of chemicals is not popular. The crops were less immune to various diseases. Improved seeds are also not used. The cultivator would rather grow the local variety and eat less, than have a larger quantity of tasteless 'foreign' rice!

As is true for the whole State, the main means of livelihood is agriculture. One interesting feature of this village is that there are no landless households.

According to P.K. Borthakur (1989), bullocks are used for ploughing and other kind of works are carried on by manpower. As hired labour is difficult to get in the village, most of the works are carried on by family labour. Double cropping is not possible due to unsuitable climate and shortage of water and as such the yield is poor. A normal variety would give only 60 tins (1 tin = 20 kg) per acre in a year.

Horticulture is an old practice which is done by 90 per cent of the families at small scale around their dwellings. The important fruits grown are orange, pineapple, banana, guava etc. The mostly grown fruit is sweet orange which may be the most profitable practice in the present condition. Each orange tree bears around 500 fruits every year. Besides fruits vegetables are grown in their kitchen gardens. Though this is not done in a large scale, vegetables available in their gardens could meet their daily needs. Many families also sell vegetables in the Mokokchung town market to augment their incomes.

According to Jyoti Kalash (1990), Southern Nagaland exhibits wet-rice terraced cultivation side by side with *jhumming*. In the village, almost all families practice *jhumming;* side by side with this a few families also go for terraced cultivation. A few families, mostly that of government servants, practice wet-rice terraced cultivation only as it does not require much labour compared with *jhumming* though initially much labour is required by way of cutting the slopes into terraces.

From the rivulets and water splashes, the main sources of irrigation, channels of enormous length are dug to carry water and overflow the terraces. Bamboo pipes sometimes serve as supplementary irrigational means down the slopes where terraces are located.

Jhumming consists during its first stage, clearance of the shrubs, surface soil with the undergrowth at the autumn season, while the conservation of the ashes for manuring is practiced during February or March. After felling the jungle, the common practice is that trees and shrubs are exposed to sunshine, which when dried are burnt. *Jhum* cultivators have to be particular about the process of clearing the soil during cultivation.

Jhum cultivation stands on the field for two years but *jhum* cycle might have covered five to nine years. *Jhum* cycle's duration however is more limited in Nagaland than in other neighbouring hill tracts. This is because of the efforts made by administration and villages themselves to keep portions of their forests protected from undue and constant ravages. Its main disadvantage is its deleterious effect on soil fertility, so that its reproductivity is hardly ever replenished. Experience however has shown that it is difficult to set down further innovations in *jhumming* as its protagonists have argued that the traditional system is the most practical form on the steep hill sides. But the yield per acre of *jhum* lands is comparatively lesser and fluctuates; for instance while a single *jhum* field might give 50 maunds during the first year, the output next year, might have dwindled to 30 maunds.

The Naga Jhum Land Regulation, 1946, gave the original inhabitants absolute rights over their *jhum* lands and recognised their eligibility to practice shifting cultivation, clear the forests and graze cattle. Lands other than those already acquired by the Government, belong to one community which comprise one village or more than one. But the Regulation is no longer tenable owing to the enforceable Naga Forest Act, 1968 and the Nagaland (Requisition and Acquisition) Act, 1965 which give to the Government absolute rights to carve out forest reserves and acquire any plots of land for its purpose on the basis of awarding compensations to the holders.

The major Naga tribes which live on *Jhumming* system are the Semas, Lothas, Rengma, Chang, Ao and Konyaks. One advantage of it is the growth of Joba's tear and millets with which a special beer is made. These do not grow in wet rice fields or in terrace cultivation. Pumpkins, onions, maize, ginger, cabbage, mustard leaves etc. are grown.

Roughly 95 per cent depend on agriculture for their livelihood. Even government servants like teachers, Grade-IV staff etc. go to the fields after quickly performing their official duties or during holidays. Anyway their family members regularly go to the fields in the morning and come back only after sun set. During seasons when much labour is required in the fields, many government servants do not attend office, even teachers do not go to school – this has a very bad impact on the education of the students. This practice is widely prevalent all over Nagaland. The school authorities should be more strict.

There are no laws or regulations governing ownership of land in the State. The ownership of land and the individual right to use it is determined by tradition and customary laws which are uncodified. The Indian Constitution under article 371A safeguards the Naga customary law and the ownership and transfer of land.

In Nagaland, three types of irrigation systems are in vogue.

1. Gravity channels for distributing water from hill streams at higher sites.
2. Gravity channels with head works built across the stream and tapping the water from the reservoirs.
3. Lift irrigation for lifting surface water.

In Nagaland most of the villages are perched on the hill tops. Therefore, irrigation is provided only in terraced fields where facilities exist to bring water from the sources by gravity through irrigation channels. In the village under study two types of irrigation are undertaken. However, due to non-availability of well organised irrigation system only 62 hectares of land are under permanent cultivation. Besides it must be noted that irrigation facilities exist only during the *kharif* season.

Practices and implements are still primitive. Sowing is done by sprinkling the seed carefully into little hollows made usually by men with a small hoe and scraped over by the following women. One big problem faced by the villagers is that when the crop is at ripening stage, it is destroyed by birds. Traditional methods such as the scare crow, bamboo clappers and the *akheketsu* are used by them to scare away the birds. The last are bamboo ropes tied around the fields supported on the pillars and connected to a main rope on elevated ground. When the birds come, a person keeps tagging at the main rope which makes the ropes around the field to shake vigorously and thereby scare away the birds. It entails a lot of labour and is effective for a week at the most. This year the method of mixing poison (zinc sulphate) in rice and placing near watering holes has been adopted as advised by the agricultural department. This has also met only with limited success.

The traditional implements are still used and they include the following :

(i) The *amughu*, an axe used for clearing jungles.
(ii) The multipurpose *dao*.
(iii) *Akupu*, the digging hoe.
(iv) The rake made of bamboo.
(v) The winnowing *jan*.
(vi) The grain basket.
(vii) The *akhozhe*, a sieve made of split bamboo.

In *jhum,* the production of rice per hectare is about 600 kg. whereas under terrace it is 1150 kg. The reasons for poor productivity are as follows:

(i) The absence of ownership right of the individuals in the cultivated land and the farmers, lack of interest and enthusiasm to make any improvement of permanent nature to the landholdings.
(ii) Absence of cadastral survey.
(iii) Very low population pressure as compared to other States and easy availability of foodgrains from Civil Supplies Department.
(iv) *Jhumming* and non adoption of improved cultural practices.
(v) Inadequate used of inputs
(vi) Poor fertility of soil due to fast run off and erosion. Acidic nature of soil depresses the availability of

nutrients like Phosphorus (P), Potash (K), Manganese (Mn) and Zinc (Zn).

(vii) Complete dependence on rainfall during summer which facilitates only one crop.

According to Jan-e-Alam (1991), another difficulty in determining the area of a plot is that there are no written land records. Land belongs to individuals by virtue of customary usage. As there are no land records so also there is no standard unit of measurement. Nagas determine the size of the *Kheti* by its yield in tin canisters. Even the size of the tin is not standardised. Yield for paddy is 125 tins per acre in terraced cultivation and 110 tins for *Jhum* cultivated area.

The villagers have a high awareness of the importance of forests for their survival. They rightly believe that if they cut all the forest their water sources will dry up endangering their survival, hence an area of 2.5 hectares of thick forest around a major water source has been reserved by the village.

Our survey revealed that almost every household in the village has terraced fields as well as *Jhum* fields. Even part time cultivators (those who are employed) grow enough to feed themselves.

Cultivation is carried out in two seasons summer and winter. However, different crops are sown and harvested in different months. This has been clearly brought out in Table 4.4 below :

Table 4.4 : Cropping Pattern

Crop	Sown in	Harvested in	Type of cultivation
Potato	1. Jan	1. May	*Jhum*
	2. September	2. December	*Jhum* & Dry Terrace.
Paddy	1. March	1. September	*Jhum*
	2. June	2. October	Wet Terrace
Millets	March	September	*Jhum*
Maize	March	July	*Jhum*

Under terraced cultivation, paddy is grown during the wet season, and potato during winter when the fields are dry. Under *Jhum*, the forest is cut in January, burnt in February, and the crops sown in March.

Cow dung is used as manure. This is obtained from the cattle the farmers keep at home. The use of chemicals is not popular. I was told that though the yield was higher, the crops were less immune to various diseases.

According to S. Imchen (1991), as per the census data of 1991, the following data is available for Surumi village in terms of occupation.

		Total	Male	Female
1.	Total main workers	619	294	325
2.	Cultivation	548	233	315
3.	Construction workers	4	2	2
4.	Trade & Communication	2	1	1
5.	Government service	68	58	10

From the above it is evident that agriculture is the main occupation for the villagers. Here it may also be mentioned that most of those in service also have field cultivated by their spouse and children.

On the basis of the data collected from the sample survey of households in the village the level of income from different occupations is given below:

	Occupation	Income (Month)
1.	Agriculture	
	a. Landless	Less than Rs. 200
	b. 2-3 acres	Less than Rs. 200
	c. 5-10 acres	Rs. 500-1000
	d. Above 10 acres	Rs. 1000-1500
2.	Government service	Rs. 1000 to 3000
3.	Shopkeepers	Rs. 300-500

Here it needs to be mentioned that the income levels given with regard to agriculture have been arrived at by dividing the total yield after harvest by 12 to arrive at the monthly average. It goes without saying that farmers with irrigated land have a higher income compared to those with unirrigated land. Cultivators having no land and also those with marginal holdings supplement their income by hiring out their labour to the larger farmers.

It is evident from the given data that those in the services sector have a much higher income than the cultivators. It varies from job to job and some earn as much as 3,000. Besides they also cultivate their fields giving them additional source of income. Thus economically they are the most well off and there is a big craze for government jobs.

According to Sanjay Kumar (1992), the study of land ownership, its classification and measurement becomes difficult in Nagaland as there is no cadastral survey conducted before. There is no detailed official record on land in respect of Nagaland. Owing to the absence of required authentic data on land ownership system, operational holdings, land-use pattern, tenure and tenancy pattern etc., it became a difficult task to conduct a data-based empirical study on land ownership system. When Nagaland was a part of Assam, a small portion of land about 259 sq. km., was surveyed which now falls under Dimapur Mauza. Except this portion of land, no area in Nagaland has so far been cadastrally surveyed and no standard and uniform laws have been framed till date. The only legal framework for determining the right to cultivate land is the "Nagaland Jhumland Act, 1970", which has certain limitations.

Invariably the ownership of land, exercise of ownership rights controlling system, land-use pattern, land boundary and man-land relations are based on traditions, which are simply guided by customary laws. The usage of customary laws are also not yet codified. Every individual farmer owns landed property and enjoys right over it. The right is permanent and inheritable and also transferable. This type of ownership comes either by inheritance or by purchase. Right of individuals to property in land are well known and well recognised, and the rules as to inheritance and partition of such property settled by strict customary laws land, especially permanent terraced cultivation, is freely sold and bought. There are various types of ownership of land. These are:

Land under the Village Authority

In most of the newly established Naga villages, this system of ownership is being practiced. The ownership of land in Naga society is based on situation and historical factors rather than a uniform principle. The system varies from tribe to tribe and village to village even among the same tribe.

Lineage Land

This is one of the most common system that we find in a Naga society today. In this practice, the land is owned by a kin group "which neither can be termed as clan land nor as individual". For instance, if a man purchases a plot of land who has several sons, after his death, his sons and grandchildren inherit that particular land and in the long run, this is shared by a kin group.

Clan Land

Almost every clan has sites for construction of houses and plots for cultivation. The oldest member of the clan is the custodian or head over the clan land and he exercises a titular right over clan land. Every clan member has right to use that land according to seniority and also availability of land. The clan land is generally distributed by the senior members of the clan through a formal meeting of the clan members.

Rough Distribution of Land Ownership and Percentage of Angami Tribe

Tribe	Ownership Types	Percentage
Angami	Ordinary Individual land	15.00
	Village authority	70.00
	Lineage land	10.00
	Clan land	5.00
		100.00

At the present rate of population growth in Nagaland, the total foodgrain requirement will not be more than 50 per cent for the State. Though 85 per cent of the population is engaged in agriculture, the Naga farmers are unable to produce even their requirements and, therefore, they are mostly dependent on outside supplies.

Summary and Issues

- — Agriculture forms the backbone of Nagaland people. By 1950, almost 95 per cent of the population was directly dependent on agriculture. The main form of cultivation is *Jhum* and this is followed by Terrace and in some places by wet rice cultivation.
- — The *Jhum* cultivation starts in the month of November and the fields are burnt in February. The cultivation is done by hoes and spade. Because of the leaves and other decay the soil is marshy. It is so light that in some cases paddy can be grown without cultivation. Also cultivated are crops like taro, pumpkin, beans etc. Also during harvesting the fodder is not made out as the cows are never fed at home at night but they are allowed to graze in jungle during day.
- — For the *Jhum* cultivation, during the first year rice is cultivated, in the second it is maize and if the third year is used then millet or vegetables are cultivated. Terrace cultivation is practiced by Angamis, Chakebsang and Zehang tribes. This is done in July-August and the paddy is harvested in October-November. Wet rice cultivation is practiced in the plain areas of the State. This is also done in July-August and the paddy is harvested in November-December.
- — Land ownership, its classification and measurement is very difficult in Nagaland. No cadastral survey has been done in the past. Thus there are no authentic data on the land ownership system, land-use pattern, tenure and tenancy pattern. The cultural system is based on traditions, which in turn are governed by the customary law.

The cropping pattern is as follows :

Crop	Sown in	Harvested in	Type of cultivation
Potato	1. January	1. May	*Jhum*
	2. September	2. December	*Jhum* & Dry Terrace
Paddy	1. March	1. September	*Jhum*
	2. June	2. October	Wet Terrace
Millets	March	September	*Jhum*
Maize	March	July	*Jhum*

— A lot has to be done to improve the productivity of land. This can be done by training, teaching and other methodology. Some tribals still prefer paddy produced by *Jhum* cultivation as it is more tasty. The attitude and mind-set would have to be changed.

VILLAGE INDUSTRIES

According to D.K. Bhalla (1986), regarding the occupation in a village, almost every one is farmer. There are no professional or hereditary blacksmiths, goldsmiths or carpenters or sweepers etc. Some people know the various craft but almost all the people in the village can practice some sort of the smithery or constructions in their own crude ways.

Co-operatives

According to Pankaj Kumar (1987), there are four co-operative societies in the village as given in Table 4.5 below :

Table 4.5 : Co-operative Societies in Tuensang Village

Name of	Membership	Share Loan (88- Capital 89)	Society
Kangsho Weaving Coop Society	25	2000	Nil
Lomo Multipurpose	72	3500	45000
Bilashi Fisheries	52	1520	Nil
Chungphu Consumers	47	1780	Nil

The consumers' co-operative society is now defunct. A godown was constructed but bottlenecks in getting supplies of essential commodities caused its failure. Six fishery ponds were constructed by the fisheries co-operative society, but it has been inactive of late. The weaving co-operative society is also suffering because of lack of supply of yarn by the Raw Materials Co-operation based in Dimapur. Weavers are now getting yarn from the open market at higher prices. Only the multipurpose co-operative society got loans worth Rs. 45000 in 1988-89 and has been sanctioned loans up to Rs. 60,000 in 1989-90. Its activities include protection of paddy, fisheries and consumer goods.

According to Rajiv Bansal (1988), the only village industry functioning in the village is spinning and weaving. Almost all Naga ladies know how to weave their *meghla* and *shawl* and hence do the same at home. The loom used is an ancient one. It is made of bamboo. However the produce generally finds a market only within the State. The market for Naga traditional handicrafts has never been explored. One of the factors which makes weaving and spinning products very expensive is the high cost of raw material and the high cost of labour. The raw material is wool which is bought locally and is very expensive. The loom used is traditional and inefficient – practically no improvement has been made in its design over the years. Each tribe in Nagaland has a distinctive shawl and hence the most widely available shawl in Mokokchung District is the Ao shawl. Generally very few ladies weave more than their domestic requirement. Hence there is little marketable surplus. Apart from weaving there is no handicraft industry.

According to Vasudha Sharma (1987), in almost every household, some weaving is done, but the cloth so produced is used for domestic purposes only. Earlier, the women of the household used to weave not only to cater to the entire domestic requirements, but also for giving gifts or shawls and *mekhalas* to relatives and friends and guests on certain occasions. Now-a-days, however, the practice has become infrequent and weaving is done only occasionally by the younger generation of women. Men never weave. No weaving is, however, being done for the market these days.

With abundant natural resources like a fertile land available in plenty, abundant rainfall and a conducive climate, there is scope for agro based industries. Human resource base is also quite well developed, because people are educated and have started becoming aware of the value of money, although the entrepreneurial spirit is conspicuous by its absence.

According to Jyoti Kalash (1990) :

(i) Among the demand based industries, rice dehusking units are predominant. The village has three such units.

(ii) Weaving specimens from the village (as elsewhere in Nagaland) comprises a wide range and number which display themselves as pieces of the precious art treasures showing in respect of designing and processing, an accomplishment of a great measure. The costumes and apparels comprise wrappers and shawls, waist-clothes and bodies, girdles (for carrying babies), scarfs, skirts, aprons and *lungis* resplendent with skilful colour combination in their own fashion and style. Weaving is still a major undertaking as the Nagas of the villages, still rely on women-folk for a great portion of family income. But these dress materials are being increasingly supplemented by mill-made fabrics. The Naga shawls and bags with different textures are highly valued, and have found great demand outside the State irrespective of their high cost price due to the laborious processing and difficulties caused by the dearth of yarn.

The best Naga shawls having different textures are woven of yarn. The shawls on the entire length or borders are striped, each tribe having their own model of geometrical designs, as part of their embroidery. Stripes in all cases are coloured differently from the main background of the cloth.

Weaving is entirely confined to the women-folk who, besides shouldering the domestic and cultivation works, weave the traditions of weaving being handed from mother to daughter.

(iii) Knitting is also a common activity with the girls. The girls knit sweaters for all in the family, including babies. Some knit for others in the village for a fee. The high altitude of the village (in fact, the whole of Nagaland) is cool and offers a good prospect for sale of hand knitted woollens. Training in knitting is also imparted in the few Industrial Training Institutes in the State. A few girls of the village have availed this facility.

(iv) Dyeing: The villagers have several techniques of dyeing. Dyes are prepared from indigo, cultivated in their home-stead gardens, but also from tubers, sappers, leaves and plants. At present chemical dyes have supplemented those procured locally. In dyeing process, the common system is boiling the yarn or cloth or hair meant for dyeing which gives lasting colour. Even the goats hair or human hair dyed red or black or any other colour is used for decorating their weapons or resplendent parts of dress.

(v) Work in cane: Cane is largely utilised for works in craft. Picturesque cane crafts comprising bowls, mugs and containers with multi-coloured engravings on them are made by all the tribes. Other varieties such as fillets as part of ornamentation have elaborately worked out designs. Cane helmets and hat frames are many. Among the Nagas a cane rain-proof hat is also made. Mats woven of cane strings with fine texture have decorative value.

Baskets are in wide range and number with different shapes and sizes. Used for different purposes – as containers for crops and other household goods and as packages for carrying luggage and merchandise. The Japa, a package with lid, hexagonal in form is popularly used all over the district (i.e. Kohima) for storing and travelling. There are other kinds of baskets bearing symbolic expression and having numerous engravings.

(vi) Work in wood: Timber has multifarious use. Tree trunks serve as poles, pillars, battens and crossbeams for house construction. A trough used for threshing paddy is a type of hollowed trunk. The most exquisite manufactures, out of wood are dishes (with legs), saucers, platters, cups and other utensils which exhibit in their own fashion which are a splendid workmanship.

Wood-carving has more artistic than commercial value. It was, through its association with its past, connected with head-hunting, as evidenced in the use of the woodcarved human skulls in imitation of the true heads, used generations ago by head hunters. Spear shafts are also of wood.

As most of the villages in Nagaland produce the aforementioned items, there is very little scope for marketing. In towns like Dimapur and Kohima, there are private weaving and knitting centres to cater to the requirements of the town people. Moreover, as people in the villages are first and foremost cultivators, they do not have the time to open up and run industries producing these items.

According to S. Imchen (1991), the men in their spare time weave baskets, bushels, and mats out of the bamboo. However, this activity is confined to meet the needs of the family and not for the market. There are some men who weave baskets for others when an order is placed by another villager. But such transactions are limited to the village. This activity is generally carried in the free time between harvest and the clearing of fresh land for cultivation.

Moreover weaving is carried out along traditional lines and modern looms are unknown. Weaving is still done on the simple tension-loom which is time consuming as well as back breaking.

The banks however do finance government sponsored schemes like the IRLP. This has a 50 per cent subsidy component and the influential people with connection reap the benefits. Hence, the targetted group do not benefit.

Regarding credit the position is bad. There is now institutional finance available. The non-availability of credit may however be attributed to the fact that the villagers still carry out traditional farming practices which does not entail much capital in the farm inputs. Some of the villagers would like to avail credit to develop terrace fields. However, they have not approached the commercial institution due to a number of reasons. Firstly, the institution of banks as a source of credit is not known to them. Secondly, they prefer loans from the various government agencies which has lower rates of interest and half of the capital is in the form of subsidiaries.

Marketing is one of the weakest links in the chain of economic activities of the village. Commercial transactions still pay a very small role in the life of the villagers. Many reasons can be given for this. Regarding rice and maize, the staple crops, surplus is not available except to some rich men due to low productivity.

Summary and Issues

- The village industry is practically non-existent. Except for shawls which are mostly used for the household the village industry is non-existent.
- The State can do a lot in this area. Here the role of bureaucrats/leaders can be of great help. The handicraft potential is very high in the State, the only thing needed is channelization.

FOOD AND LIVESTOCK

According to Rajiv Bansal (1988), the people are non-vegetarian by way of habit. While pork and rice form the staple diet, almost every other meat is also considered edible. Generally each house has a small number of pigs and hens. Some piglings and calves are bought from the plains of Assam. The cows generally yield very less milk and 3 to 4 litres/day would be the average. A Government Veterinary Doctor visits the village from time to time.

According to Jyoti Kalash (1990), this is in consonance with the saying that Nagas keep cows not for the milk but for the meat.

Usually, just before delivery, the mother-cow goes to the jungles and does not return for a few days. The approximate location of the cow is known to the cow-boys. After delivery, the cow may come back on its own (of course, with the calf/calves) or is made to do so. Thus there is very little interference with the natural process of breeding.

According to Imchen (1991), the cattle that is at present breed is of inferior quality. Superior breeds have to be introduced and the veterinary department must extend its extension services to the village in the form of artificial insemination. Similarly better breeds of pigs have to be introduced which put on meat faster. Besides better feeds is a must. However, feeds are very costly and the villagers have to make use of local materials like maize for the same which will develop a linkage between agriculture and livestock development.

The meat is cooked with jungle leaves and vegetables. Poor people often take rice with salt and chilli. Food is cooked simply by boiling, putting salt, chilli and ginger. No other spice is used. Chilli is an important item of curry. All sorts of vegetables including jungle leaves, cabbage, cauliflower, potato etc. are used.

The market for chicken, pork and beef exists but the marketing mechanism is weak. In fact one of the main reasons why commercialisation has not taken place is due to this factor. For instance, the pigs reared in the village is generally to meet such contingencies as marriages, deaths and festivals. On rare occasions some livestock is butchered and sold within the village. The majority being farmers, they cannot take to livestock rearing on a full-time basis. Besides it is considered to be demurring to make a living as a butcher. Thus marketing is essential if livestock rearing is to be set up along commercial lines.

Every family in the village with the exception of the very old and infirm rears some pigs, and chicken cattle is reared only by a few rich men in the village. However, the stock is of poor quality and the animals are left to scavenge in village. The cows are generally set free to graze in the jungle and the owner does not spend anything on food. With regard to the pigs they are generally fed the husk of rice and in the case of rich households ground corn.

The potential for development of livestock is very great. There is great demand for meat and milk in the district and the demand at present is met by bringing these from outside the State. However, though the potential exists, the need is to make the people undertake these activities on commercial lines as opposed to a purely domestic activity at present.

According to Jan-e-Alam (1991), bullocks and buffaloes are not used in agriculture. The only use in this regard, however indirectly, is the dung, which is used as manure.

Local milch cows are reared for the milk. The average milk yield is about 5 litres per day.

Summary and Issues

— Rice is the staple food of the Nagas. The people take food three times – morning, noon and evening. Noon meal is taken in the field here. The food is taken generally with one curry – jungle leaves and vegetable or meat.

— The people like meat more than anything else. Beef is common as it is cheap but pork is relished the most. Beef includes meat of cow, buffalo and mithun. Mithun is a semi-wild animal halfway between cow and buffalo and very much prized as animal for sacrifice and big feast. Fish is also liked but unfortunately it is not available in plenty.

— Silkworm, wood worms, pupae of bee and wasp are also very much relished. The pupae are easily available and are sold at very high price.

— One should respect their food habits. The livestock breed can be improved. This in turn would give more meat to the Nagas.

HEALTH AND SANITATION

According to Pankaj Kumar (1987), there are about 6 or 7 community latrines. More are needed. Few houses have their own latrines. The sample survey showed that 7 (11.7%) households had their own latrines while 5 (8.3%) households had a bathroom. The houses are spaced close together on either side of the road or side lanes. Only 6 (10%) houses had drainage facility.

People are susceptible to TB which is not as much reported as it is widespread. Only advanced cases are reported. Gastro-enteritis is a common ailment in the beginning of the rainy season. Cases of malaria are not many. The rate of infant mortality is not available. However, the sample survey revealed that 100 children had died in the 60 households surveyed. The main reasons are multigravida and nutritional deficiency among mothers.

According to Vasudha Sharma (1987), tap water is available in the village for drinking and domestic purposes. Because of education, economic condition and abundance of water, the standards of personal hygiene in the village are quite high.

According to P.K. Borthakur (1989), it appears that the people of Chungtia are generally healthy and also no endemic reports available in the village in the recent past, though the village sanitation is not satisfactory. Malaria is a common disease and about 40-50 people suffer from malaria every year. Incidence of cholera/gastro enteritis is few. About 3-5 people suffer from these every year. At present, there is no one in the village suffering from T.B. Deaths due to road-accident, snake bites are of the level of 2-3 annually.

The villagers don't have latrines attached to their houses. There were open public latrine both for men and women separately all along the village outskirts which is hidden by the rocks and nightsoil is consumed by the pigs. There is also a side platform (sunglong) made of bamboos attached to every house and there is a provision of small space to be used as latrine which is not hygienic.

According to P.K. Borthakur (1989), a typical farmer gets up early in the morning and takes a good meal before going for his work. The dinner is taken at about 5 p.m. in the evening after the day's work is over.

According to Jyoti Kalash (1990), safe drinking water is available almost throughout the year.

Among the insanitary habits of the people are (i) relieving oneself, anywhere outside the house, especially at night; (ii) though many of the latrines (which are usually located in the kitchen garden) have provision for underground accumulation of excreta, some people still have raised latrines with pigs let loose below.

Infant mortality is a very rare phenomenon in the village.

Summary and Issues

— Nagas believe and observe cleanliness. For this they have used the natural and animal sources also. The incident of malaria are low, the infant mortality is less than the national average and other tropical diseases are unheard.

— In the northern part of the State, sanitary conditions like pucca toilets, drainage etc. would have to be improved.

— The medical facilities available to an average Naga are of a very low standard. There is a strong need to open new health centres in the State.

SOCIAL LIFE

According to D.K. Bhalla (1986), it is a classless society with no hierarchy of castes. Even the development process has not created any privileged class except that few have become richer than the others by becoming Government contractors for construction and supply works under the departments like PWD, PHE, Electricity, Supply, Forests etc. But they do not enjoy any special privileges in day to day social life, conferred by the society. The classic example of such classlessness is found in a Naga kitchen where all sit and eat together including employees and servants. A Naga kitchen has a central *chulha* which is a big fire place simply made of 2 iron bars on a raised platform below which the fuel wood keeps burning throughout the day. It is always full of smoke but warm. All sit huddled around the fire, everyone contributing his or her own share in the cooking or washing. Above the fire place having few cane or bamboo sheets on which fish or meat pieces or chilly are spread. They are being dried up and smoked. They taste awfully good. The atmosphere of Naga kitchen sums up the whole society here – relaxed, slow, traditional, deeply entrenched in many old customs, classless, casteless, warm, loving, aggressive but not always hostile, hospitable, gay and laughing, uninhibitive. This is Naga society.

According to Vasudha Sharma (1987), there was another factor which more or less used to equalise the income levels in the community in the past. Giving of feasts to the whole community by rich people is an age old custom which is becoming infrequent these days, but which exists still and used to act towards narrowing down the gap between the rich and the poor in the village. Community feasts cost a fortune, but added tremendously to the prestige of the family. They also created good relations and maintained the bonds among the rich and the poor.

According to G.V.V. Sharma (1987), Lotha customary law is practiced in the village as guaranteed by Article 371A of the Constitution. Oath taking by the accused binding a strand of his hair with a piece of earth is practiced. An appeal from a decision of the village court lies to the area court from where it goes to the District Dubashi court. Though it is possible to go further upto Magistrates court, only a small fraction of cases really do so. The old beliefs of lycanthropy – a person said to be capable of wandering in the form of a tiger and of the spirit of a dead person travelling along a defined zigzag path visible from the village hill are still vaguely present though all the villagers now are wholly Christians.

According to S. Aparna (1988), the village society consists of family units which are grouped into several exogamous units known as clans. The clan is spread over several villages of the tribe, but the members of a particular clan living in a village are said to belong to one *khel.*

The villagers had been practicing the animistic religion since time immemorial in these areas. Animism, in simple terms refers to the belief system that all things that were created by a Divine creator, who also appointed the good and evil spirits are ruled over by these spirits. As the evil spirits can harm or even kill men, they have to be propitiated or exorcised by offerings such as egg, fowl, liquor, meat, cloth, iron etc. The Nagas also follow an unwritten code of moral behaviour and observe rituals and ceremonies to keep the good spirits happy and to prolong life, ward off evil, to obtain children, to achieve victory etc. They also believe that not observing these laws could lead to destruction, evil consequences and punishment after death. The rituals, taboos, etc. are, therefore, observed scrupulously by the animists.

The age-old customs that every villager recognises as their right way of life, from the basis of harmony and justice within the village society. The village society reveals a blend of easy familiarity and courteous consideration in the dealings among the members. All issues are deliberated at great length and concluded to the satisfaction of the majority.

The tribal law is an extension of this concept. There is implicit trust that all actions will be carried out within this framework of legality. But when the law is violated, the culprit, if caught, accepts the inevitability of the punishment. Punishment is usually in the form of fine and in graver offences such as causing death by accident, the culprit can be exiled from the village for a duration. The thief is penalised with a fine worth seven times the article stolen. Rape and murders are rare.

The social hierarchy is determined not solely on the basis of wealth or land-ownership, but also, to a great extent, on the qualities of honour and generosity. Thus, a person who provides a ceremonial feast for the entire village earns a honourable position in the society. One finds houses of men of such social standing bearing the prestigious carvings of mithun heads on their frontage. In the contemporary village community, persons of the salaried class and well-placed individuals are also expected to help their brethren by virtue of their position. In fact, this feeling is in part responsible for the nepotism and adhocism that one finds in the government.

According to Temjen Toy (1989), the average number of children in a family is five, with some having as many as eleven! Family planning is not really followed in these areas. The people at large prefer to have a large family as long as they can afford it. Thus, while the birth rate is high, the death rate is very low. The actual death rate could not be established.

Caste is non-existent in Nagaland, and the only division can be made on the basis of religion. In Jakhama, 85 per cent are Christians whereas the remaining 15 per cent are 'Non-Christians'. The term 'Non-Christian' represents the Animists, or the religion followed before the advent of Christianity.

According to Jyoti Kalash (1990), though the village area is big enough to enable double the present population to practice *jhumming,* houses are built in close proximity to one another. This is a common feature of villages in Nagaland. Probably, its origin may be traced back to the days of inter-tribe and inter-village feuds when the feeling of insecurity was very much present. This style of housing has at least one danger – when one house catches fire it rapidly spreads and a good part of the *Khel/Ward* is gutted.

In the State, the family is the unit of farm holding. Joint family system is practically non-existent in this State. A person immediately after marriage is supposed to become self-supporting by way of operating a separate farm holding. Therefore, farming still is a subsistence occupation for every individual household.

From ancient time, as in other Naga village, the nuclear family system is prevalent. The family consists of the father, mother, unmarried daughters. Once a man gets married, he establihes a new household and brings his wife to his new house. House is constructed with the help of his clan members. Residence after marriage being patri-local, the wife has to move into the husband's house.

Monogamy has been the rule and today there is no case of bigamy in the village though at times there had been some cases.

Descent is traced through the male parent i.e. society is patrilineal. It is also patriarchal in the sense that the husband is the head of the family. But this does not mean that the wife is relegated to an inferior position – husband and wife function as equals but in different departments of life. The husband ultimately decides policy matters of the family whereas the wife is the undisputed queen of home affairs. Socialization for the children starts at home – among the values, respect for elders, love for parents and siblings, honesty etc. are considered most important. Peer-group socialization is through playmates in the neighbourhood. After a child goes to school, it is also much influenced by it.

Clan exogamy is practiced. All girls and boys of one's clan (i.e. patri clan) who are of one's age-group are considered to be one's brothers and sisters. One can marry a cousin from one's mother's clan – though this practice is not very common, it is not despised but considered normal.

Names of clans in the village are Kent, Kemp, Khing, Thong, Seb, Nyenth etc. The system of *phatries,* i.e. interrelated clans exist, e.g. Thong and Seb are considered to be brother-clans.

Though much cohesion exists even at the village level and community feeling is very strong, the clan is the unit which is most important. The prestige of a man partially depends on the prestige of the clan and on the reverse a person, through accomplishments contribute to the honour of the clan or spoil its name by negative acts. During life-cycle rites like birth, marriage and death, the clan as a whole shoulders the responsibility though immediate relatives obviously do it to a greater degree.

Marriage by negotiations is the general rule. It starts initially when the boy sounds to his parents his desire to marry suggesting a girl with whom life parternship he wants to enter. Traditionally, when a girl reaches 16 to 17 years of age, she is considered eligible to be married. For boys 20 to 21 years usually qualifies him – but there is no hard and fast rule, with the coming of modern system of education, the age of marriage has raised among those who study in colleges. These days parents indirectly sounding a boy to get married is not uncommon.

As soon as their son's intention to get married has been divulged, a go-between or intermediary, preferably a senior *khel* or clan woman, is engaged to convey the proposal. If the proposal is accepted, it is conveyed to the boy's parents. They meet in the girl's place and fix the date and the wedding feast expenses. The boy's side provide the cash and materials to the girl's side which arranges the feast.

The society is a chain of both love and family arranged marriages. It is a well known fact that much of the indigenous oral poetry is inspired by love. There are many love stories and fictions, apart from the ballads and lyrics which show the blossoms of romanticism among the people.

Traditionally, the house construction ceremony is performed when the groom in the presence of the bride and her mother, lits a fire in the new house followed by the taking of meals, all these rites are done in silence. Other ceremonies follow when the bride in the company of her attendants is brought to a new house, symbolising the marital partnership. During the first few nights, the couple do not have connection as she remains with her girl attendants in his house. It is after overcoming shyness, when her companions are no longer necessary, that the couple are left alone.

Today, the marriage ceremony is perfomed in the church and even the dresses used are as in the West. This is followed by a feast at the bride's residence. On the first night, the bride sleeps with bridemaid and the groom with his best man. On the following day, the bride is given a farewell by her parents and relatives and thereafter she goes and lives in the husband's place. Sometimes, for convenience, the bride is taken to the groom's place on the first day itself after the feast. Traditionally marriage was more of a social event; today because of the coming of Christianity, the spiritual aspect is dominant.

Though a Christian marriage is supposed to be irreversible, the cases of divorce do occur. The reasons for divorce are usually infidelity and barrenness.

The role of women in society is uneven. There are, however, some social restrictions, viz. :

(i) she cannot inherit the father's landed property,
(ii) she cannot join hunting party,
(iii) she cannot wear male shawls,
(iv) she cannot sit cross-legged,
(v) she cannot become priest,
(vi) she cannot touch spears and shields.

According to S. Imchen (1991), the society in the village is patriarchal and hence women suffer a number of disadvantages. Women cannot inherit any property like land though she is entitled to a third of her husband's movable property. Women have no representation in the village council and the village chiefs are invariably men. One woman member is appointed as Village Development Board (VDB) member only due to specific Government orders to that effect. Moreover the lady member hardly has any say in decision making and she quietly acquiesces in the decision made by the men. Even in the family, the major decisions are taken by the father.

The women in the villages are loved and respected as mothers, sisters and wives. In fact, the very fact that they are women make the males treat them with more consideration and concern. Moreover, women is this village have no restrictions in their movements and the practice of dowry is unheard of. The women also have a large degree of freedom in the choice of spouses and in the village there are many instances of love marriage.

Marriage may be arranged or a love marriage but clan exogamy is enforced strictly. Marriage is a solemn occasion and a sacrament performed in accordance with Christian rites.

Clans play an important role among the villagers. It pervades the life of an ordinary villager influencing the choice of his wife or friends. The importance of his clan to a man can be understood by the fact that he draws sustenance from land held in common by the clan and also falls back on his clansmen in times of need and trouble.

Religion plays an important role in a society. It can be a binding or a divisive force as the situation may be and also influence the thought and action of its members. The people of the village were animists before the advent of Christianity. Today, all the villagers are Christians by faith.

In the beginning all the villagers belonged to one Church. However, in the mid 1980 a new sect, the U.R.F. (United Revival Fellowship) was established besides the existing Baptist Church. This led to a lot of friction and tension between the different members and was a great divisive force. However, in October 1992, the two groups decided to merge and give up their differences and the appointed re-union day was celebrated with great joy.

In the villages, the Church occupies an important position. The Church building is located at the highest and is the most imposing building in the village. The father is a salaried post while members of the later are chosen from among the prominent members of the village. They command a great deal of respect from the villagers.

Apart from the services held on Sundays and other days, the services of the Pastor are indispensable for other occasions like births, marriage and death. Today Christian rites are an important part and they lose sanctity without the blessing of the church. The church also provides members with solace by way of prayer and support on occasions like death and illness. The Church is binding force among the villagers. Besides the teachings the church act as guided values and actions of the members. The importance of the church can be gauged by the fact that a villager is judged and his standing in the community determined by the degree of his conformity to the standards fixed by the church.

Old beliefs however die hard and many villages still believe in things which have no place in the church's techniques. Villagers fully believe and adhere to the teachings of the church and also fully believe in superstitions like Centhrophy.

The State of Nagaland was declared a dry State on 30th March, 1989. The movement for imposition of prohibition was spearheaded by the Nagaland Mothers' Association, a very active voluntary Association. However the movement has died down now and liquor is available in black at five times the price than in the open market. The consumption of drugs and incidence of addiction are very high in the State. A number of voluntary agencies have been set up to combat this menace.

According to Jan-e-Alam (1991), Naga society is highly egalitarian as is evident from the absence of hierarchical caste structure as also any rules or regulations advocating discrimination to any group of people living in the village, even the Non-Christians participate in the social and political affairs of the village.

According to Sanjay Kumar (1992), the total number of rural households in the Block as per 1981 census was 15,494 out of 33,195 of households in the district. The average size of a household in Nagaland is worked out to be 5.18 persons per household, Kohima district, 7.19 persons and Medziphema Block 5.45 persons per household. The average size of household recorded in Kohima district is comparatively bigger, because of the prevalence of joint and extended families in the district. This practice is found mostly among the non-Naga communities. Normally Nagas do not have the practice of joint family or extended family and prevalence of nuclear family is the norm. Therefore, the average size of household in this Block is found medium, consisting of 4.55 persons to 6.91 persons per household. Five dominant Naga tribes were selected to examine the size of their households and the result is presented here below in the table.

Comparative Average Size of Households Selected Tribe/Community

Sl. No.	Tribe/Community	Average Persons		Females per 1000 males
		District level	Block level	
1.	Angamis	5.61	4.93	882
2.	Kacharis	6.91	6.91	647
3.	Kukis	5.95	6.11	981
4.	Semas	4.55	4.55	859
5.	Mixed tribes	–	4.76	723

Source : Based on 1981 census.

The above table indicates that the size of household among the Kacharis and the Kukis is slightly bigger than the other tribes. The reason being that they prefer to live in joint and extended types of families. The Kacharis of Medziphema Block are mostly concentrating in Dhansiripar circle and, the average size of their household remains the same in both the district and Block levels, i.e. 6.91 persons per households, which is incidentally the biggest size of households in our study. Ninety-nine per cent of the Sema Naga population in Khoima district is living in this Block and the size of their households also remains the same, i.e. 4.55 persons per household, which is the smallest recorded size among all other tribes in this study.

The sex ratio in a Block has worked out as 818 number of females per 1000 males. This is also much higher than the district sex ratio of 790 females per 1000 males, but lower than the State sex ratio, which is 863 females per 1000 males as per 1981 census. The sociological factor found in this analysis is that among the Kacharis and the Kukis, the sex ratio was quite different than other tribes. Among the Kacharis it is 647 females per 1000 males, whereas among the Kukis it is 981 females per 1000 males. And it appears that the productivity and survival of female population is very low among the Kacharis, whereas it is found to be highest amongst the Kukis.

According to Sanjay Kumar (1992), courting and marrying after pregnancy or childbirth is very common. But there are cases where the couple do not marry in spite of child birth. Formerly, and still now in some villages, the father of the child is required to bear the cost of bringing up the child and even pay some fine. But now-a-days social control being loose, it is difficult to impose and exact such fines. In some cases the father accepts the paternity whether he pays the upbringing cost or not, but in some cases the father refuses the paternity too, and in that case the child becomes absolute responsibility of the mother and is known by his or her mother's name, and society accepts it as a normal thing and does not look down on any such child.

Though there is freedom for women among the Nagas it is essentially a patrilineal society and it is so much so that the women do not inherit any property. When the father dies his landed property and movable valuables are divided among the sons but not daughters. (The Hindu Law does not apply to the Nagas, even Non-Christians). The daughters do not get any share of the property. The widow also do not get anything except her personal property such as weaving apparatus, clothes, her own cash and her ornaments which are given by her parents but not those given by her husband. So long she remains in the house of her deceased husband she enjoys all the facilities including use of the ornaments, but if she goes away to her parents or remarries she is to go bare headed. She gets share of the domestic fowls and ducks but not other livestock such as cows and pigs. Her share in the domestic poultry varies from one-third to half. These movable properties are a small thing and so it is divided according to convenience and natural justice, but she does not have any right to landed property or cash of the father or husband. Lion's share of the property goes to the youngest son. He gets not only the greater share of the landed property, livestock and cash, but also inherits the paternal house. The justice involved in this system is this that the elder sons are already established whereas the youngest is not, and moreover he lives with his parents and looks after till they die.

If a girl is given some landed property by her parents she enjoys it during her lifetime but it goes to her sons only and not daughters on her death. But if she dies without any son it reverts to her father or brothers, if the father is dead.

Summary and Issues

— Nagas lead essentially a community life. They work in groups, eat in groups and sleep in groups. There is no individual cultivation or harvest or house building. Every year generally in winter the houses are built turn by turn by the public free of cost. Village is a social unit. Within the village *khel* is a sub-unit. Then comes family as a unit.

— The society is based on patriarchal system. Only male members can inherit the family property. Also among some Naga tribes polygamy was prevalent. While the father is the head it is the mother who performs the entire family work, such as feeding not only children but also the domestic animals like pigs, poultry and cattle.

— There are no beggars in Naga society. It is shame to shirk hard work. The women have no legal rights yet they are very influential with the menfolk including their husband. There is a tremendous respect for women in the society. Women are actively involved in social reforms and social services.

— The social life, like in other parts of the country is in turmoil. There is a strong western influence which sometimes does not fit into the traditional customs. Nagas would have to take care that their individual identity should not be lost under these western influences.

GENERAL ECO CONDITIONS

According to Rajiv Bansal (1988), the State of Nagaland is 100 per cent electrified. Almost all houses in the village have electric connections. However electric supply is available only for a few hours in the day. On the whole the general economic condition of the people is good. There is no incidence of bonded labour in the village.

According to P.K. Borthakur (1989), the scenario of unemployed in the village is also not encouraging. In the absence of any industry etc. to absorb manpower the normal tendency is to look forward to Government jobs as the only source of employment.

According to Temjen Toy (1989), the general economic condition of the village is encouraging. As all the people have their own fields to cultivate, the question of unemployment does not arise. It is only when one looks at employment or the lack of it with respect to steady jobs in the Government that one can measure the degree of unemployment. To that extent, about 20 per cent of the residents are employed in Government service.

According to S. Imchen (1991), even those employed in Government service, though better off, have not inculcated the value of saving.

In general the villagers are strong and healthy. This is because of the nature of work that gives them ample exercise and a diet that is fresh and free from harmful toxins.

However, the hard work that agriculture entails make onset of ailments like stiff joints and backache. In terms of sanitation much is wanting. Personal hygiene also leaves much to be desired and consequently skin diseases are not uncommon. The most important aspect however is that the villagers do not use dug pit latrines but answer nature's call in the jungles bordering the village. The pig and cattle also scavenge freely in and around the village. Since the water source is at a lower level than the village, the water in the wells get contaminated and the villagers are afflicted by diseases like typhoid, cholera and especially dysentery during the rainy season.

VILLAGE ADMINISTRATION

According to D.K. Bhalla (1986), the law which operates at the base level all over Nagaland is Customary Law. This is the law of the '*Dubashi* courts'.

(i) In case of sexual affairs between a boy and a girl (premarital of course), if they plead not guilty, one of them has to bite the pubic hair of the other and pledge by it and it is believed that the person who pledges wrongly does come to a harm by the superhuman forces.

(ii) In case of theft, if the thief pleads not guilty, he has to bite the stolen goods and pledge by them.

(iii) In case of a land dispute, the asserter has to bite the soil or the tiger's teeth and pledge by that.

The operation of this law is very smooth and most cases are settled out. Only sometimes the complainant or the accused prefer to go in appeal to the Magistrate's Court. Thereby the litigations, mortgages and indebtedness are nowhere seen in the land which had destroyed the villagers in all other parts of the country in pre-independence days and even now sometimes it ruins them.

According to Vasudha Sharma (1987), Panchayati Raj system as applicable to the rest of the country is not existing in Nagaland. However, the Angami Society has been traditionally a very democratic society. Grass root democracy at the village level is truly visible in Kohima district. In Nagaland traditional village councils have been given a legal sanction by passing of a legislative act – called the Village and Area Councils Act. The village council, composed of elders, has both judicial and executive functions. They lay down rules and see that they are followed. They settle disputes arising among individuals and families in the village.

In Nagaland, the tribal councils were functioning even before the 1945 Regulation of Assam Frontier (Administration of Justice). The British appointed *Gaon Burras* (GBs, who were included in the village councils. The GBs were not paid, but were given a red blanket to denote their status and were expected to function as liaison between the council and the government. The Village and Area Council Act of 1978 gives powers to the village councils. The VDB which is the development wing of the village council functions as explained elsewhere above.

In development works also, progress is speedier, because, unlike some other villages where the development grants are to be distributed *khel*-wise, whether or not they remain sufficient for the feasibility of the development project, in Botsa, all the funds are utilised for implementing development projects by consensus.

According to Rajiv Bansal (1988), the traditional leadership system, i.e. the *Putu Menden* or the Village Council is the all important village body. The Village Council acts as the interface between the government and the villagers. Under the Nagaland Village and Areas Councils Act, 1978, the Village Council is empowered to formulate village development schemes, to assist the government agencies and to ensure administration of justice. Apart from this, the Village Council has also been vested with very wide powers. The *Putu Menden* stays in power for a duration of 30 years or one generation.

According to Ms. S. Aparna (1988), the Village Council, an elected body, which is the traditional authority has been vested formally with legitimacy under the present day political system also, with a codified frame of rights and responsibilities. The major functions of the Village Council are administrative, traditional and judicial.

The administrative functions include liaison with the district administration, construction and maintenance of community assets, planning the use of resources such as land, forests, water sources etc., that belong to the community as a whole, and management of the village fund. The traditional functions of the village council includes representing the village in tribal meets, arbitration in internal disputes, performing the required role in feasts and festivals, etc. There is a judicial board which is part of the council, and this board decides cases of civil and criminal nature under the unwritten customary law.

The GBs are a legacy from the days of British administration, and are responsible to the administration for law and order in the village. The GBs receive a red blanket (shawl) from the district administration once in two years as a token of recognition, as well as a commission from the village house tax, which is their duty to collect and remit to the government. The

GBs in Angami villages such as Chiechama are selected clan-wise either through a show of hands or by consensus and hold their post life-long. Generally, the oldest man in the *khel* who is considered wise and capable is chosen. The GB is expected to the spokesman for his people in all village matters. In recent years with the percolation of money power to the village level, the role of the GB has diminished in economic and political matters. However, in traditional and social issues, the GBs continue to play a vital role. The district administration also attempts to use this body as a stabilising factor in the changing village scene.

According to Temjen Toy (1989), each *khel* of the village is represented by a GB. All the GBs together form the Village Council. Though there are only eight *khels* in the village. Jakhama has nine GBs. This is because Phema *khel* is represented by two GBs.

Chieftainship was, therefore, a very important factor, in Naga polity. In areas where kingship/chieftainship prevailed, one just could not become the village Chief, however, influential or powerful he might be. Selection of the King/Chief involved series of religious rites and worship to their gods. In normal course the leader of the first settlement would have become the Chief. According to their tradition and custom the would-be King/Chief was required to obtain the sanction of gods to his kingship, otherwise nobody would obey him. To prove that he had the sanction of the gods, the would-be Chief had to perform certain rites and then sow paddy seeds. If this seed did not grow well, the proposed Chief had no right to claim the chieftainship. If the paddy grew well, then he was again subjected to another test, i.e. the sowing of kidney beans which would not grow so easily. If the kidney beans grew well, then followed the third test in the form of living animals particularly the cock. If the cock grew on time and in full harmony of high and low sounds, then it was believed that the gods had favoured him to be King/Chief of the village. In case of any dispute between different parties, the same process was repeated and the one who successfully passed all the three tests was taken to have had the sanction of the gods. He must be the first to sow, to plant, to pluck and to harvest, and first in all the religious rites/festivals of the village-states to ensure the prosperity of the village.

Except in a few tribes like the Aos and the Lothas etc. the chieftainship was hereditary in most of the Naga tribes. Since the chief had the sanction of gods to sow and harvest first, nobody could challenge him when he passed on his chieftainship to his eldest son (but never to a daughter) because, divine sanction had been given to that particular family.

The village Chief had a dual function as the religious and secular head of the village. As the religious head, the Chief is the first man to sow seeds, the first to plant and the first to harvest. Although the actual religious worships and sacrifices etc. were performed by the village priest, yet his presence in any religious ceremony was prominent. He presided over all religious festivals.

As the secular head, his functions were numerous. At the time of head huntings his primary concern was for the defence of the village. As the Head of the Administration, his duty was to summon and preside over the meetings of the village councillors who were by custom the representatives of the various clans. In the day-to-day administration of the village, the Chief was assisted by the councillors. In case of dispute, the Chief's house served as the court except when the councillors with his approval wanted to hold the hearings in the open space. The village Chief was, therefore, the religious head, the Chief Judge, the Chief Administrator and also the Chief Commander at the time of war and head hunting.

With all the powers concentrated in his hand, however, the village Chief could not be a Dictator as he was bound by the various tribal customs and unwritten laws which were rigidly followed. The Chief had no power to over rule them. In any disputes, he had hardly any choice as he had to bow down to the precedent cases, the customs and the practice of the society. Since most of the tribal customs and laws were based on religious practice and faith, the Chief had no power to use his discretion except in a few cases where religious customs and traditions were not clear. In fact, the King (Chief) was to use pleasant and sweet words in conversation and in public functions etc. There is a Naga saying that "No cock hurts the chicken and no King speaks roughly". Hence gentleness was a great quality of the village King/Chief.

The village King/Chief was the nominal land owner. The land actually belonged to the people. Each family had the right to possess paddy fields, gardens, and wood lands as much as he could barter/purchase. In the *jhumming* areas, the *jhum* land belonged to the people and the village Chief, in consultation with the village councillors, decided as to which side of the village, *jhumming* should be. This is one distinct point at which the Naga and Kuki tribes differ greatly. In the case of the latter, the village Chief created hurdles in the way of speedy implementation of the tribal schemes and projects. This has led to proposals that Kuki chieftainship should be abolished but the tribal customs die hard.

In the society of Ao, Lotha and Sangtam, there existed from the very beginning a republican type of government. In the Ao villages, one could become the chief by virtue of his own character and merit. They had the *Tartars* (Councillors) who were the representatives of the people; and in Lotha society the strongest in battle and the greatest performer of feat of merit could become the head of the administration. The Aos, Sangtams and Lothas had no love and regard for monarchy. They had no permanent and hereditary system of kingship. The ablest and the wisest ruled the society and were chosen on the basis of merit such as head trophy, intellect, influence, and wealth.

It is difficult to imagine, as to how the administration was run in the Angami society where extreme type of democracy existed. The independent-minded Angamis did not attach much importance to the chieftainship, as one Angami was considered as good as any other Angami. They had no Village Council. Any urgent problem or dispute was taken to a public meeting convened by any influential leader. In that meeting which reminds one of the ancient Greek public meetings, discussion was usually opened by the village Kemevo (religious and political head) and then joined by the influential leaders and those interested in the case/problem. At the time of war or head hunting, a particular warrior was selected by the village warriors to be their C-in-C and another warrior for the next occasion if the village so decides.

The functions of the Village Council even today are broadly executive, administrative and judicial. The councillors are the real body in whom the highest power of the village-state is vested. They are at the helms of affairs of the village. They formulate the policy of the village in war and in peace; they make and amend the unwritten laws which are then rigidly followed.

Since the laws were customary and divine in nature, there was no necessity of separation of powers. The councillors, therefore, did not only execute and administer the laws, they also sat as judges as this was the highest court of the village-state. Therefore, in Naga society, the court and its judges were within easy reach of the poor people. Since the poor people compulsorily belonged to one clan or the other, they were well represented by the ablest of their clan who looks after the interest of his clan. Thus no one was ignored in any court case.

The principle of administration of the village-states, the hereditary system and the divine nature attached with the kingship/chieftainship, the representative character of the village councils etc. are basically same in all the Naga tribes. However, in application of actual laws in the day-to-day administration, there are variations from tribe to tribe.

According to S. Imchen (1991), despite the dilution of his powers, the *gaon burras* continue to yield considerable influence in their respective *khels* and the village. It is a fact that the *gaon burras* own the bulk of the land in the village and each year they distributed lands among the villagers in his *khel* for cultivation. Thus a relationship on land exists between the *gaon burra* and the villagers which is similar to that of feudal lord. This relationship makes for great power and prestige in the hand of the *gaon burra* and he is entitled to a fixed number of the labour every year. The *gaon burra* of his position as Chief is automatically a member of the village council and the village development board. By virtue of being permanent member in these statutory bodies he can influence the decisions made therein.

The following data regarding the elected members of the Village Council is revealing.

Land Status	Representation in	
	VDB	Vil. Council
1. No land	–	3
2. Below 5 acres	2	6
3. 5-10 acres	3	4
4. 10 and above	2	3

The above data clearly shows that the villagers with land are predominantly represented in the Council and Board. Those without land though the most numerous in terms of household are least represented even in numbers not to speak of proportional representation. In the VDB, the body responsible for economic development, they are not represented at all. At the same time, the bigger land owners are represented in excess of its numerical strength. The chiefs (*gaon burras*) who are the biggest land owners are co-opted as members in both the VDB and Village Council and the dominance of the rich and big land owners is complete.

The Village Councils have been empowered to undertake various functions and duties by the Nagaland Village and Area Council Act, 1978. The Council performs the following functions and duties:

1. Formulates the village developments schemes,
2. Helps government agencies in development works in the village,
3. Provides surety for the repayment of loans by residence of village,
4. Constitutes the village development board,
5. Initiates preventive measures in cases of epidemic,
6. Administers justice within the village in accordance with customary law,
7. The council is auxiliary to the administration and has full powers to deal with internal administration of the village, and
8. No transfer of movable property shall be affected without the consent of the council. Written records of this shall be maintained by it.

Summary and Issues

— The administration of the village was carried on by a council. It had a council of elders representing a clan. The chief's house is the Court of Law and office of administration. In Naga society the courts and judges are within easy reach. The customary laws are still followed.

Sometimes the village council acts as an interface between the government and the villagers.

- Naga customary laws and other laws were strictly enforced. Every Naga obeyed these laws as he felt that he himself had made the laws. Breaking of laws was linked with the coming of natural calamity. Thus the society came down heavily on any such infringement.
- As far as possible, these local laws should be emerged and respected. The social pressure is there to obey these laws as compared to the Indian Penal Code.
- Democratic decentralization is already existing in the village. By reaching directly to these villages, the State can strengthen grassroots development.

GOVERNMENT PROGRAMMES, VILLAGE DEVELOPMENT BOARDS AND DEVELOPMENT

According to D.K. Bhalla (1986), the Village Development Board (VDB) in the village is playing the central role for the people's development. It is VDB which resolves on how to utilise grant-in-aid for each year, the Village Council exercises the supreme authority over the VDB by having the power to countersign all the resolutions of VDB without which they will be invalid.

It is very obvious that :

(i) The society of the area is simple in its ways. The modernisation has not changed the ways of life or value in any way except that the old ways and inter-tribal fights are gone. Christianity is the major religion. The people still belong to their villages even if they are employed in towns. The family ties are still very strong. The patriarch still controls the family and the village although in villages no longer the GB enjoy the same authority as was in the old days. The people are acutely aware of politics, politicians, political process and what flows out of all this, for them. The old traditions are still not forgotten.

(ii) The economy of the area has a major handicap, i.e. no market, which means the asset endowed under development process cannot generate incomes and thereby they will finish in the long run and development cannot be a self-sustaining continuous process.

The only chance, lies in agricultural development, horticulture, plantation crops, fruit crops and tree farming etc. Also if processing units could be established for tinned foods etc., they will fetch a sizeable income for the area.

According to G.V.V. Sharma (1987), a sum of Rs. 1,52,000 was spent by the government for various developmental activities in the last 6 years. Most of these schemes were implemented by the Village Council. Besides the above some of the villagers were covered by IRDP, TRYSEM, and other centrally sponsored schemes. The selection of the beneficiaries is also done through the Village Council and is generally considered to be fair in case of IRDP given the constraints of tradition which defines whatever is decided by the Village Development Board, unlike many other villages. An average amount of around Rs. 4,000 was annually deposited by the villagers for the VDB. The works executed by the VDB include construction of roads, footpaths, church building, loans advanced to needy villagers etc. The perception of governmental developmental programmes by the villagers is hardly encouraging. The disconcerting feature is that there is a growing tendency to look upon the government as a reservoir of money and development schemes as cash relief. Government has not been able to make people generate additional resources. Money is spent for consumption purposes rather than for creation of long term assets, which would imply more mobility, diversification, skills and entrepreneurial abilities as well as integration with outside market.

The common complaint heard in the village with regard to governmental activities is that the Village Council is not being given its due place in selection of benifeciaries for many schemes. Though the practice of selection through Village Council is well established for IRDP, it is not the same case with other schemes. Villagers do remember instances of selection for social forestry of coffee plantation schemes done on explicit recommendations from political leaders. The baseline survey for identification of the poorest of the poor is also considered defective by the villagers.

According to Vasudha Sharma (1987), one beneficial effect that VDB has is that the village people can get loans from banks for improving their economic status or for any other productive scheme against the VDB fixed deposit.

According to Tenjon Toy (1989), the Village Development Board (VDB) of Nagaland is perhaps the only one of its kind in India. It is a unique experiment in bringing about development in the rural areas of the State. At the heart of the VDB is the policy of grassroots planning and development. In a nutshell, money is given to the villagers to be used in development schemes selected and undertaken by the villagers themselves.

The Naga village of today still retains its original character of compactness which brings about unity, oneness, sense of belonging and commitment among the villagers, and a sense of pride to be a member of the village community. Apart from individuals, the village as a whole owns property – common property. This common property is used in the best interest of the village as a whole and is jealously guarded against individual exploitation.

It is against such a background that the VDB came into existence in 1980. The Government, by way of grants-in-aid created a common fund for the village. The use of this fund was meant for the development of the village, it was left to the villagers to decide among themselves as to how it should be used. As such, maximum opportunity and initiative is given to the villagers to develop their own villages. The creation of VDBs has not only encouraged the participation of the people in developmental activities but has also educated them in the fields of banking, entrepreneurship, etc.

The primary condition to be fulfilled before a village can form a VDB is that the village should be a Government recognised village. The Village Council fills up the "Formation of Village Development Board" form (Annexure II), and submits four copies of it to the Deputy Commissioner, who is the Chairman of all VDBs in the district. After the Deputy Commissioner's approval, the copies are sent to the BDO, area

Administrative Officer (EAC) and the Bank where the VDB plans to operate its accounts.

The Deputy Commissioner then sends the list of households (of the village) paying house-tax to the Rural Development Department. The department then initiates the process for allocation of funds, etc.

In the meantime, the villagers will have to select the VDB Management Committee. Now, all permanent members of the village are members of the VDB and they form the General Body of the VDB. They select members among themselves. These members form/constitute the Management Committee of the VDB and are entrusted with the management of the VDB and its funds. The size of this Committee is determined by the Village Council. However, it should not be less than five members or more than twenty-five. Women members are also selected and their numbers should not be less than one-fourth of the total membership. From among the members, a literate person is selected as the Secretary.

All decisions of the VDB should be in the form of a resolution signed by not less than 51 per cent of the total members of the Committee. The detailed duties of the Secretary and the VDB as a whole is given in Village Development Board's Model Rules, 1980.

After having formed the VDB, the next step is to go about opening appropriate bank accounts.

It is over ten years now since VDBs were first introduced in the villages of Nagaland, and by now the people at large are more or less well acquainted with its purpose and benefits. In all the villages the people were overwhelmingly in favour of VDBs. When asked why, they gave several reasons. The first reason was that it gave the villagers the opportunity to decide for themselves various schemes for their village. They find it a good idea that since they know what they need the most, it is only logical that the choice of schemes should be left to them. An even more interesting reason for favouring VDBs was that they had now given up for the Ministers and high officials in lifting up the lot of the common people, especially in the villages! Whatever the reason, all the villages seemed to have benefited a lot from VDB programmes. What was more, all of them, without exception, showed keen interest in its working.

We have discussed in a previous chapter about the different bank accounts maintained by VDBs. We have also discussed that money can be withdrawn from the Special Savings Account without any clearance from the BDO or the Area Administrative Officer (EAC/SDO). In other words, the use of this money is left to the discretion of the villagers, without the need for approvals (except that of the Chairman). It is in the use of this money that one can gauge the level of enterprise of the villagers. For instance, at Zisunyu village, the VDB had started grain banks, the likes of which had been introduced with great fanfare in the Koraput district of Orissa. Whereas here, the villagers had thought of this by themselves and had been operating it for the past six to seven years. Here, the VDB buys grain from the villagers during the harvest season when people have excess paddy. During the lean months, they lend the paddy at a nominal rate of interest. The loan is paid back in paddy. These 'grain banks' were well accepted by the villagers. As the 'interest' was also paid in kind, the size of the granary grew each year. Thus at times, excess paddy had to be sold for cash.

Besides grain banks, VDBs also run piggeries. The VDB buys pigs out of its funds. These pigs are then given to households to be looked after. When the pigs multiply, the litter is equally divided between the VDB and the household. The VDB then distributes the piglets, thereby covering more households. It should be noted here that the households are responsible for looking after the pigs. This is indeed a novel way of increasing the income of farmers.

The VDB also runs fisheries and weaving centres where the produce are sold in the local market.

The effectiveness of VDBs varied from village to village. Some villages showed greater interest in the activities of the VDB while it was not the case in some VDBs are more successful in the more backward villages, that is, there was an inverse relationship between the success of a VDB and the level of advancement of a village. This was probaly because the more advanced villages had less need for basic 'development schemes'. However, this should not be taken as a rule. Indeed there were 'advanced' villages such as Jakhama where VDBs were doing extremely well. All said and done, perhaps the success of VDBs depends more on the Secretary and the members than anything else.

One problem which is emerging among many VDBs is the misappropriation of funds by the VDB Secretaries. On the face of it, misappropriation appears to be somehow not easy.

However, a quick recount over the procedures will reveal the loopholes by which deceitful Secretaries misuse the common fund.

According to Jyoti Kalash (1990), the formation of the Village Development Board (VDB) in all the villages has done a commendable work in involving people at the grassroots level in the formulation of the area specific plans to suit a particular village. It has certainly ensured people's participation at the grassroots level and thus fulfilling the idea and concept of democratic decentralisation. Cases of thefts, assault etc. have been almost nil in recent years.

According to S. Imchen (1991), the VDB's are in exercise in decentralised planning whereby the villagers decided the schemes to be taken up as per their felt needs and aspirations.

Jawahar Rojgar Yojna (JRY) is essentially a scheme to provide a minimum number of mandays of labour annually to unemployed persons. However, this is not understood by the villagers. In fact, they do not know that the grant under JRY is to provide employment to unemployed. Hence JRY funds are being misused by the leaders of the village. In 1992-93, under JRY scheme taken up were social forestry (20,000) and construction of approach roads to the Church (Rs. 40,000). In social forestry the beneficiaries were four *gaon burras*. They did not do anything but showed existing forests as the work undertaken and no employment was provided.

According to Jan-e-Alam (1991), though every VDB in Nagaland is statutory required to have one female member, their participation in the VDB affairs in limited to preparing tea and cooking food for the participants in the VDB and VC meetings.

These GBs have a distinct attire and are easily recognisable by their big, plain red blankets.

However, VDBs have become highly politicised and a lot of irregularities are reported in their functioning.

According to S. Imchen (1991), the schemes introduced by the village studied by him have benefited only the richer and influential people. There are several reasons given for this. These are :

(i) for any given development, land is needed. So only those people benefit who have land,

(ii) the landed elements control the VDB and Village Council. Hence the schemes and projects they finalize directly or indirectly benefit them only, and

(iii) these schemes entail some amount of paper work in the district headquarters and interaction with various government officials. The simple villagers are not in a position to do so.

Also the work done by these VDBs was mostly on paper with no creation of tangible assets. In few cases where the work has been done it was very shabby and the intention of spending the minimum of the money sanctioned and pocketing of the rest was done.

The government programmes have set up a number of infrastructural facilities such as schools, a dispensary, play ground and roads linking the village to the outside world. The programme of universal immunization has helped control killer diseases especially among the children who have had the benefit of immunization. Villagers have also come to know about horticulture, terrace cultivation, fisheries and other activities.

One of the most lamentable consequences of the development programme is on the moral and psychological fabric of the villagers. The search for easy money has corrupted their minds. The youngsters are not willing to work in the fields and search for easy money. There is also a dependency syndrome among the villagers on the Government programmes.

Summary and Issues

— *District Planning and Development Board.* A supra-village body called the District Planning and Development Board (D.P.D.B.), chaired by the Deputy Commissioner of the district, had also been formed by an executive order of the State government. From 1980 to 1990 the chairpersons of the area councils were members of the D.P.D.B., thereby providing some linkage at the village level. With the elimination of the area councils in 1990, it was left to the Deputy Commissioner, who was also the ex-officio chairperson of the V.D.Bs. in his district, to safeguard the interests of the rural areas. However, it appears that the Deputy Commissioners had not exercised their powers over the affairs of the V.D.Bs. to the extent visualised in 1980, when the statutory rules for their functioning had first been promulgated.

— A study made by the Guwahati centre of the National Institute of Rural Development (N.I.R.D.) in 1989-90 had revealed that considerable slackness had crept into the functioning of the village development boards. Simultaneously in this report it is mentioned that the Development in this region may be done through an amendment to the V.D.B. rules. Under this amendment, the words "village development board" applied to all the households which comprised the village, and the earlier V.D.B. members were redesignated now as the managing committee of the board. Members of the managing committee continued to be chosen by the village council and the Deputy Commissioner continued to be the chairperson of the managing committee.

— Since Nagaland has been left out of the purview of the Constitution (Seventy-third Amendment) Act, 1992, it is for the State government to work out a viable system of local self-government to draw the people more actively into administrative and development activities and towards the democratic process than the existing system permits.

— An average Naga still aspires for the government job. This thinking has to be changed. For this, alternative sources of employment would have to be generated.

— VDBs, which came much before 73rd and 74th Amendments of Constitution of India, are under constant threat from the politicians and bureaucrats. Corruption has also started creeping in. The State Government can review its functioning and take necessary steps to streamline it.

INDEX